The
Politics of
Population
Control

The Politics of Population

Thomas B

Control

Littlewood

University of Notre Dame Press
Notre Dame ~ London

To my children,
Linda, Lisa, Leah,
and Thomas Stewart.
No finer family could
a family planner plan.

Library of Congress Cataloging in Publication Data

Littlewood, Thomas B
The politics of population control.

Bibliography: p.
Includes index.
1. United States—Population policy. 2. Birth
control—United States. I. Title.
H0766.5.U5L57   301.32'1'0973   76-51619
ISBN 0 -268-01523-6

CONTENTS

PREFACE

This book is the legitimate offspring of a union of journalism and social science. Despite the reciprocal prejudices of their practitioners, the standards of journalism and scholarship need not be incompatible. A reporter is trained to ask the right questions, a scholar to find meaning in the answers. What follows is a description and analysis of the changing politics of population in the United States beginning in the 1960s. My research ranged over many years—in the Statehouse at Springfield, Illinois, in the committee rooms of Congress, in a public housing project in Raleigh, in the stacks at Harvard, and in many other places. Relationships are spelled out where I believe they exist. The reader is forewarned, though, not to expect neat four-cornered explanations for everything that is described. My primary objective is to provoke thought about sensitive, controversial, and very important subjects of public policy that have not been openly discussed in the public arena. Whatever else it is, the reader will find that this book is not a tract. There are no preconceptions to be proven, no axes to grind.

My interest in the politics of birth control began as a young newspaper reporter in Springfield. I am grateful to Don Herzberg, then director of the Eagleton Institute of Politics at Rutgers University, now dean of the graduate school of Georgetown University, for encouraging a reexamination in depth of the events that are recalled in chapter 3. Later, as a Washington correspondent, I had an opportunity to observe the operation of the Economic Opportunity Act and the evolution of federal population policy in

vii

the late 1960s. Then in 1975 it was my special good fortune to receive a fellowship at the Institute of Politics in the John F. Kennedy School of Government at Harvard. Fellows are turned loose to roam the classrooms, libraries and faculty offices of that remarkable educational institution in pursuit of whatever interests them. Most of the cerebration for this project occurred and the actual writing started there.

I am indebted to Jonathan Moore, Janet Fraser, Elizabeth Fainsod, Graham Allison, and Elihu Bergman at Harvard. Thanks is also due Representative Paul Simon, John Reidy, Victor de Grazia, Douglas Mackintosh, Dr. Charles Arnold, Jeannie Rosoff, the late Paul Tillett, Dr. Gary London, my wife Barbara, and many others for their extraordinary assistance along the way.

More than the customary expression of gratitude is owed the publishers of this book. The role that the Catholic church plays in the scenes that follow is less than a heroic one. But Jim Langford, the director of the University of Notre Dame Press, encouraged my project and assisted me at every step of the way. The spirit of free discusson is alive and well at Notre Dame, and I am grateful.

CHAPTER 1 Introduction

How many voters there are, where they are, and how they are bunched together or scattered around can help to explain how some groups of Americans are able to exercise more influence in public affairs than others. In a more-or-less freely operating representative form of government, the birth rate is the Dow Jones index of elective politics. It was that way in the Boston of Honey Fitz and Mayor Curley. And it is that way today. Witness the recent statement of a highly regarded young black spokesman, Julian Bond of Atlanta, who said he was looking forward to the time when "we may, as we are about to do, take over the major cities of this country and hold them as enclaves against increasing repression, charging admission fees to suburban whites who must come to the city for jobs and income and who must depend on the city as a source of police protection and utility service."[1] Mayor Richard Hatcher in Gary and Cesar Chavez in the lettuce fields of California are as capable of understanding the arithmetic of representative government as the long-departed politicians of Tammany Hall.

School children are introduced to the classical elements of political demography woven through the fabric of American history almost as soon as they master finger painting and dusting the erasers. The red-skinned inhabitants of North America were shoved aside, cheated and mistreated by the first white settlers, some of whom purchased black slaves from Africa to do their most disagreeable work for them. This is as much a part of the national heritage as Lexington and Valley Forge. In an immigrant

1

nation that fought a destructive civil war over the slavery question, it is not strange at all that the most intense social and political struggles should be racial or ancestral ("ethnic") in nature. The competition for supremacy in the largest cities between the "native Americans," Puritans at first, and the more fertile Catholic immigrants from Europe is an epic illustration of that conflict. Recently arrived immigrant groups joined with their hated puritanical competitors to enforce a blatantly discriminatory immigration system that reflected their shared prejudices against Orientals, swarthy southern Europeans and other less readily assimilated peoples. Once the southern Negro was freed, instead of deporting him, which would have caused a severe dislocation of the low-cost labor supply, the states of that region simply excluded him from any participation in the political processes. All across the country, meanwhile, public officials deliberately distorted, or "gerrymandered," representative districts to foster the values of the virtuous and check the power of potential sources of venality. Although the Constitution explicitly guaranteed equal protection under law, the courts steered clear of this "political thicket."

Of all the many facets of population politics, the most fundamental is concerned with the social institutions and public policies that regulate reproduction. Within the confines of political subdivisions, the relationship between numbers of people and their electoral weight is a natural one. If there were a lot of Catholic voters in Philadelphia, for example, the voice of their church would be louder there than elsewhere. On the other hand, if Negroes concentrated in the Mississippi Delta, or Mexican immigrants in Texas, could not vote, much less run for elective office, their power would be minimal. In this young nation, thriving population growth meant more workers and more consumers; it was very good for business. In such a big country, there was plenty of room for expansion; ample supplies of labor and customers made the economy hum along nicely.

From the beginning, the values of the American family were uppermost. Public policy honored and incorporated the opposition of churches, particularly the Roman Catholic church, to "artificial" contraception. Laws were enacted making it illegal to sell or use contraceptives, or to tell anyone else about them. In some cities, birth control clinics were raided by the police. Municipal hospital doctors in New York and Chicago, cities with large Catholic populations, were prohibited from prescribing a birth control device for any patient, regardless of the religious beliefs of doctor or patient; nor could the doctor tell the woman where she could go for assistance.

Toward the end of the 1950s the dynamics of population and fertility control politics began changing dramatically in the United States. The white majority perceived a need to "help" racial minorities control their fertility. Following behind, public officials were converted over the next decade to a cautiously sympathetic appreciation of the need for government programs of birth control assistance to the poor and uneducated. How and why that happened is the central theme of this book. For many years, while blacks and other lower-class minorities were being systematically dealt out of the electoral processes, the Catholic church played an important role in the political involvement of Catholic ethnic groups, especially in the urban centers such as Philadelphia, New York, and Chicago that (because of their size) were so influential in state and national politics. One of our focal points, therefore, will be the interaction of the church, as accustomed political force. and the black population, as emerging political force.

There is no single unified population policy in the United States and never has been. Congress and the executive branch sidestepped every opportunity to impose some direct coordinated population policy on so pluralistic a society. This is not to ignore the countless indirect policies at the federal, state, and local levels: public school education is supported not by user fees but by general taxes . . . income taxes are higher for single than for married people . . . tax exemptions are based on the number of dependents in the family . . . wives working outside the home pay social security payroll taxes but do not qualify for equivalent retirement benefits . . . federally insured mortgage loans were responsible for much of the post-World War II growth of the suburbs . . . the metropolitan segment of the interstate highway system encouraged the dispersal of central city employment . . . unlocking the doors of state mental hospital wards has increased the fertility rates among patients. There are many other examples of population-related policies.

Still there is no unified policy. What is wrong with the existence of this nonpolicy—besides the unwillingness of politicians to face up to it—is the compartmentalizing of most of the academic inquiry. The Public Health School ponders infant mortality figures. The Business School delves into the economic growth implications. Physical scientists fret over the damage to the ecosystem. Sociologists and statisticians tinker with other pieces, but hardly anyone is fitting them all together into a clear picture.

In attempting to do that, we will be exploring issues that politicians do not ordinarily orate about in legislative arenas or at party rallies except in stainless clichés. Whether and how the government should concern itself with the reproductive practices of its people has never been the sort of topic that an elected official tackles enthusiastically. Family planning policymakers and professionals have been reluctant to irritate the leading "funding sources," foundations and government agencies.

Fertility control and population policy are far too important nonetheless to be left entirely to demographers, theologians, ecologists, and the galaxy of interest groups formed on all sides of the subject. Demographers are so often immersed in their statistical data, their cohort analyses and projections, and their technical jargon, that the practical significance of what they are doing slides past most of us. Indeed, the raw material of their studies—which is the number of babies that couples have—is so personal and sensitive that the discussion of fertility control policy has been monopolized by zealots of equal determination in either direction. A Catholic Right-to-Life chapter and the Ford Foundation approach population control with roughly the same degree of detachment. Little that is both objective and understandable seeps through to the public at large.

The general citizenry could scarcely have known very much about a population debate that seethed sporadically in the pages of *Science* magazine and at academic and medical meetings in the late 1960s and early 1970s. None of the contents entered the mainstream of the day's political rhetoric. The pages of the *Congressional Record* were not filled with arguments for and against the "delivery" of contraceptives to the poor. Some political scientists have since suggested that a coalition of insiders—the so-called population lobby, which consisted of like-minded government officials, wealthy foundations and philanthropists, demographers, and other population scientists—deliberately kept the debate within self-construed bounds of political feasibility that would not threaten their own preoccupation with making contraceptives more available to more people.[2] According to this thesis, the economic elite employs the expertise and symbols of science to spread the impression of a "contented consensus" while suppressing any consideration of solutions that are deemed unrealistic.

Objections to this single-minded concentration on the mechanics of contraception were founded on three quite different concerns. First, there was the moral criticism of a policy that holds down births, the traditional Catholic position which denies the existence of either a macro or micro population problem. Another view is represented by the demographers Kingsley Davis and his wife Judith Blake who argued that Americans will not be persuaded to have smaller families voluntarily until there has been fundamental social change beyond technology. Observing that "a class-directed birth control program, whatever its intent, is open to charges of genocide that are difficult to refute," Blake saw the government policy as a response to "an ill-concealed mandate from the well-to-do."[3] Challenging the assumption that excess fertility was due to births that couples would have preferred to avoid, she cited opinion polls which indicated that the poor wanted larger families and were unenthusiastic about birth control. Blake recommended a *lifting* of pressures to reproduce—by changing the occupational roles of women ("the social organization of reproduction")—rather than an *imposition* of pressures *not* to do so. That the poor have large families for reasons other than the mere unavailability of contraceptives was not a novel thought. Sociologist Lee Rainwater's interviews, for example, persuaded him that the poor have a different concept of time: they are so occupied with the problems of obtaining food and shelter today that they do not easily focus on or worry about the future. The long-range implications of having another mouth to feed, five or ten years from now, are too remote to command much systematic attention.[4] Other studies have examined the psychological satisfactions of childbirth to a mother who is troubled and alienated from society. A third dissenting position was registered by the previously mentioned political scientists who faulted the population establishment for locking the Environmental Radicals out of the debate. Implicit in their criticism was the more radical assumption that some type of government coercion would eventually be necessary to curb excessive population growth.

While the scholars quibbled, it is clear that public attitudes about birth control assistance for the ignorant and the poor continued on a shifting course that had begun changing as far back as the 1930s. In her *Science* article, Blake cited a Gallup Poll in 1937 which showed that over two-thirds of the American people approved having the government make birth control information available to married couples desiring it. In the 1950s and 1960s, many "good" Catholics disregarded their spiritual training by using contraceptives themselves. According to one interesting survey conducted in 1967, a majority of Catholics viewed population growth in the United States as a serious problem, whereas a majority of American Jews did not.[5] In the same study, 86 percent of the respondents, including a large majority of Catholics, favored the easy access of birth control information to married persons.

The reasons for the growing acceptance of a government-supported birth control program targeted at the poor and less-educated range across a vast spectrum. Because this is a subject upon which all do not speak their true minds, we can only speculate about true motives. For whatever their reasons, humanitarian and bigot can find room under the same tent, while the poor and the powerless are left standing outside.

At the top of the rationality scale, it might be said, is the Equal Opportunity Concept. Americans who can afford to pay their own medical bills usually have the capacity to regulate the births of their children, but the poor suffer untold undesirable consequences and are dragged down further by their inability to control the size of their families. This is the logical public health ideal based on maternal and child health considerations that are difficult to challenge when put forward by a demonstrated humanist-idealist. Historically, this hard core of support for organized birth control has been bolstered in the United States by elements of the very rich who fear that the capitalist system would be threatened by lower-class overpopulation.

Next is the Quality-of-Life argument put forth usually by those who are comfortably fixed and worried over metropolitan overcrowding, the shrinkage of pollution-free open space available for recreation, and the global population crisis. These are middle-class Americans who want to conserve their values and preserve social stability. Some feel endangered by lower-class black proliferation in the cities, a category that would encompass many urban Roman Catholic constituencies. Others approach the subject on a more intellectual plane: it is in the community interest for individuals to have fewer children, they maintain, and it may be that the community will some day have to police the size of families. A few are sincerely sickened by the world population-hunger problem, and want the U.S. to set a good example for the rest of the world, even though this is a food-exporting nation with serious overpopulation only in a few metropolitan centers.

At the lower end of the spectrum (by my calculations at least) are the eugenic engineers who are convinced that undesirables—blacks particularly—are propagating wildy, that they won't support themselves out of sheer laziness, and that this expanding "underclass" is determined to transfer wealth from productive workers to parasitic loafers.

I suspect that the actual motives of most Americans are more a blend of the above than we are willing to admit even to ourselves. So long as poor health and comparatively high death rates held the securely segregated lower-class minority populations in check, the voters preferred not to be reminded of birth control politics; it made most of them uncomfortable.

That era came to an end during a succession of social earthquakes that shook the landscape. Supported by the federal courts and a series of monumental civil rights decisions, black people and other minorities demanded equal opportunity and then some, to make up for decades of past discrimination. Congress passed the Voting Rights Act of 1965, which made it possible for more blacks, and then more citizens of Latin American origin, to participate in the political processes. The authority of the federal government shielded them from the demonstrated retaliatory genius of the white majority in those states.

Under the Economic Opportunity Act of 1964, the war on poverty, federal "community action" funds were used to coach the poor to take full advantage of their eligibility for public assistance payments. In a time of generally high employment and economic vitality, Aid to Families with Dependent Children, the largest of the federally assisted welfare programs, increased rapidly.

In the meantime, white families carried on with their mass exodus from the central cities to the expanding suburbs, leaving behind a rearguard of troubled, predominantly black, low-income urban dwellers. In New York, Chicago, Detroit, Philadelphia, St. Louis, Baltimore, Cleveland, and other commercial centers, the black population multiplied both because of natural increase and movement from the rural South. Better jobs and higher welfare payments spurred the migration of Negroes from Mississippi to Chicago, from Alabama to New York City. The gulf between separate but unequal societies widened—one poor and black and urban; the other affluent and white and suburban. Out of all proportion to reality, white citizens agonized over the excesses of a welfare class that was thought to be propagating wildly in untended urban seedbeds of rampant crime, dependency, and other variations of social pathology. With the black population segregated in the central cities, Julian Bond's goal of mobilizing black voters to take political control of communities they were permitted to live in, and to claim fair representation in legislative bodies, conformed to the accepted American Way. The Supreme Court's one-man-one-vote edict meant that rural representatives no longer could dominate federal and state legislatures, the final step in the long-delayed shift of power away from the small towns and farms. While blacks, Puerto Ricans, and Chicanos were migrating to northern cities, whites flocked to the "Sun Belt," booming communities in Florida, California, Arizona, Texas. Jobs and investment capital moved South, too, to regions where labor unions were not yet entrenched. Over the years, congressional committee chairmen from the one-party South had located federal projects in their districts, stimulating economic growth. Although welfare standards were higher in New York and Detroit, per capita income rose at a faster rate in Charlotte and Little Rock.

Other social currents converged. Less complicated and more reliable methods of preventing pregnancies were developed. Couples learned how to control the size of their families. Unmarried men and women could indulge in sexual intercourse with much less danger of unplanned pregnancy. Adult women refused to be content with their traditionally subservient occupational roles. The Supreme Court read the Constitution as giving women the right to terminate a pregnancy in the early stages by submitting to a surgical operation; the state could not interfere with this demonstrably efficient if morally arguable method of birth control. The authority of the institutional church declined. No longer could the Catholic church enforce its ban on contraception for many of its parishoners. Standards of behavior washed away. Society bubbled turbulently.

Many thoughtful Americans, moreover, were now expressing a concern that the national population could not keep on growing at prevailing rates without affecting the comfortable lives of the metropolitan middle class. In fact, birth rates had been falling. More couples were electing to have two-child instead of three-child-and-more families. Many others were waiting longer before having their babies. Even with smaller families, though, the population would continue to increase, if only because the many children of returned World War II veterans were themselves about to reach the age of motherhood. Metropolitan congestion and a new awareness of the hazards of polluted air and water inspired various growth limitation proposals, a reversal of the growth philosophy that was presumed to have Made This Country Great.

This desire to protect natural beauty, provide more space for recreation, and keep land-use regulation close to home where the economic power of the dominant majority is more reliable, coincided with the desire to help the urban poor control their births.

The impetus to increase birth control programs in urban areas grew at just about the same time that black leaders, disenfranchised until recently, were expressing interest in "taking over" the big cities and "holding them as enclaves against increasing repression." Whites had an interest of their own in protecting their downtown commerical investment without having to pay the "admission fees" that Julian Bond mentioned. One way of doing this was to encourage more birth control. Another was to do what they could to minimize the effectiveness of minority voters.

After the Voting Rights Act was passed, public officials throughout the South tried to manipulate the artifacts of representative government (e.g., how legislative districts are cast, how municipalities annex surrounding territory in biracial metropolitan areas). In the "new politics of population" there are obvious relationships between evolving fertility control policy and such issues as the double standards of morality in sex education, and

the procedures and regulations governing voluntary sterilizations. Beyond that, it may be that we can arrive at a truer understanding of the political climate that nurtured Louisiana's national model family planning program, one that was directed
primarily at blacks, by reviewing how city council districts are
drawn in New Orleans (denying fair representation to blacks).

The voting rights law was an important population-related statute enacted at about the same time Congress was attaching special priority to the family planning projects administered by the
Office of Economic Opportunity. Another was the Immigration
Reform Act of 1965, which did away at last with the selfishly
motivated national origins quota system, altering patterns of immigration. Soon thereafter, immigration from neighboring
Mexico became a controversial issue. For many years, Mexicans
flowed freely across the border, satisfying a demand for cheap
labor in the fields and back shops of the Southwest. However,
when Cesar Chavez and others started organizing farm workers
into labor unions, and Chicano voters were mobilized for political
action, new concerns were heard. Mexican immigration had to be
curbed. More had to be done to prevent illegal aliens from taking
scarce jobs in this country. The AFL-CIO demanded restrictions
against the employment of illegal aliens, but the Catholic church
opposed deportations that would separate families already in the
United States. The birth rate among Mexican Americans and
Puerto Ricans in this country has always been much higher than
the average among both whites and blacks. Compared to urban
whites, the marital fertility rate of Mexican Americans in 1957-60
was 51 percent higher; for Puerto Ricans living in the U.S. it was
20 percent higher; for blacks living in the North it was 13 percent
higher; for black Americans as a whole 24 percent higher.[6]

The strange electoral college method of electing a president
in the United States—actually a series of separate state
elections—places a premium on so-called voting blocs, groups of
similar voters who vote alike for much the same reasons. What
makes the electoral vote system unrepresentative is that all of a
state's votes (based on the number of senators and representatives in Congress) are awarded to the candidate who wins in that
state, even if he wins by a single popular vote. The votes of a
thousand black citizens in Ohio, therefore, are of considerably
more importance than those of a thousand black cousins in Kan-

sas. Why? In both states, nine out of ten probably supported the Democrat. But in Ohio their voting strength may tip the balance and give Ohio's larger number of electoral votes to the Democratic candidate, whereas in Kansas, where there are not as many black residents (or as many Democrats), their votes will most often be submerged by a white Republican majority. Within the national Democratic party in recent years the claims of black leaders for recognition and rewards were enhanced by the heavily Democratic "black vote" in large, closely contested and therefore pivotal states. In the presidential election of 1976, newly enfranchised black voters in some southern states as well as some of the northern industrial states were credited with the margins of victory for the first president from the Deep South since before the Civil War—James Earl Carter. The big states where the "black vote" can be crucial—New York, New Jersey, Pennsylvania, Ohio, Michigan, Illinois—happen to be among those in which Catholic European ethnic groups once could turn a national election around. Where groups of like-minded voters live and vote, comparative population growth, and patterns of migration from one state or region to another can change the balance of national power, though not overnight certainly.

Out of such dull stuff as birth rates, immigration quotas, sterilization guidelines, zoning ordinances, and redistricting maps, the fascinating New Politics of Population comes alive.

CHAPTER 2 Prelude to Change
Black Birth Rates . . . and
the Powerhouse

The Puritans who got to the shores of New England first did not want a lot of unpleasant foreigners coming along and taking over their country. And they were not bashful about saying so. There were no antidefamation leagues or Sons of Italy organizations around then. Contemporary Yankee sentiment shortly before the Civil War can be illustrated by this quotation from a book about the dangers of immigration:

> Rapid propagation . . . preserves and perpetuates the habits, customs, peculiarities and distinctive characteristics of the immigrants. . . . The foreign element will, at no very distant day, infuse itself into every department of the government and warp and bias its direction. The horde of foreign immigrants is pressing upon us. Shall we close the portals of entrance? Or shall we curtail their political power and privileges?[1]

E. L. Godkin commented similarly in the pages of the *Nation:*

> The purses of the rich cities are everywhere passing into the hands of the ignorant, the vicious, and the depraved, and are being used by them for the spread of political corruption, for the destruction of the popular faith in political purity, for the promotion of debauchery and idleness among younger men of the poorer classes.[2]

Although the struggle dragged on into the next century, the Yankees could neither close the portals nor curtail the political power of the immigrants. The competition between them set the ethnic framework for American political behavior to this day.

Colonial families were sizable, averaging about eight children, although many of the youngsters died at a young age. Succeeding generations of New Englanders had much smaller families. In the fertility contest, the Protestants were no match for the newcomers. By the early 1900s, a majority of the school children in the big cities were of foreign-born parents, auguring the future course of urban power and privilege. Some of the early birth control crusaders contended that the Catholic clergy fought so hard to suppress contraceptive services in order to enlarge its parish rolls and nourish its political power.[3] If it is assumed, however, that most of the Catholic faithful would obey the dictates of their church anyhow, making it possible for more non-Catholics to practice birth control effectively would only widen the numerical gap between them.

Their common agreement that the dissemination of contraceptive information and materials should be branded an obscene and therefore criminal act made strange under-the-bedfellows of Puritanism and its archfoe, the Catholic clergy. Compared to the northern European countries from whence came many of the immigrants, Catholicism in the U.S. developed a moral code in some ways more puritanical than the principal Protestant denominations. Fornication, the temptations of the flesh, represented evil in the eyes of the Puritans. Catholics believed artificial birth control to be contrary to God's law, an immoral interference with the family. There would be many other social issues to divide them, but backwoods Protestant fundamentalists cooperated with urban Catholic parishes to impose ascetic standards of sexual morality on a young nation of many differing cultural strains. Puritanism, in the person of the founder of the Committee for the Suppression of Vice, Anthony Comstock, demanded the passage of laws in 1873 that banned the mailing or shipment from abroad of contraceptive literature and appliances. There was adequate precedent in English common law for treating the discussion of birth control as obscenity, even though human knowledge is seldom kept buried for long by force of any kind of law.

The federal courts chipped away at Comstock's laws over the years, and by the 1930s most of the provisions had been effectively abrogated. In a law suit labeled *U.S.* v. *One Package of Japanese Pessaries,* it was decided that the government could not prevent physicians from prescribing contraceptives for legitimate medical reasons. The recurring legal controversy itself undoubtedly helped spread information. Comstockery did have the effect, however, of making it more difficult for the uneducated lower classes to learn about and obtain birth control assistance.

Running against the tide of human behavior as they did, the federal laws and the miniature Comstock statutes enacted subsequently by twenty two states were observed and enforced irregularly. Even in Massachusetts and Connecticut, the states with the most stringent laws against the use of contraceptives, diaphragms were available to women who knew about them and could afford to pay a doctor who would prescribe them. At the same time though, government and the medical profession studiously considered the child-bearing habits of the lower classes none of their business. The Catholic church insisted on it.

Elected officials at all levels of government had enough problems without inviting the retribution of the politically uninhibited Catholic hierarchy. Candidates saw no profit in an issue that could only incite one or another segment of the electorate. In New York City, politicians called the church "The Powerhouse." In smaller communities as well, private birth control clinics sometimes were closed by the police. Catholic charitable organizations pressured community funds and welfare councils to exclude Planned Parenthood. Catholic hospitals dismissed from their staffs Protestant doctors who dared become affiliated with Planned Parenthood associations. As recently as 1961, a pharmaceutical company was forced to withdraw an advertisement for contraceptive products that showed two women talking over a back fence and contained this advice: "Don't plan your family over the back fence."[4]

Even though the anti-birth-control laws had been whittled away by judicial decree, and weren't consistently enforced anyway, legislators were reluctant to take the symbolic step of actually repealing them. In 1942 and again in 1948 there were bitter referendum campaigns to remove the statutory restrictions in Massachusetts. From the pulpit, Catholics were reminded of their duty to "defend the law of God and turn back the attempt to thwart the purpose of marriage."[5] Both repeal efforts failed. Invariably, whenever the issue was raised in the open, general public opinion drifted toward a more permissive policy. After a while, nevertheless, Massachusetts Republicans discovered that a referendum on birth control always brought out the Catholic (read Democratic) vote and complicated their difficulties up and down the ballot. So they lost stomach for any more showdowns. Regardless of the church's local influence, or lack of same, a typical member of Congress wanted nothing more than for the controversy to disappear. "The subject is embarrassing, that's all. Whatever you do, don't get mixed up in any sex stuff," one of them groaned.[6] (President Gerald R. Ford had occasion many years later, in 1975, to remind his wife Betty of that political axiom after she had discussed their daughter's sex life on a television program, touching off a storm of criticism from the American Heartland, but enhancing Ford's popularity among young people.)

But there were always a few crusaders who would not let the controversy subside. Margaret Higgins Sanger was perhaps the best known and most influential of these, the sixth of eleven children fathered by an Irish-born stonecutter who lived to be eighty. Her mother died at forty eight, a victim, Margaret thought, "of my father's passion." A true pioneer of the feminist movement, she preached that "the marriage bed is the most degenerating influence in the social order," and urged her sisters to "look the whole world in the face with a go-to-hell look in the eyes." As a young nurse on the Lower East Side of New York, Margaret heard a familiar complaint from the pregnant women in the neighborhood—"it's the rich that know the tricks." She devoted herself thereafter, from 1912 until World War II, to the cause of birth control for the poor. And, until his death in 1915, Comstock devoted himself to the harassment of Mrs. Sanger for violations of "his" laws. After he was gone, the Catholic church took over the role of her antagonist. Mrs. Sanger thrived on controversy. She relished being in the center of public commotion.

Try as she might, Mrs. Sanger could not undo the birth control laws even as the Great Depression of the 1930s swelled the ranks of the poor. The American Federation of Labor opposed birth control proposals because of the impact that declining birth rates might have on new construction and building trades jobs. Mrs. Sanger argued in return that large families were aggravating the heavy financial cost of poor relief. According to one account, Speaker of the House Sam Rayburn of Texas was "brought to his feet with enthusiasm'' when a discussion of birth control focused on rural southern Negroes. ''Now you're really talking, when you're getting birth control to them,'' he is said to have exclaimed.[7] Despite such scattered spurts of inspired interest, plus the wholehearted idealistic support of the president's wife, Eleanor Roosevelt, the U.S. Public Health Service did not become involved in birth control programs until the onset of World War II, when it occurred to government leaders that unwanted pregnancies would interupt the badly needed work of women in war industries. That was the rationale behind PHS's half-speed action.

Early in her own career, Margaret Sanger was a radical socialist. Radical doctrine then held opposition to birth control to be a capitalist-papal conspiracy designed to preserve abundant supplies of (1) underpaid laborers and (2) worshipers. By 1920, however, her movement had attracted the support of the wealthy suburbanites who would constitute the future cadre of the Planned Parenthood Federation of America. Her distress turned to the large families that the lower classes were producing. Having been introduced to eugenics by her close friend the sexual psychologist Havelock Ellis, she warned of the problems caused by ignorant, unclean immigrants from southern and eastern Europe. She now considered ''the chief issue of birth control'' to be the goal of ''more children from the fit, less from the unfit.'' In 1922 she said that if society regulated reproduction as efficiently as stockbreeders did there would be no need for programs that were ''fostering the good-for-nothing at the expense of the good.''[8] One of the officers of the National Committee on Federal Legislation for Birth Control, the lobbying organization that she directed, added that he was in favor of birth control because ''my family on both sides were early colonial and pioneer stock, and I have long worked with the American Coalition of Patriotic Societies to prevent the American people from being replaced by alien or Negro stock, whether it be by immigration or by overly high birth rates among others in this country.''[9] Her movement, as David Kennedy has spelled out in an excellent book that rearranged Margaret's halo a bit, changed from ''a radical program of social disruption to a conservative program of social control.''[10] Birth control would rescue the rest of society from the prolific poor.

Social control, since Reconstruction, has been associated most often with race. Hunger and deprivation threatened the social order in the Depression. But the mass migration of the American Negro from southern cottonfields to northern city sidewalks took the race problem to the North with special urgency during and following both World Wars. Urban black ghettoes burst their seams in the 1950s, spilling over into other sections of the cities. Old Catholic neighborhoods were transformed almost overnight, and with them the politics of the older big cities of the East and Midwest.

Because black population figures are subject to so much myth and misunderstanding, some statistical perspective is essential. Not long after the American Revolution the ratio of blacks to whites in the U.S. population was higher than it is now or ever has been. By the time of the Revolution there already were 750 thousand Negro slaves in the original thirteen states. Lately, the nature of family living among field slaves on southern plantations has become the subject of scholarly revisionism. Although slave owners seldom worried themselves over the marital circumstances of their chattels, there is convincing evidence that the slaves endeavored under difficult conditions to maintain stable two-parent family relationships. Genovese refers to the "attempts of some masters to mate their slaves like cattle."[11] Where they occurred, slave marriages lacked legal sanction. Families were sometimes cruelly separated at the marketplace. Mothers could identify their children but frequently not the fathers of their children. No social stigma was attached to illegitimate births. In a slave family, obviously, the father could not easily carry the traditional responsibilities of parenthood. Variations of "extended" family units were formed to protect the young. Masters and their sons used Negro women spontaneously as concubines. In Virginia, slaves were bred for sale, an economic response to the halting of the slave traffic from Africa in the nineteenth century. It was not until the much later slave insurrections that the whites began to take steps to limit the growth of the slave population. We know that the number of slaves doubled with every generation prior to the Civil War, despite the cessation of slave traffic from abroad. We know that less than 400 thousand imported Africans had by 1860 become an American black population of more than 4 million. The fertility rate for blacks during this period is estimated at around 250 per thousand. In other words, one out of four black women of childbearing age gave birth in any given year.

In the early 1800s, the years before the Civil War, almost 20 percent of the U.S. population consisted of Negro slaves—one slave for every four whites. By 1900 that figure had dropped to 12 percent, which is still above the 11.2 percent counted in the 1970 census. Negro fertility rates dipped to around 100 per thousand by the 1930s Depression. Dismally poor health conditions account for the reduction in black births. According to sociologist Reynolds Farley, one out of five black males was infected with syphilis or gonorrhea in the 1930s.[12] Pellagra, a dietary deficiency disease, also caused sterility among black people.

In most northern cities the black death rate rose during the early 1900s while the birth rate was falling, resulting in a less than zero rate of increase. Accordingly, as the American frontier was pushing west, the proportion of blacks in the national population went down steadily to below 10 percent during the Depression years. Until the economic strain of the Depression, black family stability existed in both North and South, against formidable odds, according to the recent documentation of social historians.

The Negro matriarchy, the social tolerance of illegitimacy, and the prevalence of the "extended" black family did not end with emancipation, or with the urban migration. Often it was only the woman in the family who could find work as a lowly paid domestic servant, and it was the woman who supported the household. Precisely what family structure should be regarded as normal for the American Negro is itself a source of emotional argument among black and white sociologists. Daniel Patrick Moynihan, Harvard scholar, adviser to presidents in both political parties, and later a member of the U.S. Senate, ignited a furor in the 1960s by calling attention to "the unmistakable crisis" in the Negro family.

In any event, the black fertility rate shot back up after World War II, reaching 160 per thousand in the 1950s. One obvious cause of this was the improved health conditions that made lower infant and maternal death rates possible at last. Furthermore, black women started their childbearing earlier and had children more rapidly then than in the years immediately following emancipation. Of greater significance demographically was the decline in the death rate. Life expectancy at birth was forty-eight for a black in 1930. In 1966 it was sixty-four.

Births recorded as illegitimate are far more frequent among blacks. According to recent statistics, almost one-fourth of all black women bear their first child before their eighteenth birthday. Nearly half of all first births to blacks are recorded as illegitimate. Among women first married between 1965 and 1969, 5 percent of the white women and 32 percent of the black women who were sampled told the census bureau that they had given birth before being married. These numbers are substantially higher than for the previous generation. The National Fertility Study of 1965 reported that one-third of all black births in the previous five years were unwanted.[13]

Ten years later, in 1975, more than half the babies born in Washington, D.C., were illegitimate, the first time in any major U.S. city that more babies were born to women who were not married than to women who were. The national illegitimacy rate in that year was 47.1 percent among blacks, 6.5 percent among whites. At every income level, the black rate of illegitimacy was more than triple the white rate.

"There seems to be a greater tolerance in the black community for out-of-wedlock births, particularly among those who are low-income," observed Dr. Wendy Baldwin of the National Institute of Child Health and Human Development. "If you don't see so many opportunities ahead of you, you probably evaluate a pregnancy differently."[14]

Between 1960 and 1961 the black population increased by 431,000 or 2.57 percent, while the white population grew by 2,510,000 or 1.57 percent. The "rate of natural increase"—the excess of births over deaths—was 23 per 1,000 blacks, and 13.5 per 1,000 whites. The number of births was 32.9 per 1,000 blacks of all ages, and 22.7 per 1,000 whites of all ages.

As noted previously, fertility rates—that is, the rate of births to women between fifteen to forty-four—have been going down for all races in the United States. More women are waiting longer before marrying. More women are using contraceptives successfully. More women are working outside the home. More women are divorcing. Again on a per thousand basis, the fertility rate for whites dropped from 113.2 in 1960 to 82.4 in 1969; and for blacks from 153.5 to 113.6. Since 1961, the rate of natural increase in the black population went from 23 (per 1,000) to 15 in 1970 and 12.3 in 1973. During the same time frame, the decline for whites reached 7.5 in 1970 and 4.8 in 1973.

Here is an updating of the marital fertility figures cited at the end of the previous chapter, showing the changes in the 1960s compared to urban whites (using 1.00 as the rate for urban whites).[15]

	1957-60	1967-70
Black total	1.24	1.10
Northern black only	1.13	1.04
Puerto Rican in U.S.	1.20	1.31
Mexican-American	1.51	1.43

Percentage wise, black population is still increasing at a faster rate than the white population even though women in both races are not having as many babies, and even though the figures for Chicanos and Puerto Ricans living in the United States remain comparatively high. The gap between the higher nonwhite and the lower white fertility widened most among the least educated in the 1950s. For all races, total fertility in 1975 was only half the 1957 rate.

Between 1960 and 1970 the number of blacks in the national population increased from 18,871,831 to 22,672,570, a growth rate of about 20 percent, compared to an increase for the whites of about 12 percent. Five years later, in 1975, the black population was estimated by the census bureau to be 23,800,000, or 11 percent of the total. Black organizations made the "undercount" (the number of people missed) an issue after the 1970 census. The census bureau conceded afterwards that it had probably missed about 2.5 percent of the total population, or about 5.3 million people, and that blacks and the poor were disproportionately represented in the undercount. Congressional representation for the inner city, and an assortment of federal and state financial assistance formulas, are based on census data, so the magnitude of the undercount is of considerable importance. Despite the protests of black spokesmen, the census bureau insisted that it was unable to distribute the 2.5 percent undercount at regional and metropolitan levels.

Although life expectancy is still about seven years less for a black American, the higher growth rate of the nonwhite population is almost certain to continue until at least 1990. According to projections by Ernest B. Attah of Atlanta University, if white fertility soon drops to replacement levels (meaning no natural increase at all), and black fertility levels off more gradually so as not to reach replacement rates until after the year 2000, the black proportion in the national population at that time would be almost 30 percent. If both groups attain replacement level fairly soon, the black proportion would go from 12 percent to 14 percent by the year 2035 (because the present black population is considerably younger).[16]

Birth rates do not tell the whole story, of course. The movement of blacks from the rural South to the urban North, where they were forced to live in certain inner-city neighborhoods only, was just as important. As recently as 1910, nine out of ten lived in the South, most of them in the rural South. However, the need for workers in defense plants spurred the northward migration during World War I. Mechanization of southern farms and the fading out of the sharecropper system accelerated the trend. About 1.5 million blacks moved from the South to the North in the 1950s and again in the 1960s.

As of 1970, fully one-third of the black population lived in fifteen cities. New York City alone registered a net black migration gain of 435,840 in the 1960s. Even with the acknowledged undercount of blacks in the 1970 census, there were forty-eight cities with Negro populations of over 50,000. The growth of the black population in five big cities, measured by the percentage of total population in those cities, is shown in the chart below.

	1910	*1960*	*1970*
New York	1.9%	14%	21.2%
Chicago	2.0	23	32.7
Detroit	1.2	29	43.7
Cleveland	1.5	29	38.3
St. Louis	6.4	29	40.9

These happen all to be centers of commerce that were built by immigrants, many of them Catholic immigrants from Europe. For decades the Catholic church had been a prominent force in the affairs of each city. And although Comstockery might have been but a bizarre aberration in the social history of the nation, the other half of that coalition—the Catholic church—was both politically active and unrelenting in its opposition to the use of tax funds or tax-supported facilities for birth control services, even by non-Catholics.

In July of 1958 a gynecologist at Kings County Hospital, a tax-supported municipal institution in Brooklyn, endeavored to fit a patient with a diaphragm, then the most reliable contraceptive device. The woman was a Protestant and a diabetic. Two of her three children had been delivered by caesarian section. For many years the government of New York City and the Catholic archdiocese carried out an unwritten but well understood ban against any type of birth control assistance for anyone in the twenty municipal hospitals where almost half the city's babies were born.

You can't fight the archdiocese—the legendary Powerhouse— the doctor was warned by the city commissioner of hospitals, Dr. Morris A. Jacobs who ordered him not to go ahead with the procedure. An earlier series of articles in the *New York Post* had publicized the existence of the de facto regulation against birth control services. To the physician, Dr. Louis M. Hellman (who would later serve as the first director of population affairs in the U.S. Department of Health, Education and Welfare in the Nixon administration) and to the Planned Parenthood Federation of America, conditions seemed appropriate for making a political test of the case. For the next two months, while the controversy flared in the newspapers, Planned Parenthood mobilized the metropolitan non-Catholic community as it had never been mobilized before. The Protestant Council of clergymen, the New York Board of Rabbis, the American Jewish Congress, and the obstetrics department chiefs of all six of the city's medical schools were enlisted in the new coalition. To "do the job of social engineering that is going to guide this coalition," Planned Parenthood arranged for spokesmen who could present the arguments "less tiresomely and more effectively," according to Frederick S. Jaffe, an executive of the federation.

"We refrained from taking the easy course . . . and issuing press statements every other day, by having most of the statements made by others. Not only did it prove more interesting to the city editors and their public, it also showed to even the thickest ward-heeler in City Hall that the entire non-Catholic community was aroused. And when the entire non-Catholic community is really up in arms, City Hall often acts."[17]

The Catholic community, conversely, did not speak with one voice out of the Powerhouse as it often had in the past. *Commonweal,* the lay Catholic magazine, questioned the wisdom of the church's stand:

> It is evident that beliefs, teachings, attitudes and opinions have changed greatly for many people over the past several decades. Where consensus once existed, it no longer does. Or more correctly, it has shifted ground. Other citizens cannot expect Catholics to change their beliefs or their practices merely to conform to the new consensus. But neither can Catholics expect to control the beliefs and practices of others . . . . There are many sound and compelling reasons why Catholics should not strive for legislation which clashes with the beliefs of a large portion of society. In so doing, they do not only strain the limits of the community and considerably lessen the persuasive force of their teachings, but they almost inevitably strengthen, in the minds of non-Catholics, already present worries about Catholic power.[18]

In his subsequent analysis of the strategy used by Planned Parenthood, Jaffe thought the *Commonweal* article revealed "how some Catholics are aware what a terribly high price the Roman Church will have to pay for the continued use of its political power to maintain bans on contraception among non-Catholics. Certainly the price is *too* high, some Catholics feel, in terms of a desirable Catholic public posture, and in terms of the aspirations of Catholics for high public office."[19]

Eventually the New York City Board of Hospitals capitulated, voting eight to two to lift the ban on contraception. Dr. Hellman described the decision as "a turning point in American thinking on the subject."[20] Another student of the case, Professor Harry Giles of New York University, said the public officials thought they could "pull in our ears and close the doors and windows for a while, and it would all blow over. But it didn't. In fact, capital was made of the political hedging by a show of voters' strength, if I may bluntly call it that."[21]

The same principles were at issue, meanwhile, in a Washington controversy over the recommendation of a presidential commission that the U.S. supply birth control assistance as part of its foreign aid program to any friendly nation on request. President Dwight D. Eisenhower rejected the proposal, saying he could not "imagine anything more emphatically a subject that is not a proper political or governmental activity or function or responsibility."

At the end of 1959, the U.S. Catholic bishops issued a statement denouncing "the promotion of artificial birth control" as "a morally, humanly, psychologically, and politically disastrous approach to the population problem." In New York City, the archdiocese ordered Catholic doctors not to cooperate with the new policy there. The church evidently had no thought of voluntarily relaxing its grip on public policy: the power and resources of the government would not be utilized for the advocacy of birth control by anyone anywhere, if the church could prevent it.

By now there was a serious Catholic contender for the Democratic presidential nomination of 1960. John Fitzgerald Kennedy promised in that campaign always to put the national interest ahead of his personal religious principles. Conveniently for Kennedy, Eisenhower's statement helped to blunt the birth control policy question as an issue in the election of the nation's first Catholic president.

Came the dawning of the 1960s. The social climate was unsettled in the United States. Blacks were moving into and within the big central cities, cities that were being evacuated by middle-class whites. The civil rights revolution gathered momentum. Politicians and laymen alike were conscious of a developing "new consensus" in favor of making birth control assistance available to the poor at government expense. What happened thereafter can be illustrated by recounting the events in another urban state: Illinois.

CHAPTER 3 Illinois: The Politics of Church and State

On a pleasant September Sunday afternoon in 1962 the governor of Illinois accompanied the Roman Catholic archbishop of Chicago to the ceremonial blessing of a new parish center on the outskirts of the nation's biggest Catholic diocese. For the state's chief executive to appear at a public function with the most influential ecclesiastical leader in Illinois was in no sense peculiar. Traditionally, two No. 1 automobile license numbers were set aside in the state—official No. 1 for the governor's limousine, another No. 1 assigned to the Catholic prelate in Chicago, visible symbolic recognition of his power in the civil affairs of Illinois. For many years there had been a mutually beneficial working relationship between the Democratic party of Cook County and the then 447 parishes of the archdiocese representing almost 2,300,000 communicants. Buttressing the party organization were sturdy ethnic voting blocs, beginning with Catholics of Irish, Polish, Italian, German, Czech, Lithuanian, and other national backgrounds.[1]

There was, however, something distinctly extraordinary about the conversation that afternoon between Governor Otto Kerner and Cardinal Albert Meyer. Almost as an afterthought, while they were leaving the parish hall and strolling to the governor's car, Kerner asked the cardinal what he would think if the state of Illinois began supplying free birth control services to some of the forty-five thousand mothers whose children were supported by the Aid to Families with Dependent Children welfare program.

Cardinal Meyer was stunned by the question. Matters of public

25

policy did not ordinarily arise at parish center dedications. But Kerner was not your orthodox workaday machine politician. A proud, handsome, rather vain figure of a man, he had been a military officer and a judge in Cook County, the model showcase candidate the ward-heeling spoilsmen in the Chicago Democratic organization liked to put out front. Kerner was a Protestant. His grandparents were Czech immigrants and his father had been attorney general of Illinois. His wife was the daughter of his father's close friend, Anton Cermak, mayor of Chicago in the late 1920s and early 1930s, and a strong party leader. The Cermak and Kerner families were heroes to the Czechoslovakian voters of Cook County. Kerner's nomination for governor had been arranged by the then party boss, Mayor Richard J. Daley of Chicago. A forceful leader in the Cermak tradition, Daley assumed that Kerner would follow his orders amiably without any embarrassing public conflict. Once installed in office, however, the governor felt a need to establish his political identity and reinforce his standing outside Chicago by displaying a modicum of independence, without—of course—disturbing the stability of the party.

Startled by the inquiry, and preoccupied with his departure that very evening for Rome and the Second Vatican Council, all the cardinal could think to do was to refer the governor to the director of the diocesan Cana Conference, the church's marriage and family living agency. Cardinal Meyer was a scholarly theologian considerably more liberal than most of the clergy under him in Chicago. At dinners where politicians were present, he always tried to be flanked by priests at the table. In the cardinal's absence, the diocese would be left in command of a more seasoned politician-cleric, Monsignor George J. Casey, the Vicar General. An old-guard diocesan bureaucrat, Casey shared many of the conservative social attitudes of the Irish and Polish parishioners in the diocese.

Of crucial importance, Kerner came away from that day's conversation with the clear impression that the birth control balloon he had casually floated would not arouse the active resistance of the Catholic church.

He miscalculated. Before the matter would finally be settled two and a half years later, the Democratic party of Illinois would be subjected to the internecine strife that a multiethnic political party is always anxious to avoid; the entire public assistance program would be reorganized; and the new politics of birth control would be vividly played out on the public stage.

For several years before, the Planned Parenthood Association and the Church Federation of Greater Chicago, an inter-denominational Protestant council, had been endeavoring to upset an unofficial prohibition against contraceptive services in Cook County Hospital, the huge tax-supported institution operated by the county of which Chicago is the central city. In Chicago, the "charity" hospital system comparable to New York's municipal system was established by the county government. Although 65 percent of the patients were non-Catholic, the hospital superintendent would not permit Planned Parenthood to open a privately financed clinic on the premises. He insisted that birth control was a "socio-economic and not a medical problem." The Cook County Board of Commissioners refused even to hold hearings on the request.

Lately though, Planned Parenthood and churchmen of all faiths, among them the director of the Cana Conference, Rev. Walter Imbiorski, had commenced what they described as "dialogues" on birth control policy. The sessions resulted in the formation by a woman physician, Dr. Lonny Myers, of a committee called Citizens for the Extension of Birth Control Services. Meetings were arranged with representatives of the Cana Conference for the purpose, she said, of "simply wanting to make our motivations clear and avoid unnecessary misunderstandings." It was at this stage, Imbiorski later recalled, that he realized an "organized campaign" would soon be forthcoming. To "keep our ears out" in anticipation of the birth control campaign, Imbiorski assembled a strategy committee of his own consisting of the vice-chancellor of the diocese, the church's lobbyist at the state capital, and a delegation of legal and theological scholars from the Catholic universities in the Chicago area.

From the beginning of his term in 1961, Kerner's administration had been plagued by dwindling balances in the state treasury. State officials in both parties were alarmed by rising outlays for public assistance. AFDC alone was costing $12 million a month in Illinois. Within ten years the number of children on AFDC rolls had increased from 59,000 to 200,000. During 1962, 15,000 babies were born to public assistance recipients in Cook County Hospital, of which approximately 13,000 were recorded as illegitimate. Politicians fretted because they recognized that AFDC was perceived by many citizens as an unduly expensive dole for southern Negro migrants who were incapable of supporting themselves under the best of economic conditions. Mindful of this sentiment, Kerner vacillated in his public pronouncements between a vow that "businesslike" procedures and more efficient administration would put a stop to the waste; and, when his liberal advisers had his ear, an appeal to the legislature to "stop badgering the unfortunate and relatively helpless recipients of public aid."

Since 1931, public assistance had been administered in Illinois by a commission made up of seven unpaid citizen members appointed by the governor and confirmed by the state senate—no more than four from the same political party. Three ex-officio members (who happened now all to be Democrats) also served on the commission: the independently elected state auditor and state treasurer, and the state finance director appointed by the governor. The theory behind this bipartisan commission system of administration was that members who did not have to stand for election could function better as a buffer between the electorate and the needy but powerless poor.

His friend and generous campaign contributor, the wealthy Chicago industrialist Arnold Maremont, was chosen by the governor to be chairman of the Public Aid Commission. Maremont took the job with the understanding that he would be allowed to screen Kerner's other appointments to the commission.

Whatever else could be said about Maremont, he was not a hypocrite. In the course of accumulating his industrial empire he had managed to acquire a reputation in the business world for ruthlessness. Margaret Sanger, the birth control pioneer, was not a business tycoon, but some of the same adjectives were used to describe her—intemperate, uncompromising, arrogant, power-driven publicity hound.

There were some, no doubt, who may have been influenced by the fact that Maremont was Jewish. An organization that relies on a coalition of ethnic interests must balance its candidate slates and its patronage rewards with great care. And in the summer of 1962 many Democrats in the echelon below Daley were grumbling about the many Jews who had been endorsed for important offices (e.g., Rep. Sidney Yates to run against Sen. Everett M. Dirksen).

A few days after the conversation between the governor and the cardinal, Maremont met briefly with Imbiorski. The priest stated emphatically that the church could never hold still for the distribution of contraceptive materials to unmarried women. But Maremont was more interested in reading Imbiorski's mood and he judged (like Kerner had) that the church did not want a "head count" on the issue and would try to avoid a public confrontation.

Almost all the welfare funds for Chicago consisted of either federal or state aid channeled through the state commission. Maremont was determined, therefore, to strip the Cook County welfare director, Raymond Hilliard, of his nearly autonomous administrative power. Before coming to Chicago, Hilliard had been welfare commissioner in New York City but was forced to resign after a 1953 controversy over whether Planned Parenthood would be admitted to the metropolitan welfare council. "I got burned by Planned Parenthood," he explained later. "There were big fights and big mistakes. I resigned. I had to as a Roman Catholic. If I hadn't, I would have been fired." Having a welfare director who is wired in to the Democratic organization and to the chancery office was important enough in Chicago that Maremont's move against Hilliard exacerbated the birth control disagreement.

For chief administrative officer of the state commission, Maremont selected a career member of the staff, Harold Swank, a Protestant from a rural downstate county who was handicapped by his lack of first-hand exposure to metropolitan welfare problems.

When, at last, Maremont publicly announced his plan for a birth control program, Swank added the personal footnote that he thought sterilization should be available at state expense to those on welfare who wanted it and whose physicians considered it desirable. Mention of sterilization prompted the church's counter-strategy committee to mobilize for action. Monsignor Casey was consulted. Dr. William Brice Buckingham, a Chicago physician and the chairman of the Cana Conference, issued a statement attacking the planned program:

> The proposals for the State to involve itself actively in persuading the indigent, particularly Negroes and Puerto

Ricans, to reduce their numbers by making birth control and sterilization free and easy and acceptable are an invasion of individual liberties. . . . When the State pays for birth control services, it is in effect advocating these practices. This means agents of the State advising, suggesting and to some extent determining who shall have children and how many they are allowed.

One of Maremont's supporters on the commission, William L. Rutherford of Peoria, recommended in addition that the laws be changed to provide for the compulsory sterilization of any woman who bore, or any man who sired, more than one illegitimate child. Even before Buckingham's statement, the four Catholics who were among the ten members of the public aid commission denounced the "Maremont program." All the members of the commission received telegrams from Casey that he said were meant to "make the Catholic stand perfectly clear."

We object most vehemently to the use of public funds to subsidize the operation of an organized campaign of artificial birth control. We object most vehemently to making birth control the endorsed public policy of the welfare department of the State of Illinois. These policies ignore and dismiss the deepest convictions of a great segment, and perhaps a majority, of the citizens. They cushion injustice and tranquilize the social conscience.

[Promoters] of the program have recklessly stirred up public controversy [in their attempt] to bring about a sweeping change in public policy which is abhorrent to a substantial section of the population. . . . They have risked community strife to achieve their own sectarian goals while at the same time trying to blame others for the controversy.

. . . [The commissioners] carry a grave responsibility to the public good, even as the elected official who appointed them must bear full and certain responsibility to the public good and the electorate.

As politicians go, Kerner may have been unorthodox, but the scarcely veiled threat in that last sentence was not lost on him. The governor telephoned Maremont at once and asked if he thought it wise to go ahead. Maremont replied that it was too late to turn back.

One of the Catholic commissioners, James Ronan, was Daley's stand-in as state chairman of the Democratic party besides being Kerner's state finance director. He recommended as strongly as he could that the program be abandoned. Ronan felt, as did some others on the staff, that even if the objectives were meritorious they could be accomplished administratively with far less commotion. Maremont was accused of having a compulsive need to be constantly in the center of a storm, an allegation made often against Margaret Sanger. To the contrary, Maremont maintained that the quiet "administrative" approach was precisely how the church had been able to wield such influence behind the scenes. At any rate, Kerner did nothing to interfere. When the dust settled, he assured friends, the church hierarchy might be pouting but Catholic voters would not much care one way or the other. It was fully understood by Maremont that he would act as the lightning rod throughout and that the governor would remain publicly disassociated from the conflict as best he could.

While the public debate continued, proponents and opponents organized letter-writing campaigns and other forms of pressure. Much the same as in the New York controversy, Planned Parenthood played a coordinating role, leading the forty-some social service and other organizations that were rounding up support. State Treasurer Francis Lorenz, an ex-officio commissioner and of Polish-American parentage, attended a mass in his own church at which the priest instructed parishioners to write letters and asked Lorenz, from the pulpit, to explain where the letters should be sent.

A few black leaders helped in the Negro community. But neither now nor later did any broadly based pressure develop that would make it necessary for Democratic aldermen and committeemen in the black wards to move either way. In Chicago, the South Side ward committees answered to their longtime leader, Rep. William L. Dawson. They were highly practical politicians, not social reformers. The typical Negro precinct captain knew only that the Catholics were quite sensitive about the subject and it would be prudent to stay on the sidelines. Besides, the absence of easy birth control meant more opportunities to do more favors for more voters. The lethargy among South Side interest groups puzzled Planned Parenthood. "We were constantly confounded," one of the association officials recalled later, "by the fact that they [the Negroes] did not seem to view the controversy as one in which they had an important stake. They did not see themselves discriminated against as a group by the denial of these services. Of course, they were deeply involved during this period in other more tangible pursuits of equal opportunity." Already some younger black leaders were beginning to view the entire venture as a plot to reduce the numbers of blacks, although this had not yet become a prominent part of the public debate.

Two months and ten days after the governor's conversation with the cardinal, the public aid commission voted six to four to legalize birth control services for welfare mothers who wanted the assistance. The four Catholic members voted no. A welfare birth control program had become public policy in Illinois over the opposition of: (1) the Catholic church; (2) all but one of the elected state officers; (3) the Democratic state chairman; (4) most of the governor's staff.

A few weeks later, however, in early January of 1963, the Illinois General Assembly convened for its biennial six-month session. The president pro tem of the senate, Arthur J. Bidwill, a Republican from suburban Cook County and a Catholic who was educated at the University of Notre Dame, pronounced the policy immoral and unconstitutional. He predicted ominously that Maremont would have great difficulty being confirmed by the senate for the chairmanship of the public aid commission. The chairman had been serving on an interim basis because the legislature was not in session at the time of his nomination.

Even more ominous (to Maremont) than Bidwill's warning was the introduction by Senator Morgan Finley, Democrat of Chicago, of Senate Bill 66. S.B. 66 would nullify the birth control policy by statutory enactment. Finley was more than a mere senator. He was Dick Daley's senator. His district near the stockyards in a white neighborhood on the edge of the black ghetto had once been represented in the state senate by Richard Daley. The mayor was considered Finley's political godfather; he was the mayor's protégé. Both men were Irish Catholics. When Finley spoke, other Democratic senators assumed they were listening to the words of the mayor.

Ronan, Lorenz, Bidwill, Finley. All Catholics. All determined that the Maremont policy not be carried out. How to explain such unity of purpose? Was someone coordinating their responses? Evidently not. One of those who participated in Imbiorski's strategy committee meetings was Claire Driscoll, an attorney for the archdiocese and for twenty-two years the legislative representative (lobbyist) for the Catholic Welfare Committee of Illinois. Bishops of the six Illinois dioceses were represented on this committee, which existed as an umbrella mechanism for making known the church's position on legislative issues. Driscoll did not engage in the intrigues that a race track lobbyist might. He carried no black bags, bribed no legislators. What he did do was represent the voice of the Powerhouse in Illinois.

On questions of moral conscience that involved Catholic principles, public officials of that faith tended to react instinctively in Illinois in the 1960s. This was especially true of those who were educated in Catholic schools. Discussing the case later, Driscoll insisted that Catholics in public office were troubled by the birth control issue and came to him for counsel, rather than the other way around. Finley explained it this way: "If you are a Catholic and reasonably intelligent you ought to be able to recognize that the church wants you to proceed in a certain way without signals being given." Imbiorski phrased it differently: "The role of the church is to form the consciences of these people. Then they go."[2] Hot lines between the chancery and the state house were unnecessary.

Nor has the church ever been as monolithic a structure as the powerhouse analogy leads us to believe. The pastor of a Polish congregation on the Northwest Side of Chicago might exercise considerable independence of the cardinal's office on most matters, including lay politics. In all his activities, Driscoll had to reconcile the views of the more conservative—indeed, even anti-urban—bishops of the downstate dioceses with those of the huge metropolitan archdiocese. Therefore, the stance that the church's statewide committee assumed in Springfield had to take into consideration the attitudes of the downstate bishops for whom public assistance and other big-city problems were remote.

Protestant clergymen were much less united in Chicago than they had been in New York. Historically, contraception had always been a difficult moral question for many American Protestant faiths, particularly Lutherans and Episcopalians. Shifting the marriage emphasis from procreation to companionship and sexual pleasure occurred only gradually and over many years. Some Protestant leaders were bothered, too, in earlier years by a concern that birth control would contribute to the shrinking birth rate of the Protestant "native American" stock.[3]

In the Illinois case, moreover, there was a moral dilemma posed by the state's subsidization of birth control services for the unmarried. Dr. Myers, founder of the organization that was promoting the extension of birth control services, offered this comment: "We all agree that the ideal way for women who do not live with their legal spouses to avoid pregnancies is to abstain from sex and divert their sexual drive into more constructive and socially acceptable channels, such as bridge parties, teas, and great book clubs. But what chances has an AFDC mother to attain this ideal? The result of our naive desire to settle for nothing less than abstinence is random reproduction and irresponsible parenthood."

Maremont, meanwhile, had several concerns to keep juggling. He had to hold intact his majority on the commission; rekindle the support of the hesitating Protestant and Jewish groups; convince Negro leaders that the program would benefit their people; prevent the Finley bill from passing the legislature and putting the governor in the unwelcome position of having either to sign it or veto it. And, finally, he had to keep the governor from changing his mind about the whole business.

What about Mayor Daley? Although Maremont talked once with Daley about the birth control question, there is no evidence that Kerner consulted the mayor before the program was initiated. During their single meeting, Daley suggested to Maremont in an offhand way that the expedient solution all around would be for Maremont to make a sizable contribution to Planned Parenthood for the operation of private clinics to serve welfare clients. Throughout the entire episode, Daley emerges as the consummate political leader, ever mindful of the complications of binding diverse ethnic constituencies together in a political organization. This was one of the secrets of Daley's seldom understood effectiveness. He was an expert at the oblique response. Maremont wants to give contraceptives to poor people. Maremont is rich. So why doesn't Maremont give a wad of dough to Planned Parenthood and not get messed up in the risky affairs of government? (Interestingly, President Kennedy took a similar tack in 1962 when the foreign aid birth control issue was topical. "Why doesn't the Ford Foundation concentrate all its resources on the population problem around the world?" he suggested to a visitor who was reporting on overpopulation in Brazil.)[4]

Finley understood well the necessity of not trying to advance his bill in the senate until after the April 2 mayoral election in Chicago. Daley was a candidate for reelection to a third term against Republican Ben Adamowski, a Polish Catholic who had been a Democrat earlier in his career. The mayor did not want the issue popping up in his own campaign.

Every Sunday afternoon during this period, Finley met to discuss tactics with Daley's administrative assistant, Ray Simon, who was active also in the Cana Conference. Before Finley was to make a speech before the influential City Club of Chicago about his opposition to the Maremont plan, for example, Simon helped him prepare and rehearse answers to the questions that would probably be asked. Simon also served on Imbiorski's strategy committee, so he was the convenient conduit from the church through the Cana Conference to Finley via City Hall and the interest that Daley and the Democratic organization shared in the controversy.

Unwilling to let the matter drag on until after the Chicago election was out of the way, Maremont demanded that the commission begin paying for contraceptive services just before the election. His timing angered Daley, who instructed Finley to press for passage of his bill immediately. "I'm for Finley's bill," the mayor declared at his press conference. "It's a forward step in parenthood legislation."

There weren't nearly as many Democrats and Catholics in the senate as there were Republicans and non-Catholics. So Finley willingly accepted an amendment restricting the services to married women living with their husbands. This concession did not please the downstate Catholic bishops because of its compromise with Catholic doctrine. But it did increase the chances of winning support from rural downstate Protestants. A bothersome complication for Maremont all along had been how to implement the program without repealing or violating a section of the criminal law which classified sexual intercourse with a female under age eighteen as contributing to the delinquency of a minor. By limiting the services to married women, that problem would be taken care of; but thousands of unmarried AFDC mothers, for whom the need was greatest, would be disqualified.

Daley won reelection, though by a smaller plurality than had been predicted. On the day before the election, Republican candidate Adamowski sued in the county courts for an injunction that would bar the public aid commission from dispensing contraceptives to unmarried women. On the day after the election, the Illinois attorney general, William G. Clark, a Chicago Democrat and a Catholic, intervened in the suit on Adamowski's side in his capacity as lawyer for the state auditor, Michael Howlett, an anti-Maremont ex-officio member of the commission. Clark issued a legal opinion that the Maremont plan was unconstitutional, whereupon Howlett announced that he would refuse to process state checks for the services to unmarried women. Maremont retained independent counsel, Thomas McConnell, the son of a Presbyterian minister, who alleged in court that Clark was "following the dogma of his own religion" rather than the Illinois Constitution. Clark protested angrily that he had been "accused of being a Catholic."

As such rhetoric was adding fuel to the argument, most Democratic professional politicians in Illinois wanted nothing more than for the dispute to go away. Newspaper readers were made aware that all Catholics on the public aid commission tried unsuccessfully to turn back a birth control program that the Democratic governor apparently wanted; that two state officials who were Catholics (Howlett and Clark) had then collaborated to stop it; and that the attorney general had been charged by a lawyer for Maremont with making public decisions according to the dictates of his religious faith.

By now Finley's bill had passed the senate, forty-two to five, and was pending in the house of representatives. But the prospects in that body were different—for an unusual set of circumstances not explained in most political science textbooks. Although two more Republicans than Democrats had been elected to the house, the Democratic governor might have arranged to peel away two or more semiloyal Republicans from the majority and install a minority Democrat in the speaker's chair. It had been done before in Illinois. Instead Kerner decided to throw his weight behind one of the several Republican candidates for speaker, one who promised as his part of the deal that no "hot" bills would be allowed to reach the governor's desk. Kerner told Maremont that the heat from the Finley bill was becoming unbearable. So Maremont saw to it that the Republican speaker, John Lewis, used his arbitrary powers as presiding officer to prevent the measure from being put to a vote.

Much earlier in the session, the senate confirmed the other public aid commissioners but deferred action on Maremont until after the Finley bill had been disposed of. Now that the legislation had cleared the senate, the nomination was approved, thirty-five to seven. Finley asked Daley whether he should vote to confirm Maremont. Not caring to prolong the controversy, Daley advised him to do so.

A short time later, the terms of two pro-Maremont members of the public aid commission expired. Kerner reneged on his promise to Maremont and filled one of the two vacancies with a Catholic physician who had testified against the birth control plans at the commission's hearings. The heat was beginning to get to the governor. He was balancing up the commission, an omen of trouble ahead for Maremont.

In the meantime the appropriation of funds for public assistance was nearly exhausted. Kerner had to plead with the legislature for a deficiency appropriation to continue welfare payments until the end of June when the new biennium would begin. The Republican majority in the senate demanded, however, that specific individual grant limitations be written into the legislation before the money would be allocated, a condition that Kerner and Maremont resisted. Whether to write into the law ceilings over individual family grants became an issue that threatened to snarl the legislature with more weeks of disagreement and delay.

Maremont was never one to submerge disagreements in gallons of gooey rhetoric, a trait often useful to play-acting politicians. On the contrary, he had a well-developed knack for provocative comments. A few weeks before, he confided to a newspaper interviewer that "many Catholics I know must be using birth control devices. I think it's strange that some of my Catholic friends have only one or two children, since I understand the rhythm method is not too reliable."

Upset now by the new conflict with the senate over statutory grant ceilings, he held a press conference at which he excoriated

. . . Republican senators who are getting even with

> Negroes on AFDC because the Negroes helped to elect
> Mayor Daley and are generally Democratic. Seventy per-
> cent of the people on relief are Negroes. Republican senators
> are anti-Negro and have set out to injure Negroes. If the
> recipients were white, there would be no problem. The
> Republicans want the backing of white citizens who feel
> taxes are too high, and they are using the Negro to get this
> support. It is cruel and inhuman and smacks of Hitlerism.

Such a blanket characterization of the Republicans in the Illinois senate as Hitlerian could not have been intended to smooth
troubled waters. But Maremont did not immediately recognize
the opening he had given enemies who were waiting in ambush.
Bidwill quickly discovered that formal notification of Maremont's confirmation had not yet been sent to the governor. By
changing its rules the senate would "de-confirm" Maremont
retroactively, an action without precedent in Illinois law. The
governor was warned by Bidwill, furthermore, that his entire
legislative program would be in jeopardy if he tried to salvage
Maremont. Smelling blood, Ronan and the Chicago Democrats
leaped on the prey.

Only one public official defended Maremont—and that was
Mayor Daley. Maremont ought to be forgiven, Daley said. "God
knows we all make mistakes. After all, we ask for forgiveness in
our prayers."

"Daley doesn't have to deal with the senate every day," the
governor told Maremont that evening. "I do." When Maremont
suggested that Attorney General Clark be persuaded as a loyal
Democrat to issue a legal opinion that the de-confirmation proceeding was illegal, which it probably was, Kerner said Clark
would not possibly agree to do that. "You don't understand,
Arnold," Kerner explained, "it's a religious question." Kerner
did nothing to save Maremont, and the chairman of the public aid
commission was expelled from the administration by *unanimous
vote* of the senate.

Within four months of the commission's decision to begin the
program, the state auditor had refused to make payments for
contraceptives to unmarried women, legislation to support that
refusal had passed one of the two houses of the legislature, and
the sponsor had been driven out of the government.

Since his return from Rome early in the year, Cardinal Meyer was kept apprised of the situation regularly by Imbiorski. The decision that he now had to make was whether to "mobilize the Catholic vote," as Imbiorski later put it, in an outpouring of pressure on Kerner and on the Republican speaker of the house that would overturn the program in its entirety and establish that birth control was not the public policy of the state of Illinois.

A priest at Loyola University in Chicago, Rev. John A. Rohr, wrote a timely article warning Catholics to employ the "large segment" argument only with their eyes wide open. In effect, this argument holds that birth control devices should not be distributed at public cost in Illinois because it is considered immoral by "a large segment" of the voting populace, namely the large number of Catholic taxpayers in Illinois.

> Obviously, the argument would be meaningless in North Carolina where there are few Catholics and where, incidentally, publicly supported birth control programs have taken root and flourished. . . . Such a [political threat as was made by Monsignor Casey to Kerner] would be absurd, if not foolhardy, in North Carolina or Arkansas. Thus, the real question for Catholic leaders in states similar to Illinois is whether to fight a holy war over birth control, a war in which their cause will probably triumph, or whether to acquiesce in the name of pluralism and ecumenism. The decision must be made on prudential grounds that will vary from state to state.[5]

In Illinois the church acquiesced—in steps. Against the advice of the downstate bishops, the cardinal decided against mobilization. Private citizen Maremont had one last tactic of his own in mind to try and keep the program intact. He floated a trial balloon proposal that signatures be obtained on petitions for a statewide public policy referendum at the 1964 election on the birth control proposition. Maremont suspected that the last thing the first Catholic president would want in a state he carried by only six thousand votes the first time would be a referendum on a religious issue. Maremont believed (incorrectly) that the White House would be so alarmed by the implications that the president would prevail on Daley and Kerner to back away from the issue. Again one can see how Maremont's plan of action (assuming it was he who sold Kerner on the idea in the first place) still theorized that neither the church nor the Democratic party would risk an above-board "head count" on birth control policy.

After nine weeks of deadlock, meanwhile, Kerner capitulated and accepted legislatively imposed ceilings over public aid grants. And, following Maremont's departure, a pending bill easily passed both houses and was signed into law dissolving the public aid commission. Many other governors before had tried to transfer public aid administration into a department directly under their control. At last the political conditions were ripe for it.

After those two bills were passed, a birth control compromise was worked out with Daley's help. For at least two years the program would be limited to married women living with their husbands. During that period, a bipartisan commission chaired by Finley would inquire into the "legal, social, moral, health, and financial implications" of birth control services for any welfare recipient. Thus the showdown would be deferred; any changes would occur gradually, less dramatically. Immediately the Chicago Board of Health began making referrals to Planned Parenthood clinics, something that had never been permitted before. And finally, after months of hearings, Finley's commission recommended legislation extending the services to any mother receiving public assistance, fifteen years of age or older, regardless of her marital status.

One Catholic state official who had been zealously defending the "Catholic position" remarked to another who had done the same: "Well, the boys in the black suits pulled the rug out from under us."

Finley said church officials "did a complete flipflop." After the controversy died down, he acknowledged in an interview that the episode awakened Catholic leaders of the Democratic organization to the political implications of racial birth rates. At one of the legislative hearings, Philip M. Hauser, a distinguished demographer at the University of Chicago who is usually identified with the aforementioned population establishment, testified about the comparative rate of natural increase in Chicago. In 1940 it had been higher for whites than nonwhites. Twenty years later, in the 1960 census, it was two and a half times higher for nonwhites. At this rate of increase, Hauser projected that the nonwhite population of the city would double every twenty-five years without in-migration. He said the nonwhite birth rate of Chicago in 1960 was only a point or two below that of India. In every way he could, Hauser had been trying to alert the American public to the dangers of "a population crisis that promises to become a national catastrophe." In a magazine article published by *Look* in 1961, he said:

> Today the Negro population is increasing at a rate 60 percent ahead of the white population. This contributes to the frictions between whites and Negroes in our large cities. And the poverty of city Negroes contributes to keeping them a depressed ghetto group living in the midst of crime, poverty, broken homes, and social disorganization.[6]

A bill to establish the new policy was quickly and handily approved by both houses of the next legislature. Kerner signed it into law. The same attorney general and the same auditor agreed to honor its provisions, although the same conflicting criminal statutes remained on the books. To maintain some semblance of consistency and to mollify the downstate bishops and other Catholic traditionalists who understandably might have been confused, Driscoll reaffirmed the church's official position in his testimony before the legislature. To subsidize the purchase of contraceptives for unmarried women would promote "evil consequences to the public good," he said. Privately he put the church's stamp of approval on the policy.

I have discussed this episode in such detail because I believe it illuminates forces that were taking shape in the country at large. The works of Aristotle are not on the book shelves in the headquarters of the Cook County Democratic Central Committee, but there is every reason to deduce that what he said in *Politics* ("A neglect of an effective birth control policy is a never-failing source of poverty, which is in turn the parent of revolution and crime") was well understood in terms of the 1960s. Finley's (and Daley's) Eleventh Ward stood on the western edge of the black frontier in Chicago. Many of the old Irish Catholic parishes were in the path of black neighborhood expansion. Daley's ward committeemen and precinct captains knew that more and more of the wards in Daley's Chicago—and, of course, in the Catholic parishes in the archdiocese—would become predominantly black if the white population of the city continued to decline while the black population kept on growing. That much could be understood without reading Hauser or Aristotle. There were other reasons, to be sure, for what was happening. An important one, no doubt, is that spokesmen for the church could see the abortion issue looming before them and wanted to keep their powder dry for that battle.

The policies that kept birth control services out of tax-supported medical institutions in New York and Chicago were nourished by silence. Exposure to the light of public scrutiny had to cause them to wither. It could be no other way in a society where Catholics were a minority.

Did social forces then predetermine the course of events in Illinois, as some would suggest? Was the outcome inevitable? Arnold Maremont, for one, thinks not. From his viewpoint, the result was a vindication of his unorthodox political personality and methods. Sometimes it takes a Sanger-like persistence to force a sensitive issue to the surface of public consciousness. Maremont's Hitlerian reference, he realized later, was "a blunder in the heat of battle. Still, I could have survived it, were it not for the fact that I rocked the political structure. There really is no new magic that has come upon the scene. It simply is true in birth control as in other initially semipopular innovations that the people out in front are frequently the casualties."

By the late 1960s birth control services were a regular feature of the public health programs in New York City and Chicago. In 1969 approximately one hundred and twenty thousand clients were being assisted at a hundred family planning clinics operated by New York's health department centers and municipal hospitals. And at last the bar was lowered in Chicago's Cook County Hospital. Planned Parenthood representatives now toured the maternity wards routinely in quest of clients. During the first five years, forty thousand new mothers were referred to one of the city's free birth control clinics. Partly as a result, the number of births in the charity hospital declined from twenty thousand in 1963 to twelve thousand in 1969.

Nevertheless, when the identical issue of birth control for welfare recipients arose in Pennsylvania in 1965, the archbishop of the Philadelphia diocese, Cardinal John J. Krol, elected to stand and fight hard against the proposal in the state legislature. The Pennsylvania Catholic Conference distributed a grossly misleading pamphlet entitled, "Betty and Jack Talk About Government Birth Control." A woman was pictured hugging a baby and remarking: "Gosh, I wonder how many people realize that government birth control is intended eventually to tell us how many children we're allowed to have? Sort of frightening, isn't it?" A full-page advertisement signed by all the Catholic bishops in Pennsylvania appeared in sixty newspapers across the state attacking the program as "no business of the state." The compromise reached there involved important concessions by Planned Parenthood that were not made elsewhere. Contraceptives could not be supplied to unmarried women; nor were caseworkers permitted to bring up the subject of birth control on their own.

In Massachusetts, Cardinal Richard Cushing took a more liberal stance when a bill came before the legislature of that state to legalize the sale of contraceptives. Predictably he opposed the legislation because he said it lacked safeguards to protect the morals of the young. But the cardinal conceded that "it does not seem reasonable to me to forbid by civil law a practice that can be considered a matter of private morality." His ambiguity puzzled kneejerk Catholic legislators and some of their constituents, particularly those who were having difficulty accepting the recent reforms in the Catholic liturgy.

As a national organization, the Catholic bishops continued to hold the line against public policies of birth prevention. Citing the "inherently coercive character of government action," the bishops issued a stern statement of warning that is reminiscent of the telegram Monsignor Casey had composed in Illinois: "Basic to the well-being of the family is freedom from external coercion in order that it may determine its own destiny. . . . Let our political leaders be on guard that the common good suffer no evil from public policies which tamper with the instincts of love and the sources of life."

CHAPTER 4 From Eisenhower
to Nixon: The Evolution
of Federal Policy

Just before leaving the White House for the last time, Dwight
D. Eisenhower told a wealthy friend who was active in the birth
control establishment that "Kennedy can do something about it,
but I can't."[1] A far more astute politician than he is given credit
for, President Eisenhower sympathized with the birth control
cause (he became an officer of Planned Parenthood soon after),
but he felt that the subject was a "divisive issue" which the first
Catholic president could deal with in a far different light than he
could. As it turned out, President Kennedy chose a waiting game
during his unexpectedly brief time in office, being in no position to
invite unnecessary conflicts.

After the assassination of Kennedy, his brother-in-law, Sargent
Shriver, became the first director of the Office of Economic
Opportunity, the agency created under the Economic Opportunity Act to wage an innovative war on poverty. Like his
predecessor, the new president, Lyndon B. Johnson, lent rhetorical encouragement to family planning goals but proceeded
with great care. Johnson insisted that everything be checked out
first with the Catholic church. Although the act authorized grants
to public and private agencies for "social programs and assistance," Shriver dragged his feet.[2] His wife (Kennedy's sister)
Eunice objected to the inclusion of birth control services because
of her personal religious conviction that artificial contraception
was immoral. So, at first, grants under the Community Action
Program were not only small in number, they also were weighted
down with administrative conditions. Only married women living

44

with their husbands could be helped. The monthly ration of pills or other items could not exceed twelve dollars per recipient, an amount considered inadequate by Planned Parenthood. Steriliza-tion—a terminal method of permanent birth control available to both sexes—could not be performed with family planning funds. Eunice also was said to have demanded safeguards against "pub-lic propaganda" promoting the services. The first direct OEO grant for family planning services—a piddling $8,000—went to Corpus Christi, Texas, in a state with a large population of low-income Mexican-American families. A year after the first grant, OEO had only fourteen programs going in five states with a total annual budget of $437,000.

Against Shriver's better judgment, and contrary to the advice he was getting at home, other forces were pulling his agency, kicking and screaming, as it were, into the birth control business. OEO's slightest accomplishment looked statistically impressive alongside the old-line health agencies that were administering the so-called formula grants for family planning. In the Department of Health, Education and Welfare, funds for family planning were administered by the Children's Bureau, an agency of the Social and Rehabilitation Service devoted for many years to prenatal care and maternal health but crusted over with HEW's bureau-cratic barnacles. HEW Secretary Robert Finch noted with dis-may that the average age of Children's Bureau personnel in 1969 was "about fifty-eight." Whereas the Children's Bureau dedi-cated itself to healthy, bouncy babies, OEO dared experiment with ways of bypassing the health bureaucracies and "deliv-ering" family planning services directly to the poor. OEO's char-ter went beyond healthy babies. That agency asked not only will mother and baby be healthy, but can the family afford shoes for the children?

In North Carolina, where publicly financed birth control pro-grams had been operating since 1937, many obstetricians and gynecologists refused to cooperate with the OEO programs in the 1960s because they were afraid that the government clinics would interfere with their freedom to charge fees for services.[3] Steriliza-tion of welfare recipients impressed many of them as a com-mendable, foolproof method of birth control, whenever possible, but they did not want to risk losing the opportunity to prescribe contraceptives for a fee in their private offices. In that southern state, according to Anthony Measham, the early programs were motivated more by eugenics—curbing the breeding of undesirables—than by public health considerations. In some counties, the opposition of the organized medical profession was overcome by enlisting the political support of community groups most concerned with the high cost of welfare. Referring to the general public apathy and ambivalence about family planning programs, Measham described how public policymakers often deliberately avoided publicity. Seldom were issues debated publicly. He quoted a staff member of the state health department who encouraged "a positive breeding of better family children, more of them, and the curbing of the breeding of undesirables." Another survey by Measham (published in 1971) of physician attitudes in a southeastern urban community showed that almost half favored compulsory sterilization of unmarried women after a third illegitimate birth.[4]

If one assumes, as Margaret Sanger did,[5] that only medical doctors could ensure safe and effective contraceptive use, the record of the medical profession in the history of birth control in the U.S. is a dismal one. She pleaded in the 1920s and 1930s for medical acceptance of contraception yet could not bring herself to tolerate medical control of her clinics. Most medical societies then feared "quackery" if contraceptives were to be prescribed in the absence of "pathological conditions." The Illinois Medical Society objected in 1925 to the idea of what was called "sociologic" contraception. Sanger's interest in eugenic sterilization probably accounted for her unwillingness to permit too much medical supervision of the clinics. As a result, much of the medical profession in all parts of the country remained ignorant of the latest contraceptive developments, even after the American Medical Association endorsed birth control as a legitimate professional activity in 1937.

For change to occur in the 1960s, therefore, it was first necessary to shake up the public health doctors. A committee of the National Academy of Sciences helped by recommending in its study of "The Growth of U.S. Population" that family planning be made an integral part of public medical programs. Philip Hauser of the University of Chicago forecast in the N.A.S. study that "the magnitude of the explosive growth of the Negro population will undoubtedly make the problems of intergroup relations even more difficult in the coming years." On through the seventies, the impetus for change came from outside the health system, in response, according to Frederick Jaffe of Planned Parenthood, to two principal concerns—poverty and the problems of population growth. "Health institutions and health professionals have not collectively distinguished themselves in pressing for a change of policy," he said, reflecting the views of Margaret Sanger's heirs in the birth control movement.[6]

Jaffe and two other prominent birth control establishmentarians collaborated in 1967 on a study of how HEW's family planning operations should be reorganized. He and Oscar Harkavy, population division officer of the Ford Foundation, and Samuel Wishik of Columbia University, wrote a report that criticized the structure, staffing, and financing of the program.

Contents of the Harkavy-Jaffe-Wishik intradepartmental report to the Secretary of HEW were made public by an elderly senator from Alaska, Ernest Gruening, who compiled seventeen volumes of published testimony during three years of hearings on "the population crisis" before his Senate subcommittee on foreign aid expenditures. While a medical student at Harvard in 1909, Gruening's exposure to the overcrowding and poverty in the Boston slums first interested him in birth control. Later, before beginning his political career, he had been a crusading newspaper editor. The bill that furnished the excuse for his subcommittee's elaborate inquiry would merely have established assistant secretaries for population problems in the Departments of State and HEW. But the legislation, dismissed as unnecessary by the Johnson administration, never got out of the subcommittee. The hearings served nevertheless as an instrument to force Congress to pay attention to the subject at least. Then, as always, congressional resistance to birth control projects was more successful outside the public spotlight. HEW appropriations, for example, had to contend with the chairman of the HEW-Labor appropriations subcommittee of the House, Rep. John Fogarty, a Catholic from Rhode Island who did not approve of government financing of contraception.

We saw earlier how it remained for the courts to bring birth control law closer to the realities of social behavior. That happened again in the 1960s and 1970s when the Supreme Court declared unconstitutional the last state laws that endeavored to ban the use of contraceptives. In 1961, the director of the Planned Parenthood League of Connecticut, Mrs. Estelle Griswold, was arrested for opening a public birth control clinic. The Supreme Court held, seven to two, that Connecticut's 1879 law forbidding the use of contraceptives even by married couples violated a right of marital privacy older than the Bill of Rights. By denying the government's authority to intrude into the privacy of the bedroom the court's opinion in *Griswold* would have profound future constitutional significance. Soon after, the doctrine established in *Griswold* was used in the abortion case, *Roe* v. *Wade,* to "encompass a woman's decision whether or not to terminate her pregnancy." And before long the court erased the distinction between married and unmarried women in the contraceptive control laws. William R. Baird was arrested and sentenced to ninety days in jail for violating a Massachusetts "Crimes Against Chastity" statute which banned the sale of contraceptives to persons not married. During a lecture at Boston University, Baird gave a package of vaginal foam to an unmarried coed for which act he was convicted of unlawful conduct. On March 22, 1971, the Supreme Court ruled in *Baird* v. *Eisenstadt* that the Massachusetts law violated the rights of single persons under the Equal Protection Clause of the Fourteenth Amendment. "Whatever the rights of the individual to access to contraceptives may be," said Justice William J. Brennan, Jr., "the rights must be the same for the unmarried and married alike. . . . If the right to privacy means anything, it is the right of the individual, married or single, to be free from unwarranted government intrusion into matters so fundamentally affecting a person as the decision whether to bear or beget a child."

Many of these events that were so important in the evolution of family planning policy—the *Griswold* decision, publication of the National Academy of Sciences report, the start of the Gruening hearings, and OEO's first sizeable project grants—occurred in 1965, the same year that the Voting Rights Act and the Immigration Reform Act were passed by Congress.

Something else happened inadvertently that year of surprising significance in the fast-changing politics of fertility control. Daniel Patrick Moynihan, then an assistant secretary of labor on leave from his university faculty position, completed a report to the president on the deterioration of the Negro family. He identified that condition as the fundamental source of weakness in the

Negro community. The ideas that slavery, unemployment, and poverty were the root causes of a matriarchal black society characterized by female-headed families, welfare dependency, and illegitimate births were neither novel scholarship nor sudden political insight. Black scholars had been treating the same statistics for years. Every fourth Negro birth is illegitimate. Fewer than half of all Negro children reaching age eighteen lived all their lives with both parents. Moynihan called these facts alarming. He said the family structure of lower-class Negroes "is approaching complete breakdown."

Though the facts were well established, many black leaders were especially disturbed by the title of Moynihan's report— "The Negro Family: the Case for National Action." What kind of *national action*? they wondered. The author said he meant economic programs to make more jobs available. But the angry response seemed linked to a fear that "the government would try to impose sexual continence and fidelity—virtues which nearly all critics think overrated."[7] Floyd McKissick, director of CORE, commented: "Just because Moynihan believes in middle-class values doesn't mean they are good for everyone." At a subsequent White House Conference on Children the black caucus of delegates issued a position paper specifically rejecting "the widespread notion that the one-parent family is inherently defective" and suggesting further that "work and welfare need to be redefined in our society as equal rights." Whatever else Moynihan's report did, it did not solve the problem, if it is a problem. The percentage of black households headed by women climbed to 28.3 percent in 1970 and 35.3 percent in 1974 (for white households the comparable figure in 1974 was 10.5 percent).

To highlight the family behavior of black males, as Moynihan's report did, obviously touched a very sensitive nerve. Release of the document was followed very quickly by President Johnson's Howard University speech based on the report in June of 1965. It seemed to galvanize many thoughtful black citizens into an awareness, rational or not, that perhaps some form of "black genocide" was not all that unthinkable. Charles V. Willie, a professor of sociology at Syracuse University (and a black), said later that Moynihan

tipped off blacks about what was in the minds of whites when he described the situation as "acute" because of the "extraordinary rise in Negro population." . . . [A] leading government spokesman has declared that an increase in black people of one or two percentage points is "extraordinary." Blacks also point out that whites were not concerned about their family form and size during the days of slavery. Blacks point out that over the years the greatest contributor to family instability among the members of their race has been the death of the male spouse rather than divorce or desertion. Moreover, blacks point out that the major control upon their fertility rate in the past has been the deaths of their very young children. . . . It would seem that whites are concerned about the size and stability of the black family now only because the number of black men who are dying prematurely is decreasing and the number of black children born who survive is increasing. If you can understand the basis of the alarm among white liberals about this situation, then you can understand the basis for a charge of genocide which is made by black militants.[8]

Coming when it did, Moynihan's report unintentionally reinforced the insecurities of many black Americans; if black family style is considered abnormal enough to warrant "national action," what might the white majority try to do by way of enforcing conformity to a different standard of behavior? Eugene Genovese has described how the combination of paternalism and racism "transformed elements of personal dependency into a sense of collective weakness" which made it difficult for blacks to "grasp their collective strength as a people and act like political men."[9] Introduction of the black genocide argument into the rhetoric of fertility control served the purposes of those emerging black male political leaders who sought their enhanced power in numerical expansion.

Within the Office of Economic Opportunity, meanwhile, the family planning program was being held back by an odd alliance of bureaucrats who were ideologically opposed to it and young radicals on the staff who were influenced by the Black Power advocates in their midst.

Then, unexpectedly, the demand for swifter movement on birth control assistance for the poor and less educated began coming from a heretofore reluctant source: Capitol Hill. For reasons discussed earlier, few members of Congress have ever been very interested in the touchy subject of birth control, and even now the ones who were most concerned tended to be wealthy patricians—Sen. Joseph Clark of Pennsylvania, Sen. Joseph Tydings of Maryland, Rep. James Scheuer of New York City, Rep. George H. Bush, Jr. of Texas (whose father once lost a Senate election in Connecticut after columnist Drew Pearson "revealed" the candidate's "involvement" with Planned Parenthood on the weekend before the ballots were cast); and later Rep. Pierre Du Pont of Delaware. In 1966, Scheuer introduced two bills to repeal the federal Comstock statutes that had been invalidated by judicial decree. The bills were buried, nevertheless, in subcommittees headed by Michael Feighan of Cleveland and James Burke of Boston, both Catholics. One year later, the political winds had shifted. Congress designated family planning one of the special "national emphasis" programs in the Economic Opportunity Act.

Still more important, in the long run, the provisions of the Social Security Act governing Aid to Families with Dependent Children, the costliest of the welfare programs, were altered to: (1) require that at least 6 percent of all funds available for maternal and infant care be earmarked for family planning; (2) direct all the states to offer family planning services to present, past, and potential AFDC recipients in an effort to reduce illegitimate births and corral welfare expenses; (3) establish a ceiling over the proportion of children under eighteen who could qualify for AFDC in any state; (4) authorize states to purchase family planning services from nongovernmental providers; (5) provide matching federal grants to the states for family planning. The significance of the last provision was not recognized at the time, but it created open-ended funding by the federal government. Later, in the amendments of 1972, the federal match was quietly increased from 75 percent to 90 percent. The federal government would put up nine dollars for every one dollar produced by the states for family planning purposes, in much the same way that the national government matches state appropriations for highway building. It was a very important change in the law because Washington could no longer control outlays for family planning as budgetary conditions dictated.

At OEO, Dr. Gary D. London, head of the reproductive physiology department at Los Angeles County General Hospital, took over as associate director for family planning. "We are," he said late in 1967, "riding a thin and rather unusual line. Our crucial support is coming from both extremes on the political spectrum. On one end are the liberals who have always favored it. On the other, though, are many conservative converts who don't like the high price of public welfare and see this as a way of holding down the numbers of dependent children."[10]

In its report recommending special attention for family planning, the House Education and Labor Committee said, "additional emphasis on this aspect of the poverty program would be desirable." For many years the Catholic muscle on that committee had been effectively flexed to delay federal aid to elementary and secondary education—until, that is, the interests of nonpublic schools could be accommodated. But now one of the representatives on that committee, Rep. Roman C. Pucinski, related that a poll of his heavily Polish Catholic district on Chicago's Northwest Side indicated that more than three-fourths of his constituents supported government birth control services for the poor. Another Chicago area congressman, Rep. Edward J. Derwinski, who specialized in the cultivation of Eastern European ethnic "heritage groups" in the Republican party, agreed that lay Catholics were no longer as impressed by church rules. "These matters excite the clergy types and maybe a few superactive Catholics," he said, "but the average Catholic is just not that uptight about such things anymore."

Church officials still argued against family planning assistance on moral and theological grounds, but members of Congress had swung over to the conviction that the people back home were strongly in favor of such programs, if for no other reason than to keep the welfare rolls from expanding. From different regions of the country, community action agencies were demanding, meanwhile, that OEO's administrative strings be loosened. Shriver was swept along by the pressure from Congress. First, he had to disenthrall the regional bureaucracies of the previously operative notion that he expected them to head off the birth control applications. Demonstrating his conversion, Shriver approved a grant funded directly by his office to train Chicago public aid caseworkers in family planning procedures, bypassing the City Hall antipoverty agency and irritating Democratic party leaders in an area where he entertained personal political career ambitions. To some extent, the changing attitudes in Congress were stimulated by the outside leaders of "the movement"—the likes of John D. Rockefeller III and other members of the Rockefeller family; Hugh Moore, founder of the Dixie Cup Co.; William H. Draper, John Nuveen, Eugene Black, John Cowles, Cass Canfield, Lammot DuPont Copeland, and other wealthy businessmen, bankers, and retired ambassadors. It is theoretically possible to hypothesize that some of these men were worried about the rise of political pressure for the redistribution of income. John D. Rockefeller III prevailed on President Johnson to appoint a national Commission on Population and Family Planning headed by Rockefeller and HEW Secretary Wilbur J. Cohen. Their report, "The Transition from Concern to Action," was issued in November of 1968, just after the election that turned Johnson into a lame duck president. But he left office without trying to do anything tangible about implementing the recommendations. It was a subject he obviously cared little about.

Looking back on the events of 1968, few would deny that the destructive urban riots which followed the assassination that year of Dr. King had a bigger impact on white opinion regarding birth control for racial minorities than either John D. Rockefeller III or the report of his presidential commission.

A Republican president, Richard M. Nixon, took office in 1969 with none other than the same Daniel Patrick Moynihan as his principal social policy adviser. Moynihan told me later he was surprised by the readiness of the Nixon administration to sponsor the family planning program emphasis that he advocated. In Nixon's as in any other Republican administration the interests of the business community were almost always paramount. In the late 1960s the need for social order was perceived by businessmen and financiers as more urgent than the customary desire for perpetual population/economic growth. That change of faith is easily the most important development in the contemporary evolution of birth control policy in the United States. None of the capitalists in the Commerce and Treasury Departments intervened.

On July 18, 1969, Nixon sent a message to Congress requesting that "we establish as a national goal the provision of adequate family planning services within the next five years to all those who want them but cannot afford them." He attributed "many of our social problems . . . to the fact that we have had only fifty years in which to accommodate the second 100 million Americans." No American woman should be denied access to family planning assistance because of her economic condition, the president declared. His commitment to the five-year goal pleased the population establishment, but many of the experts in the field were disappointed by Nixon's acceptance of the inevitability of a third 100 million Americans by the end of this century. The president spoke of "accommodating" population growth instead of trying to curb the numbers. "One of the most serious challenges to human destiny in the last third of this century will be the growth of the population," the message warned. "Whether man's response to that challenge will be a cause for pride or for despair by the year 2000 will depend very much on what we do today." He asked for an increase in government spending for family planning from $48 million to an annual budget that would reach $150 million within five years. And, eight months after Johnson had been presented with his commission's report, Nixon proposed the creation of another presidential commission, this one to be called the Commission on Population Growth and the American Future. Despite the seemingly broader sweep of the mandate, at a White House briefing on the message Moynihan dispelled any thought that the commission would be expected to come up with a national growth policy. "There is not going to be a day soon when there is a national growth policy," Moynihan explained. "We would hope there is going to be a decade during which one emerges. You don't sit down and work out something like that." The team of Harkavy, Jaffe, and Wishik appended its own interpretation in the pages of *Science* (July 25, 1969): ". . . There has never been an official policy regarding the virtue or necessity of reducing U.S. population growth, much less achieving population stability. . . . It is clear that the federal program has been advanced, not for population control, but to improve health and reduce the impact of poverty and deprivation." By way of accentuating that point, when the recent HEW Secretary, Robert Finch (since moved to the White House staff), mentioned the possibility that "disincentives" to childbirth might have to be considered, the White House quickly denied that his remark represented administration policy.

Responding to the chief executive's initiative, Congress passed a bill that went further than he wanted to go. The Family Planning Services and Population Research Act of 1970 closely resembled legislation that had been introduced by Senator Tydings of Maryland. The law established a centralized Office of Population Affairs and a National Center for Family Planning Services in HEW, against the wishes of the administration. Over the next three fiscal years, $382 million was authorized to be spent for family planning services, research, personnel training, and educational activities. Adopting the president's goal of providing services on a voluntary basis to every wanting woman within five years, Congress estimated that five million women would need this subsidized help. All the important decisions were made in the respective Senate and House committees; there was little debate on the floor of either chamber. The Senate committee hearings were quarterbacked by Planned Parenthood's Program Development Center. Elihu Bergman of Harvard's Center for Population Studies has noted the conspicuous absence of testimony from the intended beneficiaries of the new services. The Senate passed the bill unanimously.

Rep. John W. McCormack of Massachusetts, the seventy-eight-year-old Speaker of the House, dubbed "The Bishop" by his colleagues because of his many years of fidelity to the Catholic hierarchy, tried for a while to keep the measure bottled up in the House committee, contending that it would be wiser to await the 1970 census data before enacting any population legislation. But the bill was voted out of committee and passed by the House, 298 to 32. Most of the few who spoke against the bill were right-wing extremists. Rep. John G. Schmitz, from Orange County, California, said: "There are people in our government today who want power over who shall live and who shall die in these United States. . . . I make a prediction: in a few years you will see [this bill's] 'may' changed to 'shall' when it is found that the objectives cannot be achieved by voluntary means."

The House and Senate conferees who reconciled minor differences in the two bills emphasized that none of the funds could be used for any program that included abortion as a method of family planning. This did not mollify the U.S. Catholic Conference. The bishops complained that "the government has taken the role of advocate. . . . Coercion of the individual takes place when over-zealous welfare workers and medical personnel attempt to pressure an individual mother to avoid further child-bearing." Referring to "psychological pressure based on information," Rev. James T. McHugh of the Catholic Conference's Family Life Division, said the bill was "morally unacceptable and politically unfeasible." "To put it bluntly," McHugh added, "we have had quite enough of the crisis rhetoric that is calculated to idealize the two-child family to the disadvantage of families of more than two children."

Nixon signed the bill into law, praising it as landmark legislation, which it certainly was. Moynihan, the social scientist from Harvard who was the administration's resident liberal, was instrumental in the White House decision to accept the measure. On one occasion Moynihan had phrased his own interpretation of the population problem this way: "Or, to put it another way, how long do we want to stand in line to go to the movie?" A better understanding of the motives of some of the policymakers in the White House can perhaps be gleaned by looking at a population report then being circulated inside the administration. Statistics were assembled to illustrate the "striking bulge" in the number of black Americans between the ages of five and nine. This group of youngsters who would soon enter their teens—"an age group with problems that can create social turbulence"—was 25 percent larger than ten years before. The percentage increase of young blacks was four times as great as whites. The document made available to the *Washington Post* [11] (probably by Moynihan) also dealt with the dependency rate—the ratio of "mouths to hands"—pointing out that Negroes have to support a fourth again as many dependents with 59 percent of the income of whites. Meanwhile, Dr. Roger O. Egeberg, assistant secretary of HEW for health and scientific affairs, told a conference on conservation and population growth that "our health-care programs are on quicksand if we don't start to do something about population." [12]

As the first deputy assistant secretary of population affairs in HEW's unfortunately labeled Office of Population Affairs, the president selected Dr. Hellman, the doctor who precipitated the 1958 showdown in New York's municipal hospitals. The reference to population affairs did little to persuade doubters that HEW was primarily concerned with better health for all. "By linking family planning with population, Congress has set the stage for enunciation of a public population policy," Hellman explained later.[13] He said it was clear that Congress and the executive branch expected the 1970 legislation to slow the growth rate, reduce the birth rate, and provide other social benefits. He recalled that a short thirteen years ago birth control services were offered in the tax-supported public health programs of only seven states, all in the South. "Acceptance of (the act) vividly symbolized the enormous revolution in thinking and practice that has taken place in the last decade," Hellman observed. Asserting that "most of us hope government (population) policy will be based on voluntarism," he went on to suggest that "long delays in the formulation of a governmental population policy can dissipate the last hope of a voluntary solution. The planners of involuntarism are already at their drawing boards."

Along with the family planning authorization and the reorganization of HEW agencies, Congress approved the creation of the commission that the president asked for, after adding some congressional members. When the president's appointees were announced, the same John D. Rockefeller III was named chairman, and the same reliable spokesmen for the population establishment filled a majority of the membership spots. Once again, the poor and minorities were conspicuous by their underrepresentation. Bergman has made a detailed study of the interlocking relationships in this Enlightened Triumvirate (to use his term).[14] Often the "High Priests" who make up what he calls the "cerebral core," academicians from the Carolina Population Center (University of North Carolina) and other campus population centers, are retained as consultants by the funding sources. These funding sources are, first, the foundations and associations (e.g., the Population Crisis Committee, the Population Council) set up by wealthy philanthropists, and, secondly, the government bureaucrats who dispense federal grants.

Until the less restrained Environmental Radicals and Zero Population Growth advocates entered upon the stage, this coalition of like-minded individuals dominated what little discussion of population issues there was. In November of 1960, *Readers Digest* published an article by Yale Sociologist Lincoln Day entitled "The American Fertility Cult—Our Irresponsible Birth Rate." In that and other writings, Day and his wife Alice Taylor Day, also a sociologist, expressed their disappointment that Americans were so complacent about being in the midst of "one of the most rapid rates of sustained population growth in the history of man.'' Another 400 years at present growth rates and the entire U.S. would be as densely populated as New York City, the Days pointed out.[15] ''Our religious climate has undoubtedly inhibited the circulation of ideas about population growth and control, as much by the fear it creates of open controversy between religious groups as by active religious opposition to the principle of population control itself,'' the Days said. They went on to predict how the conditions of life would deteriorate. There would be less open space for recreational and aesthetic enjoyment. The cost of public services would be higher for an urbanized population. Moreover, ''with growing numbers, life becomes more complex. . . . Social changes lead to an even greater need for external control over the individual, for a narrowing of the range of his unregulated behavior.''

If population growth continues, the Days warned that even more stringent controls over the use of land would have to be imposed.

> To the extent that land could be allowed to remain privately owned in a United States with double or triple its present numbers, its use would have to be further and further circumscribed. Eventually, there could be no such thing as a ''family farm'' or a ''place in the country''—or, under still greater pressure of numbers—even a backyard whose owner could be allowed the luxury of determining for himself how he wanted to use it, whether to use it for growing flowers instead of for the production of food or minerals. In these more extreme conditions, the right of eminent domain would become little more than a museum piece; the idea that a man's home was his castle, something of a wry joke.[16]

Continuing, the Days related the growth of numbers to the unhappy fact that most American citizens must resort to organized lobbying to have any influence in public affairs. ''On his own, the individual citizen has hardly a chance,'' they said. ''Yet, with lobbying, because of its very nature, some groups will have far greater access to and influence over legislators and executives than will others. It is the well-financed, well-organized lobbyists for business, veterans, doctors, the military, farmers, and labor unions whose efforts meet most frequently with success. Compared with these powerhouses, the civil libertarians, conservationists, consumer representatives, or peace groups are but 90-pound weaklings."

Conjuring up visions of an America whose citizens would not be permitted to grow flowers in their backyards is curious scholarship. It has been a long time, if ever, since an individual American citizen could influence public affairs on a par with the lobbies. The well-organized planters' lobby met with far more success in the early days of the Republic than did the scattered homesteaders on the frontier. Despite the Days' polemics and their deplorable ignorance of political reality, they were reflecting a concern of many educated Americans that there were too many of us, that the political system was becoming impenetrable, that only the powerful, organized interests could make a difference anymore, and that the size of the nation was somehow responsible.

In 1968, Garrett Hardin's essay "The Tragedy of the Commons" attracted wide attention.[17] Declaring his belief that injustice and loss of freedom to propagate are preferable to total ruin, he recommended "mutual coercion, mutually agreed upon by the majority of the people affected." On another occasion, Hardin said: "We have to take children in their earliest years and start implanting some different ideas about the good life simply constituting getting married and multiplying. We have to tell them what a good time the unmarrieds are having. But this approach has limitations. In the long run, voluntarism is insanity. The result will be continued uncontrolled population growth."[18]

Even a social progressive like Kingsley Davis suggested that "this country would be better off with half the population. With our present technology and the population of the 1930s the country would be a paradise. As it is, it's getting to be like hell."[19] Because couples, and not society, control fertility, he expressed a preference for indirect disincentives to reproduce. "Social reformers who would not hesitate to . . . force all workers in any industry to join a union balk at any suggestion that couples be permitted to have only a certain number of offspring," the Californian said. "Invariably, they interpret societal control of reproduction as meaning direct police supervision of individual behavior."

The environmental protection movement came into vogue during the Nixon years, and the population controllers did not hesitate to hitch a ride wherever and whenever they could. In 1969 the Association for Voluntary Sterilization, which had been organized and promoted by Hugh Moore, arranged a joint meeting with the National Conference on Conservation to endorse the two-child family size limitation goal. Inside the administration, the chairman of the President's Council on Environmental Quality, Russell E. Train, tried to provoke an explicit reconsideration of the time-honored devotion to economic growth. "With all the benefits from economic growth," he said, "we are beginning to question whether more is really better." Commerce Secretary Peter G. Peterson followed with a speech reminding the environmentalists not to "slip into rigid, simplistic, and confused positions."

The assumption that population must be curbed to preserve a quality of life that all Americans shared equally disturbed many black thinkers. Julian Bond considered Paul Ehrlich's popular book *The Population Bomb* a "theoretical bomb in the hands of frightened racists, as well as over the heads of black people, as the justification for genocide." Not all family planners were convinced of the good sense of coupling the population and environmental movements. In a speech to the Population Association of America, Frank Notestein took a different slant: "Pollution is related almost exclusively to mismanagement and to our high standard of living. It is related negligibly to our numbers. . . . In political terms, relating pollution to population may have done harm to a serious attack on both pollution and population to concentrate attention on the importance of stopping population growth in say twenty, thirty, or fifty years."

Some of the veneer of idealism had worn away from the population control movement. A full-page advertisement in the *New York Times* asked in large black type: How many People Do *You* Want in Your Country?

Our city slums are packed with youngsters—thousands of them idle, victims of discontent and drug addiction. And millions more will pour into our streets in the next few years at the present rate of procreation. You go out after dark at your peril. Last year one out of every four hundred Americans was murdered, raped, or robbed.[20]

At first glance, the tone of the ad smacks of a John Birch Society tract or a leftover Goldwater campaign leaflet. But, no, the names associated with the sponsoring committee, the Campaign to Check the Population Explosion, are those of the most prominent leaders of the movement: Hugh Moore and others, the chairman of the American Can Company, the former chairman of Standard Oil Company of New Jersey, the chairman of E. I. Du Pont de Nemours & Company, the chairman of Scripps-Howard Newspapers, Philip Hauser of the University of Chicago.

"There are people who feel that we ought to do something about the overgrowth of one ethnic group or another," acknowledged the establishmentarian Samuel Wishik. "It behooves the rest of us to try to see to it that these kinds of motivations do not dominate our decisions."[21]

Recent American presidents have resorted to the presidential study commission as a way of giving the interested public the impression that something is being done about a problem when it is not. Instead of confronting the sensitive issues of population policy, Nixon's commission with its diverse public and congressional representation concluded that the nation should "welcome and plan for" stabilization of the population. Beyond reaffirming the principle of equal access to birth control services, and opposing the compulsory regulation of fertility, the commission did not say how that was to be achieved. Nevertheless, the attention devoted to any commission's inquiry can be a useful halfway house that helps to legitimatize a social problem as a suitable topic for the political agenda sometime soon.

This time, though, the generally consensual contents of the report were obscured by two recommendations that were seized upon by the man who set the commission up in business in the first place—President Nixon. He criticized the commission's endorsement of liberalized abortion laws and removal of legal restrictions affecting birth control services to minors. "It is important," Nixon said in a statement issued six weeks after the report had been presented to him, "that the public know my views on the issues raised. In particular, I want to reaffirm and reemphasize that I do not support unrestricted abortion policies. . . . I consider abortion an unacceptable form of population control. In my judgment, unrestricted abortion policies would demean human life. I also want to make it clear that I do not support the unrestricted distribution of family planning services and devices to minors. Such measures would do nothing to preserve and strengthen close family relationships.''

McHugh of the Catholic Conference (now a monsignor) charged that the commission's "preoccupation with finding an effective way of eliminating the 'unwanted child,' '' led it into "an ideological Valley of Death.'' He suggested that the president treat the report with "benign neglect"—borrowing the term Moynihan had used to describe how racial problems should be dealt with. Which is what the Nixon administration did—except that some of the effects were not so benign, as we shall see in future chapters.

It was 1972—a presidential election year—and the Nixon team had embarked on a new strategy that necessitated some abrupt shifts in population policy. Moynihan had returned to academia. Charles Colson and John Ehrlichman were in charge of adapting social policy to election campaign requirements. Especially after it became apparent that the Democratic opposition would nominate a candidate of the liberal left—Sen. George S. McGovern of South Dakota—Nixon and his staff knew they could appeal to traditionally Democratic Catholic voters in the cities. "Ethnic Catholics'' such as those in Chicago were likely to be turned off quickest by the youngish McGovern supporters and by the social issues with which the Democratic candidate would be identified—symbolized by the three A's, acid (narcotics), amnesty (for Vietnam draft dodgers), and abortion. Nixon invited Cardinal Krol of Philadelphia to a well-publicized meeting at the White House. He wrote Cardinal Terence Cooke in New York City associating himself with the cardinal's struggle to have New York's relatively permissive abortion law repealed by the state legislature. Governor Nelson Rockefeller, who was chairman of Nixon's reelection campaign in New York state, did not appreciate the president's intervention in an area of purely state jurisdiction.

Only a few weeks earlier, HEW had sponsored a regional conference in New York City on "Teen-agers and Contraceptive Services.'' The keynote speaker, Dr. Frank Beckles, director of HEW's National Center for Family Planning Services, applauded the federal government's long overdue involvement in birth control assistance for adolescents. Referring to the alarming increase in venereal disease among young people, he said, "We are witnessing departures from traditional life styles that are totally misunderstood and for which we are totally unprepared. . . . Pregnant teen-agers are high risks, medically, socially, and educationally." Congress, meanwhile, put a requirement in federal law that state welfare departments provide such services to "minors who can be considered to be sexually active." After Nixon released his broadside against the abortion and adolescent birth control sections of the commission report, Dr. Hellman said HEW would, until ordered to do otherwise by the White House, continue to support family planning services regardless of age or marital status of the recipients. That order never came from the White House, which was more interested in political symbols than in substantive practices. So HEW proceeded on course. The White House did intervene, however haphazardly and ineffectively, in a related area of both symbolic and real significance—sterilization policy—with tragic consequences that will be examined at length in chapter 7.

Nixon was reelected overwhelmingly. In his second administration Moynihan went to India as the American ambassador instead of resuming his domestic policy role in the White House. Even before the reelection campaign, the president and his staff selected health and social services as a proving ground for his "Creative Federalism" concept. Under that plan, federal project grants-in-aid were to be consolidated. State governments would be free to decide how the federal dollars would be spent. Family planning programs would compete, therefore, for state health department priority. More important, eligibility for birth control services, and the amount of the individual payments, would be determined in the state capital, not in Washington. It was further decided that family planning would be lumped in with welfare services to be financed as much as possible by Medicaid and public assistance. A House Republican research task force on population policy, under Rep. George Bush of Texas, released a dissenting report urging that the states not be given control over family planning grants for at least four years. Recommending that family planning be exempt from the otherwise desirable transfer of decision-making power to the statehouses, the Bush committee said it had to be recognized that the state health departments lacked adequate systems for "delivering" birth control services to the poor. By now the congressional appropriation for family planning services had been gradually stepped up until about 3.5 million American women were receiving some type of publicly subsidized services. These services were being dispensed by 3,000 governmental and volunteer health agencies in two-thirds of the U.S. counties. The designation of a goal of 5 million women "in need" was described later by Dr. Hellman as "a wonderful political gimmick."[22] Since passage of the 1970 act, Planned Parenthood continued to "up the ante," to use Dr. Hellman's term, managing to jack up the need estimate from 5 million to 10.8 million persons. Joining the needy pool were 3.4 million females classified as barely above the recognized poverty line and 1.7 million sexually active teenagers. Dr. Hellman preferred to talk about the number of women "at risk" rather than "in need."

For research to find more reliable contraceptive techniques the appropriation was never anywhere near the authorization. The way Congress works, separate committees authorize or set the limits for expenditures before a generally more stingy appropriations committee comes along later and parcels out the cash. Although the failure rate for contraceptive use was believed still to be over one-third, contraceptive research could not hope to compete with the politically sexier heart and cancer programs.

Funds made available for services increased gradually in step with HEW's five-year plan until fiscal year 1973. Then the administration not only ordered no further increases but some of the money that had already been appropriated was withheld (impounded). While the purchasing power of the dollar shrank, the growth in the numbers of women receiving birth control assistance stopped. This happened not because the Nixon crowd was out to gut the family planning program. Other budget needs were considered more pressing, and the administration was committed to the turning back of decision-making power to the states and localities. In 1973 the authorizing legislation was extended by Congress for only one year. Tydings, Bush, Gruening, and Scheuer were no longer there, having retired or been defeated. Others were battling to prevent or reverse the impoundment of funds for health programs that excited more voters. Furthermore, after taking steps to convert the family planning program into a welfare service, hardening the economic eligibility requirements, the administration abolished the separate Center for Family Planning Services in HEW. Marjorie Costa, a black woman who succeeded Beckles as director, was shifted to another office and the family planning function was reorganized under HEW's Bureau of Community Health Services.

Coming at about the same time, the Supreme Court's ruling on state abortion laws probably cut two ways. Activation of an aroused Right to Life movement represented a threat to family planners insofar as the religiously motivated opposition to artificial birth control had been dormant and was now wide awake. On the other hand, the abortion decision presumably helped to make the "preventive action" of contraception more reasonable to more people.

In May of 1973, as a cost-cutting measure apparently, HEW proposed a rule that would have disqualified for birth control aid any women who did not have a child, or was not pregnant, or was not on welfare. To be eligible for subsidized contraception, a prospective first-time mother would have had to be at least three months pregnant, by which time obviously it would be at least three months too late. The regulation was revised in October, after it was pointed out that the restriction could not help but inspire more abortions.

Fertility control "is almost always a relatively minor concern of government," lamented Frederick Jaffe of Planned Parenthood. "It does not loom large enough among the considerations determining policy change and thus is subject to all the vicissitudes of the political process. The U.S. national family planning program had the stamp of presidential and congressional approval, was guided by perhaps the most detailed long-range plan ever prepared for any federal programs, and was succeeding in doing exactly what it was asked to do. Nonetheless, it could not be exempted from a systemwide initiative designed to change the fundamental relationships underlying all public programs. . . . To depend on government alone to implement a fertility control program is, in the face of political realities, to depend on a very uncertain foundation."

The birth rate, which began dropping in 1957, reached its lowest point in U.S. history in 1972. Low-income fertility declined too. AFDC rolls stopped rising for the first time in several years. By 1974 the birth rate started back up, not because couples were having bigger families but rather because there were more women reaching the childbearing ages. The death rate reached an alltime low in 1974, and the natural increase in the national population was estimated that year at 1,233,000. There were fewer marriages, more divorces, and over nine hundred thousand legal abortions. The sharpest decline in the number of births occurred in states where the most abortions were performed. In New York City, for example, the decline in births was three times that of the nation as a whole. There was clearly a relationship between abortion policy and the decrease in births.[23] The stated family size expectations of American wives continued to fall, according to the census bureau, but demographers emphasized that much of the decline in fertility appeared to represent merely a postponement of childbearing. More women were marrying later and more women were working "temporarily" at outside jobs after marriage.

Meanwhile, the nation experienced the trauma of scandal in the White House, an impeachment proceeding against the president, and the first forced resignation of the chief executive before the end of his term. While Nixon was still trying to hang on to his office, an important population bill slipped through the cracks in Congress, partly because of impeachment politics. How a land-use planning bill that the Nixon administration had originally proposed was jettisoned by Nixon in a desperate struggle to placate Republican conservatives will be described in chapter 12.

Twice, in 1974 and again in 1975, the new president—Gerald R. Ford—vetoed authorization and appropriation bills for HEW that included funds for family planning. Finally, in 1975, Congress succeeded in overriding the veto of a health bill that retained most of the features of the 1970 family planning law through 1977. HEW was directed to disburse project grants according to federal standards, blunting the thrust of Nixon's Creative Federalism as adopted and adapted by the Ford administration.

There were, as Samuel Wishik recognized, people around who felt that something ought to be done about "one ethnic group or another." Behind all the fashionable rhetoric about ecological purity, backyard gardens, freedom of opportunity, maternal health, and long lines at movie houses stood the often unpleasant political sociology of class and race. The policies of the 1960s and 1970s were aimed at lowering the fertility of the poor and the uneducated—particularly of blacks and Latin Americans. If the objective is to check population growth as such, then the sensible policy would be to start with "that segment of the population which already possesses motivation and technical competence in fertility control." So observed H. Yuan Tien, sociologist at Ohio State University, who went on to note, however, that if "blacks were to receive comparatively less attention in national population problems, the existing racial composition of the population would be likely to undergo an important change. Should this prove to be unacceptable, then the dilemma of population numbers will be an American dilemma for a long time to come. In a nutshell, population policy and politics are inseparable."[24] Blacks received more and not less attention, of course, which is another kind of American dilemma proving again that population policy and politics are indeed inseparable.

Our safety, our survival literally, depend on our ever increasing numbers and the heavy concentration of our people in the financial heart of America—namely in the large urban centers . . . the city has become the black man's land.

> —Daniel H. Watts in the black nationalist publication *Liberator*.

Everyone talks about population control but nobody suggests that the Kennedy women stop having children because there's respect for their freedom to do what they want.

> —Rev. Jesse L. Jackson, black leader in Chicago.

Women of any religion want a small family. It's the menfolk who are the stumbling-block.

5 Black Genocide and
Homewood-Brushton

The interests of the black man, an angry, defiant black man
tilting against the white power structure, and the interests of the
black woman, typically in this case a trouble-weary mother
scrambling day-by-day to get by on welfare, collided at the mobile
birth control clinic that had been rolled into one corner of the
black man's land, the Homewood-Brushton neighborhood of
Pittsburgh. Planned Parenthood operated the clinic without controversy in Homewood-Brushton until the local Citizens' Renewal Council requested a grant of money from the federal Office
of Economic Opportunity to pay for the service in 1966. On the
citywide community action agency that approved the use of federal funds for the family planning program in that neighborhood,
Mayor Joseph M. Barr, a Democrat, cast the deciding vote to
approve the project.

By now the male-dominated black community organizations,
those that were long established as well as the newer, more
aggressive groups of younger men, rose up in protest against the
special attention that their residents were receiving. The Pittsburgh branch of NAACP complained that the facility had become
an instrument of genocide that would be used to exterminate the
Negro people. William "Bouie" Haden, leader of a militant black
organization called the United Movement for Progress, and also
the Homewood-Brushton delegate on the citywide community
action agency, was not as polite about it. He threatened to fire-
bomb the center unless it closed. Once the government started
supporting what had been a Planned Parenthood clinic, male

spokesmen objected to the selective but vigorous (they thought) "pill pushing" by single-minded federally paid "outreach workers" who went knocking on doors only in black neighborhoods trying to entice confused women to the birth control center. In various vague ways difficult to document, the women were given to understand, by welfare caseworkers and others in positions of authority, that their welfare checks might stop coming unless they took the hint, hustled over to the clinic, and began practicing contraception pronto. Or this, at least, is what the men said.

All the OEO-funded clinics were in black neighborhoods of Pittsburgh; neither of the two heavily Catholic white poverty districts contained any birth control facilities because, according to officials of Planned Parenthood, the local residents did not want them. There and in other cities and counties across the nation, local leaders and OEO officials in Washington knew better than to antagonize the Catholic church excessively. OEO services tended to be concentrated in places where the black minority lived. Moreover, harking back to the unforgettable Moynihan report, B. William Austin noticed in his study of the black genocide issue for the national Urban League later that "the black experience in the United States became a 'national problem' only as the population became an urban one."[1]

Long before that, when most impoverished black people still lived and toiled in the rural South, black scholars and others were conscious of the significance of group birth rates. Marcus Garvey, a spiritual godfather of today's black separatists, warned in 1923 that blacks might be exterminated if they permitted themselves to be weakened by a reduction of their population. In 1939, black anthropologist W. Montague Cobb counseled the Afro-American to "maintain (a) high birth rate. . . . This alone has made him able to increase in spite of decimating mortality and hardships. If the tide should turn against him later, strength will be better than weakness in numbers." In 1945, Dr. Julian Lewis, a pathologist and former professor at the University of Chicago, predicted that blacks could survive in the U.S. only if they sustained a high birth rate. White population growth would be assured by their relatively low death rate, he said. Birth control on a wide scale, consequently, would be race suicide for blacks, it was argued. By that time the northern urban migration was underway. Columnist Langston Hughes foresaw the dispatch of a "sterilization wagon" to Harlem, sent by helpful whites who would merely be wanting to lend a helping hand to that underprivileged, over-populated section of New York City.

More recent opinion surveys by William Darity and his colleagues[2] substantiated elsewhere what obviously existed in Pittsburgh: a particular hostility toward birth control services by black males under age thirty. The young men that Darity talked to seemed to be more conscious of "alleged plots and genocide" than other segments of the black population. Now that segregation is officially unavailable, they were wary of any form of fertility control that could supply the white majority with an instrument to bring about "the final solution" to the race problem. A young, growing population, on the other hand, would be expected to keep up the pressure for social change, a requisite condition for black politicians to be effective. In a medium-sized New England city, Darity's team found strength-in-numbers attitudes among the young men. Fully half that group agreed with the flat statement that "black families should not limit their family sizes." Another study of black couples in Philadelphia and Charlotte revealed a general feeling among both sexes that sex education and contraception were okay but abortion and sterilization were unacceptable forms of birth control. Registering "strong support for the idea that birth control clinics are genocide," they favored complete community control of clinics that were operating. A majority of the respondents agreed with the statement: "As the need for cheap labor goes down, there will be an effort to decrease the black population."

In his statement to the Commission on Population Growth and the American Future, Professor Willie of Syracuse said:

> Many people in the black community are deeply suspicious of any family planning program initiated by whites. . . . The genocidal charge is neither absurd nor hollow as some whites have contended. Neither is it limited to residents of the ghetto, whether they be low-income black militants or middle-aged black moderates. Indeed my studies of black students at white colleges indicate that young educated blacks fear black genocide.
>
> Because so little trust exists between the races in the United States, when whites speak of limiting fertility or controlling the family in any way, many blacks feel that

whites are planning to return to a modified Malthusian plan which has controlled black family life in the past. Blacks know that their families have been disrupted and limited in the past because of deaths. They therefore are suspicious of any plan that does not assure them death again, individually or collectively, will not be the chief controlling variable.[3]

It has been shown that black women are generally less hostile now toward the use of contraceptives. Studies indicated not only that more of them understand and approve birth control but that more of them at all economic and educational levels are practicing it. In Pittsburgh, about seventy women members of the Welfare Rights Organization rejected Haden's lead. "Who appointed him our leader anyhow?" inquired Mrs. Georgiana Henderson. "We're getting tired of his statements. He is only one person— and a man at that. He can't speak for the women of Homewood. Birth control is none of his business. Why should I let one loud-mouth tell me about having children." Similar expressions were heard from other women in the group who said they would not tolerate male invasion of territorial rights over their bodies.[4] Most of the commotion about the clinic, the women noticed, seemed to be coming from men—"men who do not have to bear the children."[5]

Mrs. Frankie Pace, who lived in the Hill District in the heart of the city's black ghetto, said many of her neighbor women were ignorant of birth control methods and needed help. Some thought urinating after intercourse would prevent conception. Once the Planned Parenthood national headquarters in New York had sent in representatives—blacks not whites—to organize the women, it was obvious that the "consumers" of the birth control services did not see the program as a genocidal plot that would bring about their extermination.

This newly articulated tension between the sexes was not lessened any by the cocky Black Panther rhetoric. The Panthers' proclamation in favor of "pussy power," for instance, antagonized the sisterhood still more after a subsequent explanation by one of the Panthers that he was only trying to say that "you sisters have a strategic position for the revolution—prone."[6]

Shirley Chisholm, a feisty black congresswoman from Brooklyn, dismissed the genocide talk as mostly "male rhetoric for male ears." "Young black women who watched their own mothers and grandmothers struggle to raise a family alone are no longer willing to listen to a black man's cry of genocide," seconded the black author Carolyn Jones. A rare militant male who was able to understand that female point-of-view, Julius Lester, offered this comment:

> Those black militants who stand up and tell women to "produce black babies!" are telling black women to be slaves. . . . To have 11 children and a welfare check is almost akin to suicide, no matter how much black militants want to romanticize the black mother. There is power in numbers, but that power is greatly diminished if a lot of these numbers have to sit home and change diapers instead of being on the front lines where most of them would rather be.

Some of the younger black women whose knowledge of birth control practices extended beyond their own neighborhoods and personal experiences were more critical. Mrs. Naomi Gray, a former member of the Planned Parenthood national staff, presented this picture in her testimony before the study commission:

> Any hope of engaging the cooperation of blacks has been severely handicapped—if not annihilated—by the bandwagoning of a vast majority of white interests into this population/ecology movement. The question of who gets to survive is raised. So to us it's like every man for himself now, because we have no reason to expect that we won't get the worst of this [movement] too. It's like putting the cart before the horse to put family planning clinics before health care clinics. It can legitimately be said that some white interests are more concerned with causing certain black babies not to be born than with the survival of those already born. Many blacks in this country want to be left alone at this point. They are tired of being dragged along behind white movements which are irrelevant or detrimental to their interests.
>
> What few white liberal forces were left after the "backlash" have gone off traipsing after daisies and low-phosphate detergents.

At the first National Conference on Optimum Population and Environment in 1970, the caucus of black delegates walked out of the meeting after asserting that "the elimination of dangerous species such as rats, roaches, and other vermin is of more immediate concern to black people than the preservation of brook trout, buffalo, and bald eagles." The black delegates complained that they had been invited to "legitimize a preconceived plan of vicious extermination." One of them, Mrs. Freddie Mae Brown, chairman of the Metropolitan Black Survival Committee in St. Louis, said: "The whites are scared of us blacks getting control. Otherwise all their population control programs would not be directed at ghettos."

On other occasions, another black woman, Dr. Frances Cress Welsing, who is a child psychiatrist in the District of Columbia, has told black people they are sadly mistaken if they consider birth control "under white supremacy" to be in their best interests. She believes, too, that the different male and female attitudes are understandable. Both are part of a population under extreme pressure. Men who have been deprived of equal opportunity to be a success may feel their only way of demonstrating their manhood is to be a sex machine. And women who do not know whether they will wind up having to care for their children by themselves are likely to be receptive to a certain amount of family planning.[7] As a general rule, though, Austin suggests that the availability of day-care services is likely to be a more pressing need for working mothers.

Assessing the opinion of any group on a question as sensitive as birth control is tentative enough, especially when many of the people are hesitant about expressing their views or are unable to see it as in any way involving a political question. More tentative than that is separation of opinion into neat categories.[8] Black opinion can be divided into radical and nonradical groupings, separated generally by a willingness to consider the possible benefits of birth control.

Back in 1962 the establishmentarian head of the Urban League, Whitney Young, was skeptical of birth control programs on these grounds: First, many of the state administrators, in the South especially, were racists who he said could not be trusted; second, he accused Planned Parenthood of having "a single-minded interest in our welfare designed more to control population expansion and reduce taxes than to achieve a humane and social goal"; and finally there was an absence of minority representation in the local operation of the programs. Marvin Davies, an official of the Florida branch of another nonradical association, the NAACP, said simply (and honestly) that government-supported birth control was "not in the best interests of the black people. Our women need to produce more babies, not less. Our problems are mainly economic, and until we comprise 30 to 35 percent of the population we won't really be able to affect the power structure in this country."

Darity quotes in his study from remarks at a meeting of the Southern Christian Leadership Conference in South Carolina, an organization that probably belongs somewhere between the Panthers and the Urban League:

"Birth control is a plot just as segregation was a plot to keep the Negro down."

"Let's just have more and more Negroes and we'll overcome them by sheer numbers alone; we'll take what's ours."

"Birth control is compared to 'stopping the germ before it starts' and 'weeding out impurities.' "[9]

Radicals, it might be said, are less uncertain of white motives. Assuming the worst, Black Muslims and Black Panthers believe absolutely that they cannot be secure unless there is a growing black population. Muslim leader Elijah Muhammed asked, "why don't they divide the country with you, give you a few of these United States, and let you raise all the children you want?" In California, a militant organization used the acronym EROS— Endeavor to Raise Our Size.

Black consciousness of the genocide issue gained momentum in 1968 following the assassination of Dr. King and the convening of a conference on human values in family planning at Cleveland later in the year. Thereafter the genocide issue became a standard for any young black politician even mildly radical. Comedian Dick Gregory said, "My answer to genocide, quite simply, is eight black kids—and another baby on the way." Jesse Jackson, the Chicagoan who sat in a chair Mayor Daley thought would be his at the 1972 Democratic National Convention, considered family planning "a form of drug warfare against the helpless . . . whose relative increase in population threatens the white caste in this nation." "The assumption is that the so-called black migrant [from the South] is some type of foreign element in the city," he continued. "But [they] are citizens. Miami made a home for Cuban refugees who were neither citizens nor persons familiar with the language and culture of this nation. They now claim a very healthy share of the economy of greater Miami."[10]

Haden's allies in the Pittsburgh fight tell us a great deal about the politics of the issue. Throughout the controversy the most prominent spokesman for his cause was a black physician, Dr. Charles E. Greenlee, chairman of the health committee of the Pittsburgh NAACP. The doctor pursued two themes, one that "our only power is in our birth rate," the other that the government was coercing black women into practicing birth control, "to make less niggers so they won't have to build houses for them." In the course of the debate he raised some legitimate questions about the morality of distributing birth control pills to girls as young as twelve.

In black communities everywhere, the neighborhood physicians were in a unique position to be struck by the incongruity of making free contraceptives suddenly available to people who lacked basic health services. What is sometimes called the African Queen mentality—suburban ladies trooping valiantly into the fearsome ghetto bearing their kits of loops and condoms—has always been a difficult public relations problem for family planners. Outreach workers are quick to call on women who forget to renew their birth control pill prescription. But Stycos quotes a black critic: "What hospital has a policy of visiting sick people who skip their appointments? What welfare group sends volunteers to the homes of people who miss getting their check or their chance to get welfare food supplies? Do they have 'volunteers' going out and telling people about good jobs?"[11] A national conference on the status of health in the black community accused the government of promoting family planning for the poor at the expense of maternal and child health services.

At its 1968 meeting, the black medical organization (the National Medical Association) condemned the continuing high infant morality statistics. "Some of our physicians insist that Black Power is the concept most likely to . . . challenge the whole value system of American life," related one of the NMA leaders.[12] "Major teaching hospitals, North and South, frequently prevent the black M.D. from participating in obstetrical care but do allow him to work in family planning clinics. 'The best way to get Nigras is to get them before they are born' is still a common saying."

An official of the family planning program in the District of Columbia, who asked not to be identified ("funding sources do not appreciate frank talk about family planning"), told me that the regional offices of OEO and later HEW never thought of contraception as but one ingredient in a comprehensive health program. "Their only questions were, 'how many people did you see?' and 'how much money did you spend?' A pure numbers game." The same official recalled how community resistance to the development of satellite family planning clinics had been overcome with difficulty in the national capital. "I showed them the maternal mortality statistics for the previous five years. Fifty-four women lost their lives during childbirth in the District of Columbia, two of them white. So if I was really interested in something genocidal, I'd tell all the black women to go out and get pregnant, and they'll die at the rate of 25-to-1."

Haden's other important partner in that campaign, besides the black doctors, was the Catholic diocese of Pittsburgh, which contributed to the financial support of his organization. The church's contribution included a $10,000 salary subsidy paid directly to Haden. More important, the church's influence over public opinion was committed to the battle, via Msgr. Charles Owen Rice, a well-known liberal leader of the anti-Vietnam war movement and the author of a regular column in the diocesan newspaper. Catholic members of the citywide community action board had successfully resisted the birth control clinics, the clergyman noted, until "our Mayor, Joseph Barr, another good Catholic, cast the deciding vote that unleashed the Pittsburgh experiment." Depicting the clinic program as "an invitation to the Negroes to commit race suicide," Monsignor Rice wrote:

> . . . Our Catholic leadership has been wooed, unsuccessfully thank God, on many levels with the promise that "we will leave your people alone. The proliferating Negro is our target." . . . Sluicing a flow of birth control pills into poor Negro ghettos is sociological vandalism. Those ghettos are in a precarious condition not only materially but spiritually; and by spiritual I intend the broadest meaning. . . . The Pill Mill will roll for the black poor. In births, according to our rulers, White is good and Black is bad. Along the same line of policy the Negro will be shown how to indulge without fear of pregnancy, and the result ought to be twofold: one, less relief money; two, fewer black folks.[13]

Thus the church hierarchy made a decision in Pittsburgh different from the one that had been made in Chicago when Arnold

Maremont wanted contraceptives made available to the black poor—and different from the one made by the Democratic political leadership of Pittsburgh. In neither case did the church have a direct interest, most blacks being non-Catholics;[14] unless, that is, the potential growth of the black population is perceived as being against the interests of the white parishes in the central city. This, I maintain, is precisely what happened in the Chicago case. In Pittsburgh, despite the conscious "forfeiture" of the white poverty areas by Planned Parenthood, the antagonisms between the Catholic clergy and Planned Parenthood were so rigid and of such long standing that the church lined up instinctively on the side of whoever happened to be squaring off against the family planners. It is worth noting too that Dr. Greenlee's columns in local black newspapers stressed Catholic "right-to-life" arguments by referring to "kill pills," "death in a douche bag," etc.

In the meantime a family planning clinic had been burned in Cleveland. Executives of Planned Parenthood and OEO were nervous. So the Homewood-Brushton clinic, now located in a neighborhood church, closed temporarily in 1968. Then at the beginning of the following year Haden and Greenlee persuaded the Pittsburgh CAA to withdraw its support for that and five other poverty centers in black neighborhoods—the first such rejection of an OEO family planning grant anywhere in the nation.

After the clinics were shut down, the organized women kept agitating for their reopening. In this effort they were assisted by a coalition of Presbyterian, Episcopal, Unitarian, Baptist, Lutheran, and Jewish congregations, representatives of which signed a joint freedom-of-conscience statement. Bethesda United Presbyterian church, a neighborhood congregation, denounced Haden's threats of violence. "To label such a program genocide is patently false," the Presbyterians declared. "To say that coercion is used in so intimate an area is open to question. No strictures are too strong, no criticism too severe, no condemnations too harsh calling to task those persons who would thus mislead and inflame the public on this important issue."

Haden fought back hard. "The white power structure won't spend a dime to kill the rats that eat up your babies," he told the women, "but they'll spend thousands to make sure you can't have any babies."

William Austin, who reviewed the dispute for his Urban League study, said the women fully understood that there were no Planned Parenthood clinics in white poverty neighborhoods, but they still perceived the free services to be in their own best interests; and they did not appreciate being thought of as random reproduction machines that could be put to political use. "We're speaking for the women and we want the Planned Parenthood centers to stay in our neighborhood," protested Mrs. Henderson's group. The women took advantage of their strategic position in the controversy to demand a permanent location for the clinic with more privacy and cleaner facilities.

Many neighborhood blacks were distressed by the public quarreling. At one of the meetings, "black women teased and taunted Haden." A columnist for a black newspaper, Carl Morris in *The New Courier*, said "their jovial rejoinders heightened the stereotype that many whites have about blacks—a promiscuous sex life. A young black woman attempted to tell her older sisters that arguing in public before whites was an error, that black people need to get together, that they should settle their differences behind closed doors."[15]

Though the demonstration of feminine black unity was engineered by Planned Parenthood's now-battle-seasoned legions in New York City, OEO and the political leadership in Pittsburgh had to be impressed. Shortly thereafter, on a motion by the Democratic organization's ward chairman, employed on Mayor Barr's city payroll as a human services aide, Haden was removed as the Homewood-Brushton Citizens Renewal Council delegate on the citywide board. Federal antipoverty funds were restored and the centers reopened at improved locations in the black neighborhoods. The Catholic newspaper predicted that maternity wards would be closed at nearby hospitals "for at the rate the white man is winning the black genocide game there'll be no young blacks forty years from now. And the blacks assist in their own funeral march."

Greenlee and Haden capitulated, but neither the fear nor the issue of genocide subsided. Bills were introduced in many state legislatures proposing mandatory sterilization after a specified number of illegitimate pregnancies. Legislators in California, Connecticut, Delaware, Georgia, Illinois, Iowa, Louisiana, Maryland, Ohio, Tennessee, Mississippi, North Carolina, and

Virginia proposed a welfare cutoff unless mothers of two or more illegitimate children submitted to sterilization. Other bills that were introduced but failed to pass would have provided cash incentives to welfare mothers who agreed to sterilization. Rep. David H. Glass of Kosciusko, Mississippi, a sponsor of the legislation in that state, said: "The Negro woman, because of child welfare assistance [is] making it a business in some cases of giving birth to illegitimate children. . . . The purpose of my bill was to try to stop, or slow down, such traffic at its source."[16] A pamphlet quoted another sponsor, Rep. Stone Banfield, as forecasting that "once the cutting starts" (meaning the surgical sterilization) "they'll head for Chicago" (alluding to the flow of black migrants to northern cities).[17] The bill passed the house but was defeated in the senate.

Compulsory sterilization of unwed mothers was seriously debated in two successive General Assemblies of North Carolina. Supporters warned of rising AFDC expenditures and the consequences of "breeding a race of bastards," but church groups, principally the Catholic bishop of Raleigh, and other opinion leaders, notably Harry Golden, editor of the *Carolina Israelite*, rallied the opposition and successfully blocked the bill.

According to author Samuel Yette,[18] a panel at the 1969 White House Conference on Food and Nutrition considered a proposal by the chairman, Dr. Charles U. Lowe of the National Institutes of Health, that unmarried minor females be sterilized after giving birth a second time. In Yette's account, Fannie Lou Hamer, the Mississippi civil rights leader, is credited with having confronted Lowe and forcing the withdrawal of the sterilization resolution. Mrs. Hamer said on another occasion that "six out of every ten Negro women were taken to Sunflower city hospital [in her home town] to be sterilized for no reason at all. Often the women were not told that they had been sterilized until they were released from the hospital."[19]

Mrs. Hamer had herself been sterilized without her knowledge when she went into the hospital to have a small uterine tumor—"a knot on my stomach," she called it—removed.

She was recuperating from the operation when she heard what they were saying in the big house at the plantation. Vera Alice Marlow—cousin of the doctor and wife of the plantation owner—told her cook and the cook told Mrs.

Hamer's cousin who told her: Fannie Lou had been given a hysterectomy.

"For a long time I was very angry about what had been done to me. If he was going to give that sort of operation then he should have told me. I would have loved to have children. I went to the doctor who did that to me and I asked him, Why? Why had he done that to me? He didn't have to say anything—and he didn't."[20]

The Hamers had not had any children of their own, only an adopted daughter. Did she consider suing the doctor? "At that time? Me? Getting a white lawyer to go against a white doctor? I would have been taking my hands and screwing tacks in my own casket." Physicians in many northern cities still report seeing patients, young women recently arrived from the South who had been surgically sterilized without knowing it. "They mean birth control just for the poor and black women," Mrs. Hamer complained. "After all, the white folks don't need the black children to pick the cotton now and they have the defoliants to strip the leaves and pull off the cotton bolls. They're telling so many people they need to be on birth control pills. It makes me so mad when I hear them say we're becoming too many. Folks are sick that say we're too many. Only God can determine that. A God that can keep the fowl in the air and the grass green certainly wouldn't have made the earth too small."[21]

A black woman in Mound Bayou, Mississippi, remembered signing at age ten, as the only literate member of her family, a release form which allowed a white doctor to perform what she now considers an unnecessary hysterectomy on her mother. In Jackson, Mississippi, a black doctor told of two young women who came to his office after a visit to a white clinic. They had inquired about an abortion and were advised that they should also have hysterectomies, although the black doctor could find no medical reason for that.

The wave of punitive proposals directed at welfare recipients added to the climate of racial hostility. Richard Friske, a convervative state legislator from Michigan, reflected the views of many Americans when he asserted: "There is a need for curbing the growth of the drone population that weakens our society. Educated, propertied Americans need a vigorous pro-natalist outlook, but the tax pressure on the middle-class all but forbids this . . . while the ignorant dependent elements multiply.'' William Shockley, Nobel Laureate in physics, advocated cash incentives for welfare recipients to be sterilized. The pressure for punitive action was especially severe in the case of young people. When conventional persuasion fails and a teen-ager has a second illegitimate child, a court should order the insertion of an IUD (intrauterine device), U.S District Court Judge Don J. Young of Dayton, Ohio, argued in a paper presented to the National Council of Juvenile Court Judges and published in the American Bar Association *Journal*. This would allow time for social workers to ''rehabiliate'' the young person, the judge maintained. ''By now many girls with more than one illegitimate child have had IUDs inserted,'' he said, ''but so far the practice has not been the result of a court order, since the girls' parents have voluntarily seen to it that the contraceptive method is employed.'' The judge had no doubt that ''as a technical legal proposition the power of the juvenile court in dealing with children adjudged to be delinquent is far greater than the powers accorded generally to the courts for the purposes of commitment of the mentally retarded,'' including compulsory sterilization.[22]

The proportion of female sterilizations performed for ''contraceptive reasons'' as distinguished from medical reasons, was higher for black women and women of Spanish origin than for American women generally. Johan Eliot said low-income women were taking part in organized family planning programs ''because they want urgently to control their fertility.''

> One wonders whether nonwhite women, more often served in public facilities, are offered the option more frequently than white women who, for the most part, are served by private physicians in their own offices. Nonwhite Americans are not unaware of how the American Indian came to be called the vanishing American . . . . This country's starkest example of genocide in practice.[23]

Latin-American ethnic groups of poor living in the Southwest and in northern U.S. cities did not take readily to organized birth control. Their traditional Catholic cultural preference for large families complicated the mission of the fertility controllers. As we have seen, Mexican-American birth rates are double those of other Americans. But so is the infant mortality rate. Cesar

Chavez, charismatic organizer of farm workers in the Southwest, opposed birth control for the Chicano people, partly because of his Catholic faith and partly because of his belief that "smaller families would diminish the numerical power of the poor."[24] "Our only solution" Chavez has argued, "is to make the minority much less a minority and make the race multiply and progress." For the Chicano to accept birth control, said Joe C. Ortega, attorney for the Mexican-American Legal Defense Fund, would be to give up his most treasured asset, his large family. "It is for upper-class society a marvelous thing to talk of zero population growth," Ortega observed, ". . . but for the *pobre de la tierra* (poor of the earth) it is just another cliché wherein the rules of the game have been changed to suit someone else."

Among the most fascinating aspects of fertility control politics in the United States is the examination of Jewish attitudes. Jews, quite often, are being tugged in opposite directions. They recognize the problems of overpopulation, yet are concerned about the diminishing influence of their own religious group in American political affairs if their own numbers continue to decrease. In 1974 there were a little over six million Jews in the U.S., fifty-five thousand more than the year before despite smaller-than-average family size and a declining group birth rate. Throughout this century, Jews were vociferously active egalitarian leaders of Planned Parenthood and other outlets for the birth control establishment defined earlier, as philanthropists, academicians, doctors, businessmen, government officials, publishers, social workers. More recently, Jewish Americans were prominently identified with the Zero Population Growth and environmental protection movements.

Nevertheless, while Jews were in the vanguard of the campaign to check population growth and to prevent excessive births by the poor and the uneducated, their own religious leaders were reminding them of their rich cultural superiority and pleading with them to have more children and head off the impending "disappearance" of Judaism in this country.

Jews tend to be urban people. They live in big cities—over 2,380,000 in the New York City area alone; over a half million in Los Angeles. Other large concentrations are in the Philadelphia, Chicago and Miami metropolitan areas. Because Jews and blacks share a historic familiarity with injustice and oppression wherever they have lived, their coexistence in the central cities of America was destined to be, in the words of a recent book, a "bittersweet encounter."[25] While the black ghetto was expanding in many big cities, Jewish citizens hung on as money-lenders, merchants, slum landlords, school principals, and welfare caseworkers. Economic and social friction followed. Anti-Semitism assumed a prominent place in the rhetoric of black nationalism. In the 1960s, CORE and other civil rights organizations were bankrolled by Jewish contributors. Whenever some black militant uttered an anti-Semitic remark, which happened frequently, the wealthy Jews threatened to withdraw their financial support unless the leaders repudiated the offender to the satisfaction of the easily offended patrons.

Zero population growth might be a good idea for other people but it would be "a disservice to humanity for Jews to disappear," said Rabbi William Berman of New York, organizer of the Jewish Population Regeneration Union.[26] Ira Silverman, director of the Institute for Jewish Policy Planning of the Synagogue Council of America, stressed the importance of Jewish survival "through the generative, the procreative process." He said the Jewish community would be better served by the three-child model than by the two-child ideal. He could understand the arithmetic of a democracy, too, it would seem. Orthodox Rabbi Norman Lamm set his sights higher, recommending Jewish families of four or five children and adding pessimistically that Jews are a disappearing species and should be treated no worse than the kangaroo and the bald eagle. "Our goal should be constant expansion," declared Sol Roth, president of the New York board of rabbis, reasoning that "the Jewish community will not solve the world's problems by applying Z.P.G. to itself." A survey of the Hassidic Jewish community of Williamsburg in Brooklyn indicated that the residents were "unalterably opposed to any limitation of their population on moral, philosophic, and pragmatic grounds."

Pragmatism being a valued but variable concept, consistency is a virtue that ethnic group population thinkers manage to forego. Blacks say they are in a position to take over the commercial centers of America ("the city has become the black man's land") if their numbers continue to grow, even if the rest of the people have to support them ("work and welfare need to be redefined in our society as equal rights"). Cesar Chavez says the Chicanos can speak with a louder voice and demand economic justice only if their numbers expand. Jews are the first to warn against the dangers of population growth, but their religious counselors say that society would not benefit, and Jewish power would surely suffer, if Jews, who are culturally superior, keep on having smaller families.

Replying to the article in *Time* that quoted the views of Rabbis Berman and Lamm, Barry Neidorf of Northbrook, Ill., had this comment:

> Not too many years ago, when Zero Population Growth was first publicized, the black community denounced it as a racist policy. Now [the rabbis] are making these same assertions on behalf of Jews. As a Jew and a father, I don't feel it is necessary to design my family around the needs of my religion but rather around the needs of my economic status and the world at large. Any attempt at equating Z.P.G with anti-Semitism is a frightening Kafkaesque paranoia.

In his restrained report for the Urban League, William Austin concluded that family planning, in its present form, did not seem to be "overly genocidal." He noted the presence, however, of a number of "grave problems which could be extremely harmful if not corrected immediately." What American population policy there is is based on family planning directed at curbing the fertility of the poor, and not as part of a more comprehensive health policy. Nor is there any national legislative policy regarding sterilization. "Because of the wide latitude that private doctors, private clinics, medical research organizations and local officials have in this area, we consider it to have the most dangerous implications for black and poor people," Austin said. He recommended the formation of a nonprofit private corporation to operate family planning programs with government support and community representation on the board of directors; an independent national monitoring system to watch for abuses; and more nonwhites in policymaking positions within the family planning structure.

If Congress were to come right out with it and proclaim a policy of forcibly reducing the fertility of those who can't take care of themselves, would that be "black genocide"? If it is in the political interests of black people to be one out of five or even one out of four of the national population, is there some way their political leaders and representatives can make that happen? Sociologist Phillips Cutright addresses the second question by drawing a parallel between racial attitudes on birth control and the historic Catholic-Protestant experience in the United States. In the 1920s, Catholic immigration was "controlled" by the enactment of national origin quotas, he says, because Protestants were alarmed by the growing Catholic population. As recently as the Kennedy campaign of 1960 there were some Americans who believed that Catholics had more children as a deliberate strategy to capture the political apparatus in succeeding generations, a conspiratorial alliance of cleric and parishoner that defied logical analysis. The birth rate is still higher for Catholics than for non-Catholics in the United States. In the mid-1950s, Catholics representing 20 percent of the childbearing-age population had 30 percent of the babies. Catholics had to do more than have a lot of babies to acquire power, however; and that they did, Cutright points out, by living in a few large urban states and by settling pretty much on one political party. Similarly, residential segregation and not their own choice have forced most blacks to live together in central cities. There is, says Cutright, no evidence that fertility differentials have ever allowed any American minority group to rise to political power in the past.[27]

The implications of a population control policy aimed at the poor are nonetheless obvious, especially if the policy is coated with hypocrisy, as it is now. Norman Hilmar expressed it well in a speech to a Planned Parenthood audience:

> One hopes that our very legitimate concern about excessive population growth in the years ahead will not be perverted into propaganda efforts which, by design or by accident, stampede us into willingness and even eagerness to ameliorate our society's population problems by ruthless measures to force down the fertility of the poor, the politically impotent, and the unpopular among us. . . .
>
> If birth control assistance is aggressively pushed on the poor without concurrent and *tangible* efforts to improve their life chances substantially, their "antiestablishment" reactions and suspicions will with considerable justification be exacerbated.

. . . If we rely on blatant coercion or "subtle" manipulation to take from couples their options with respect to bearing children, we still cannot guarantee that the birth rate would fall before the government does. And we probably would be embarking on a course of increasingly brutal oppression which would unduly postpone if not extinguish human freedom and responsible self-government. The herd manager and the game warden are not very appealing models to emulate in the management of human affairs.[28]

CHAPTER 6 Birth Rates in the Bayous . . . the Saga of Joe Beasley

Joe Beasley will save the world—unless the government hangs him first.
— Attorney Jim Garrison

The time is early autumn of 1965, a few months after the Illinois welfare birth control controversy had been settled and while Sargent and Eunice Shriver were trying to work out what part family planning would play in the Great Society's antipoverty program. The place is the Petroleum Club in Shreveport, Louisiana. Over a sumptuous dinner of the finest Chateaubriand, Joseph Diehl Beasley, doctor of medicine, is engaged comfortably in conversation with Msgr. Marvin Bordelon representing the bishops of the Catholic dioceses of Louisiana. In that unlikely setting, the charismatic young crusader from coastal Georgia and the clergyman from French Louisiana are discussing the New Politics of Population. To be more precise, they are negotiating the conditions under which the church would permit Beasley to begin providing tax-financed birth control services to low-income residents of the state.

At that time, in the mid-1960s, it was still a felony to disseminate information about contraceptives in Louisiana much less think up ways of giving them away to the poor at public expense. The social turmoil of those years spawned many social engineers like Joe Beasley, but not many with quite so much ego-driven determination, far-down-the-road vision, organizational talent, promotional zeal, and political daring.

He was born in the little town of Glennville, not far from Savannah, the son of a professional baseball player and an aspiring opera singer who were married to one another three times and divorced from one another three times. Out on his own at an early age, Beasley worked his way through medical school at Emory University in Atlanta, at odd jobs as dishwasher, hodcarrier, bartender. He learned obstetrics and gynecology, then became a surgeon. "I really loved it—particularly tramautic surgery," he recalled later. "I couldn't think about much else—and that's very good treatment for anxiety. You could be as manic as you liked."[1] But the youthful surgeon was more intrigued by the "generic" health problems of people who lived in the underdeveloped nations. After enrolling at the University of London School of Medicine, he returned to Tulane University, primarily because of that institution's interest in tropical disease, epidemiology, and Latin America. His work with the underdeveloped countries convinced him that "the major problems involved in health care and human services didn't have much to do with what I'd been working on the previous nine years. The obvious need was more balance—population control."

If birth rates could be lowered at home in Louisiana, perhaps a more efficient system could be devised for delivering health services to the poor that would serve as a prototype for the rest of the world. "From both a political and religious point-of-view, Louisiana [is] a particularly sensitive workshop," Beasley recognized. He thought of the state as an especially challenging test of what he had in mind because of the notable lack of concern by government with the plight of the poor; the high rate of illegitimate births; the racial problems and the punitive approach to welfare dependency; and, finally, because of the influence of the Catholic church. In 1958 a committee of the Louisiana legislature had considered and rejected compulsory sterilization as a remedy for illegitimacy. One or the other of the houses of the legislature did at various times pass bills which would have imprisoned or fined both parents of illegitimate children. The high incidence of illegitimacy was a pressing issue in the state.

First the state law had to be changed by the legislature to permit birth control assistance for the poor, a goal that could never be achieved without the church's cooperation. Unlike the governor of Illinois, Beasley knew better than to put the bishops on the spot by confronting them directly. Instead he identified and sought out the lower echelons of the church hierarchy that would be more likely to understand his desire to correct the cycle of welfare dependency. Before approaching the New Orleans' archdiocesan

Family Life Apostolate (an agency comparable to the bureau that Father Imbiorski headed in Chicago), Beasley assembled data to show the correlation between infant mortality and the health of the mother at the time of conception. He documented the predictable health problems of babies born to unmarried adolescents. In this way, he tried to illustrate the medical and social problems that occur when an ill mother becomes pregnant again, or a teen-ager becomes pregnant for the first time. After making his initial contacts with the family life personnel, Beasley waited for them to inform the archbishop, John Cody (later Cardinal Cody of Chicago). One of the bishop's assistants, Monsignor Bordelon, was then assigned by Cody to negotiate the details, if possible. Beasley found these meetings in a private dining room at the Commander's Palace in New Orleans and at other fancy restaurants to be highly productive. At no time, though, did the doctor put Cody in the position of having to declare himself or the church in favor of something contrary to Catholic doctrine, which of course artificial contraception was.

There are two Louisianas: French Louisiana stretches across the southern population centers and is Catholic; by southern standards, it has a tradition of racial tolerance. Northern Louisiana has a higher proportion of rural blacks, more fundamentalist Baptists, and more racial tension. Beasley agreed not to attempt any of "the things that really bugged them [the church leaders]"—namely, the use of mass communications to advertise or promote birth control services (one of the conditions stipulated by Shriver for the first OEO grants); and no referrals by clinics to other places where abortions or sterilizations would be performed. Beasley agreed further that Catholics who came to the birth control clinics would be told about the rhythm method of contraception and would be advised to consult their parish priest. But if they returned they would be provided with a contraceptive the same as anyone else. Most important of all, he offered to begin with a demonstration clinic not in French Catholic southern Louisiana around New Orleans, but in rural Lincoln Parish far to the north. Ruston is the seat of Lincoln Parish, which has a large non-Catholic black population, an ideal choice. Grambling College, a well-known Negro institution, is located there.

The church would be given an opportunity to "review" the program before it expanded into the southern parishes. "Another thing bugging them,'' Beasley said later, ''was that Planned Parenthood might come in and do all [of what we had promised not to do]. They saw me as a lesser evil than Planned Parenthood because this would be a completely state operation. And I was able to guarantee them [because] I had previously negotiated with Planned Parenthood in New York that they would *not* come in and do these other things.''[2]

When Beasley went to the governor of Louisiana, John McKeithen, to obtain his backing for the legislation repealing the antibirth control law, McKeithen could not believe that the plan had been approved tacitly or otherwise by Archbishop Cody. As in Illinois earlier, Catholic politicians under-emphasized the church's potential for compromise. ''He picked up the phone while I was in his office and called Cody,'' Beasley remembered much later. ''When the conversation ended, Big John was amazed. And not many things that happened in Louisiana amazed Big John.''[3]

Even at that early date, the thirty-three-year-old doctor was thinking in terms of a delivery system that could be ''replicated,'' to use one of his favorite words, nationwide and eventually worldwide. Joe Beasley entertained no small plans. ''The whole concern was with how you survey the land, lay the track, assemble the railroad cars and get the train moving,'' one of his top assistants has since explained to me. ''What was in the cars was secondary. It happened to be contraceptives.'' The contraceptives may have been secondary, but it is important to understand that when Beasley made the rounds of state and local centers of political power to obtain the necessary political ''clearance'' for what he had in mind, the political and medical establishments responded enthusiastically because they were worried about black birth rates and rising welfare costs. His own objectives recognized the connection between unwanted or excessive fertility and the health problems of the poor. He was thinking of comprehensive health services for the poor, of which family planning would be only a beginning. But Beasley understood enough about white southern attitudes to know that the prospect of restricting black births would appeal to people who could make his program succeed or fail, people who had little instinctive empathy for the poor and their problems. Besides, the only federal funding then likely to be available was ticketed for family planning. Systematically, he sounded out the state board of health, the state welfare department, the state department of hospitals, the state medical society, the tri-parish medical society in the Lincoln Parish area where the program would begin, and the regional hospital there. Beasley went to some lengths, in other words, to gain the cooperation of the state's elaborate welfare-health bureaucracy, although even then he had every intention of working around them to the extent practicable.

Louisiana has a statewide system of charity hospitals, which are in effect black hospitals. Most blacks who cannot pay for regular hospital services have their babies in the charity hospital. Most low-income whites in Louisiana who cannot afford regular maternity services somehow arrange to have their babies in hospitals other than the charity hospitals. The charity hospitals are comparable to New York City's municipal hospitals and Chicago's Cook County Hospital, except that they are more racially segregated. At the outset, a decision was made by Beasley to base the Louisiana family planning program in the charity hospital system. Priority attention would be given to postpartum patients in the charity hospitals, those who had just given birth.

To calm any possible misunderstanding of his concentration on the black community, Beasley wisely arranged a formal meeting with three black leaders in Lincoln Parish—the president of Grambling College, the head of the sociology department there, and a leading black businessman—all intelligent, respected community figures who were familiar with the problems stemming from high birth rates.

Beasley describes what happened:

> . . . We sort of used the three of them as a steering group. And then we initiated a program . . . we talked with them individually and in a series of small groups. . . . And then the next thing we decided to do was to have a big open meeting at the Baptist church in Lincoln Parish. It was full of old people, young people, women with children. I was properly introduced, and what have you, by the minister, and then I gave a talk on what we were going to do—what we were going to teach everybody about contraceptives. When I pulled out the first pill and condom up there in that church, I swear it was like—it was like the first violinist in the New York Philharmonic breaking out into a boogie-woogie in the middle of Bach. It was the quietest moment I have ever seen.

Everybody, even the children, just shut up because they sensed there was something big going on. And then this old fellow in the first row said, "Amen"—and *everybody* started talking.[4]

In that part of Louisiana, Beasley was able to deal with the black preachers and work with the Southern Baptist Conference. There were no Bouie Hadens to contend with. Through his prior acquaintance with Bruce Everist, a pediatrician at Lincoln General Hospital, Beasley was able to enlist the cooperation of local doctors, the Chamber of Commerce, and officials of the city government, thus avoiding the politics of confrontation. Without much of an organization at that stage, Beasley did most of the planning himself from his position on the staff of the Center for Population and Family Studies at Tulane. A "market" survey identified 961 women who had given birth since 1960 at one of the three charity hospitals in the area. They were marked as priority customers. No OEO funds or other direct project grants were available then from the federal government, so the project was financed by a research and development grant from the Children's Bureau in HEW. At the same time, he conducted studies of "attitudes and knowledge relevant to family planning among low-income, high-risk Negro women" in both Lincoln Parish and New Orleans. Because it was thought that poor women could not be relied upon to take The Pill regularly, intrauterine contraceptive devices (IUDs) were stressed.

Beasley knew it would be essential to use the services of local physicians as a necessary bridge to the community. He could not import doctors. But neither of the two obstetrician-gynecologists in the parish believed in the use of the IUD or were familiar with it. So they were flown by Beasley to meet with the commercial developers of the two IUDs then in use for an abbreviated training and indoctrination period. The available doctors and many of the other professional personnel had what Beasley soon saw as the wrong racial attitudes, formed during their work in the charity hospital system. So he not only insisted on strict standards of privacy and voluntariness, but organized paraprofessional health workers as a buffer between patient and physician. For postpartum patients, the first appointments usually were not made until six weeks after the birth of their children and included the postpartum examination, thus emphasizing the positive health-care aspects of family planning. The importance of direct patient contact was not overlooked. Elaborate follow-up procedures were practiced for those who missed appointments. "Outreach workers" were hired who could knock on doors and maintain the direct contact. This did not occur without some problems. One of the first outreach workers had been recommended by a black community leader before Beasley discovered that she was his mistress. This caused much local consternation and she was fired, which caused still more consternation.

Nevertheless, the first clinic, which was set up in an existing public health facility, worked phenomenally well. This was due in large part to the role played by the chief public health nurse, June Moore. Her mother had been the public health nurse before her and she was respected in the black community. It was she, for example, who was able to patch up the damage left by the outreach worker-mistress incident. In the first year and a half of operation, the birth rate among medically indigent women in Lincoln Parish dropped 32 percent, or by almost one third.[5] The rate of illegitimate births declined from 172 per 1,000 births to 121. Not insignificantly, more than 99 percent of the women served were Protestants.

Already Beasley was impatient with the bureaucratic procedures. "I tried to run the program [through] the state [government] and I couldn't do it. I couldn't get the nurses and the doctors and the people and the supplies and the penicillin—and I couldn't get them all occurring at the same time. I couldn't hire the kind of people I wanted because of civil service."

So in 1966 he set up an independent nonprofit corporation—Family Planning, Inc. Subsequently, Beasley acknowledged that "real down deep in my guts, I didn't want to work with the government when I started. It's very frustrating to work with government. If you're a can-do person in a can't-do system, it frustrates the hell out of you."[6]

The longer he continued the more convinced Beasley became that the state boards of health are primarily political instruments of the medical societies. "Almost all the boards of health in the United States . . . exist to perpetuate the private practice of medicine . . . to keep the state out of the private doctor's pocket," and not to help deliver health care services to poor people. "The board of health has never really been involved with delivering human health services. They immunize kids; they purify the Mississippi River for us to drink—it's a bloody goddamn miracle, but they do—they do these sort of things. But in terms of an operating entity, the concept that I talked about was fairly alien to a lot of people in the board of health. You could have set up an agency right up next to the governor, but then the board of health would have been merely middle-management. That would have killed them.''[7]

By now Beasley's corporation was eager to spread into other pastures. Congress had attached special priority to family planning. President Johnson, and Nixon after him, spoke of ambitious goals. The two family planning bureaucracies in Washington— the new one at OEO, the rival one in HEW—were competing to see which could dispense funds faster and report the more impressive results to the congressional appropriations committees. Grants were dished out without much attention to details of how they were spent. Logic would soon demand that the various funding sources be consolidated. The bureaucracies in Washington were maneuvering for dominance. Beasley willingly used what he called "flexible capital" from the Rockefeller, Ford, and other foundations to attract federal funds from any and all sources. He landed the first big OEO grants for projects in New Orleans, Baton Rouge, Alexandria, Shreveport, Monroe, Lafayette. The Catholic bishops acquiesced in the expansion. Beasley attributed this to the spirit of "serendipity" then abroad in the church, a term defined by Webster as the "gift of finding valuable or agreeable things not sought for." "It was a political decision," Beasley suggested to me later. "They knew those women were going to do that [use contraceptives] anyway." At the time, the ecumenical mood was in vogue and it appeared that the Church of Rome might change its position on birth control.

Before long Beasley's corporation had 144 birth control clinics operating all over Louisiana. Over sixty thousand new patients a year were receiving free government-supplied contraceptives. Over a million patient visits a year were being recorded. At one time, grants were being received from thirty-one different sources of funding. "If this can be done in such a short time in Louisiana," declared the head of the corporation, "it should not be unrealistic to assume that America can provide family planning services for its poor nationwide."

Joe Beasley of Louisiana was acclaimed the conquering hero of the family planning movement—a can-do fellow in a can't-do country. In a miraculously short time span, the Louisiana program had become a model of success. His clinics reported the best record of continuation—that is, of women who continued to use contraceptives after their initial experience—of any program in the world. This is the true mark of achievement in a birth control program, but it also requires a steadily increasing supply of funds as more people ask for free contraceptives while the old patients continue to take advantage of the subsidized assistance. Beasley became chairman of the board of the national Planned Parenthood organization. He and two other Planned Parenthood officers, Alan Guttmacher and Frederick Jaffe, were said to have "sponsored" Dr. Hellman for the top HEW family planning position. HEW Secretary Robert Finch asked Beasley to take the lead in designing the new Center for Family Planning Services in that department. He and the other officials of Planned Parenthood began mobilizing family planning leaders into pressure groups that could lobby effectively at the state level. Harvard University created a special chair in Population and Public Health for Beasley's parttime attention. Truly Mr. Family Planning in America, he began talking of "a model that could be replicated all over the world." He began to have visions of a Nobel Prize dancing in front of his eyes.

And if Dr. Joe was going to save the world, he was going to travel first-class doing it. Half a million dollars of corporation funds went for the purchase of an executive jet to speed him and others on their busy schedules. For Beasley's use when he visited Washington, the corporation paid the $960-a-month rent for an apartment in the Watergate building. He lived fast and high, entertaining foundation executives and parish bosses from the bayous at lavish dinners at Antoine's in the French Quarter. Joe Beasley's charming personality is an important element in all this: he bubbled over with grandiose schemes, a shameless self-promoter, very attractive to women, a master at government grantsmanship, a politically savvy organizer whose immodest long-range planning came to take precedence—unfortunately— over his check on the daily operations of his underlings.

Just as Beasley was preparing to introduce his program to New Orleans, the Queen City of French Louisiana, the genocide issue

had attracted attention in Pittsburgh and elsewhere. Don Hubbard, rising young leader of a militant Black Power organization
in the predominantly black lower Ninth Ward of the city—called
SOUL—made it an issue in New Orleans. Throughout Louisiana,
the birth control program was perceived by whites and blacks
alike as a black program. Very few low-income whites were
served by the clinics, reflecting (Beasley said) "their resistance
apparently to an integrated service." Once the program was
underway in New Orleans with its racially and culturally mixed
urban population, over 96 percent of the patients were black. A
promotional film that was produced to sell the program featured a
fatherly black doctor, although in fact almost all the doctors were
white and not many of them were very fatherly. Intelligent blacks
resented such sales techniques. From the beginning Beasley had
devoted much of his time to reassuring established black spokesmen—generally the older preachers who were considered the
political representatives—that there would be no coercion. Yet
none of the six top officials in Beasley's corporate management
were black.

His confrontations with the young militants became more frequent and more urgent. As in Pittsburgh, outreach workers were
intimidated by Black Panthers. A white nurse was murdered in
the Mississippi delta region. Clinics were threatened with bomb-
ing. One observer described what he referred to as "the Mau-
Mauing" of Beasley's program by "a small group of well-
organized individuals in the New Orleans black community. The
time is right, the providers of the service are feeling anxious (read
vulnerable), and black militancy still scares folks."[8] For their
meetings with Beasley, the black spokesmen were accompanied
by "imported, highly-costumed, dashiki-clad, paratrooper-
booted, dark-sunglasses-wearing, bereted young street fighters
who can glare with the best of them. There is an air of hostility
artificial or not." Beasley came armed with charts and graphs.
But the black leaders announced forthwith that there would be no
more "talking at" the black community. They read off a list of
demands, dropped the paper on the table and walked out after five
minutes.

In New Orleans, almost half of the population in the 1970
census was black; yet *none* of the seven members of the city
council was black, a situation that we will examine in more detail

in a later chapter. Under the new order, a white politician who hoped to govern the city would need the organized help of black politicians. Associated with Hubbard in the SOUL organization was a talented and ambitious black man who understood how the game was played, even though he had always been on the outside looking in. His name was Sherman Copelin. Copelin and Hubbard delivered the black vote to the successful mayoral candidate, Moon Landrieu, in return tor which they were promised a share of the spoils beginning with Copelin's appointment as director of the city's federally-funded model cities program. The model cities program was another of the Johnson administration's Great Society initiatives, an effort to demonstrate how selected urban neighborhoods could be improved by the equivalent of a massive injection of broad-spectrum drugs, ranging from better garbage collection to physical rehabilitation and jobs for school dropouts.

Copelin and his friends wanted to be let in on Beasley's spoils too. They wanted seats at Antoine's and on the executive jet. They wanted to be involved in top management, and they wanted the clinics to serve all the health needs of the community and not just the sexual passions of the black people.

Without further ado, Beasley made two key decisions.

First, he decided to wait no longer before taking his family planning corporation the next step by converting it into a comprehensive health center operation. Plans called for the opening of a parent-child development center, plus three health centers that would be integrated into Copelin's model cities program serving a hundred thousand people in three inner-city neighborhoods. The city health department would be bypassed altogether. Nobody endeavored to keep a low profile. With much attendant publicity all over the state, Beasley's corporation was renamed the Family Health Foundation.

Second, he decided to try to buy off his black critics. Whereas Mayor Barr in Pittsburgh had crushed Bouie Haden, and Planned Parenthood had overridden his protests by organizing the welfare mothers against him, Beasley followed a different strategy. Political scientists call it the politics of co-option. Richard J. Daley of Chicago, who used it very successfully for a long time to the mutual benefit of (almost) everyone involved, would explain it differently, something like: "If a guy's giving you trouble, and you can't stop it, you take him in."

Patronage had always been a headache for Beasley. Many state and parish health officers had been retained as consultants on his payroll. Jobs were given to two daughters of a brother of McKeithen's successor as governor, Edwin Edwards. The foundation payroll grew to over a thousand regular employees. "We had to deal constantly on political terms with the state and federal governments," he explained to a class at Harvard at about that time. "There is pressure on you for patronage in every god-damned place. If you don't go for patronage, you get hurt politically. If you go for patronage, you hurt your morale, you hurt the caliber of your people, the whole thing falls down a bit. You are constantly dealing with people in political positions who know they have something you want. They know you can't move until you get around them, and they don't give a shit about you. So you either have to deal with them one way or another or get out."[9]

Hubbard, Copelin's wife Maxine, and another SOUL leader, Nils Douglas, were put on the payroll. Later, when Beasley's problems became the subject of legal action, his comptroller, Oscar Kramer, testified about complicated "conduits" that he said were used to get money to influential people "for whatever parasite was trying to put the bite on the foundation."

"This is a goddamned jungle," Beasley told the Harvard students in 1973. "It's tremendously frustrated by the fact that there is not a strong political or social will to have us do what we want to do. So we are always having to try to create the will, and at the same time *do* it, and at the same time get some money to do it, which there isn't much of, because there isn't any political or social will."[10]

As the payoffs and the patchwork funding multiplied, Beasley had a premonition that he was wading in over his head. "We are dealing with regulations and guidelines that are changing. We don't know frequently until after July 1st what our operational budget is going to be for a particular unit for last July 1st! We are dealing with six different funding sources in Louisiana, of which at least three of the guidelines are contradictory. We've run one program in one area with as many as three or four operational guidelines, the same kinds of money for the same program. One would say, like in Monopoly, 'Do not pass go,' while another one would say, 'Pass Go and go directly to jail,' and with another one you get Broadway. You end up with an auditor with his eyes crossed. What we have to do is get the best legal advice, the best accounting advice and go ahead."[11]

As long as Beasley was in the business of providing contraceptives to low-income blacks, the political and medical establishments were pleased with him. The white middle-class, Catholics and non-Catholics, supported the program because they saw it as a way of holding down both black birth rates and welfare dependency.

But any excursion into general health care constituted a threat to all kinds of people, beginning with the public health departments and the private doctors. Beasley saw the trouble coming. "Our biggest political enemy is organized medicine," he said in 1973. "There are certain factions of doctors in the state that hate our guts and will do everything they can to destroy us, because their basic feeling is that there shouldn't be any federal funds in the state for us. They say, 'You're going to go into general health delivery with those clinics and form a corporate practice of medicine. There's some magical way you're funding it from the federal government. Then you're going to eat our lunch economically.' The only thing more fundamental than sex is economics. When you threaten somebody economically, you really raise eyebrows. The medical society is an enemy. Anytime you threaten that particular system you're in great trouble. . . . The further we go toward health delivery, the more political opposition you get. . . . I am trying to do everything I can, but I think it's a political failure."[12] He spoke of opposition from unexpected sources—black pharmacists, black physicians in the ghetto, others who had a stake in the state's charity hospital system. ("The floor wax contract in the charity hospital is a much-sought-after political plum. There's a 15 percent rakeoff.")

Then too Beasley's network of clinics all over the state worried the politicians. Besides knocking on doors to solicit patients and remind them of missed appointments, the outreach workers could be mustered as easily into a statewide organization to deliver political messages. Beasley's growing problems with the public health establishment and the medical profession—and his alliance with Copelin and Hubbard (which he says he considered necessary to gain acceptability in the black neighborhoods of New Orleans)—made the politicization of his organization seem inevitable.

Other untimely developments aggravated Beasley's problems. His cooperative association with the Catholic bishops dissolved over the abortion issue. As a member of the national Commission on Population Growth and the American Future, appointed by Nixon, Beasley joined David Rockefeller at a press conference announcement of the proabortion recommendation. Back in New Orleans, the new bishop considered that Beasley had gone back on his word. But the doctor drew a distinction between his position in Louisiana, where he made no effort to promote liberal abortion policies, and his role as "a national leader" of the population movement. He told me later that Planned Parenthood and the other prominent actors in the national population establishment had a three-step plan:

1. To "get in family planning and get it financed."
2. To have sterilization approved as an acceptable form of family planning.
3. And then the elimination of barriers to abortion.

In any event, the church turned on him with a vengeance at a particularly inopportune moment for him. "They [the church officials] will bend on just about everything until you get to abortion," he sadly reflected in our interview. At the church parish level, there had been some unilateral excommunications of Catholics who were involved in Beasley's program (in much the same way that some Illinois priests had acted independently of diocesan authority when the Maremont controversy was raging in that state). But by and large Beasley's operation in Louisiana worked as well as it did as long as it did because the Catholic hierarchy did not choose to exercise a veto power.

In Washington, meanwhile, Nixon had been reelected and his administration was concerned about the budgetary pressure for social program spending. Caspar Weinberger, the new Secretary of HEW, and Roy Ash, director of the Office of Management and Budget, were bothered by the open-ended, uncontrollable future financing of family planning programs possible under Section 4-A of the Social Security Act. This is the provision in the law relating to mandatory services for past, present, and potential recipients of Aid to Families with Dependent Children. By juggling other sources of federal funds and "laundering" them to qualify for still more federal money on a nine-to-one matching basis, Beasley had claimed $10 million for Louisiana alone under that program. In this context, laundering is a complicated, irregular, and almost always illegal process by which public funds are mingled with private funds in order to disguise their source. Planned Parenthood, moreover, was counseling other state program executives on how they could qualify for the automatic matching funds, without, of course, going through the laundry. Weinberger and Ash could imagine outlays soaring close to $2 billion a year and out of control. Beasley would later accuse HEW of deliberately delaying the issuance of guidelines for program spending under that section of the law and then persecuting him in order to "muddy the waters" and thereby discourage other states from getting big (that is, Beasley-sized) ideas. This strikes me as an imaginatively conspiratorial notion that is too paranoid to hold much water, muddy or otherwise.

His extravagant habits and reckless disposal of public funds could not help but come to the attention of HEW's auditors. Beasley made the foundation's records readily available, however, and it was not until after the election was out of the way that the HEW auditors, for whatever their reasons, went after Joe Beasley tooth and nail.

During the years that HEW and OEO had been shoveling out money as fast as they could in compliance with presidential orders to "reach" as many low-income women as they could, Beasley's team was available and ready to take it from whatever source, even though one federal agency usually did not know (or care) what the other was doing, and even though, as we have already seen, Beasley realized that the regulations and guidelines were nonexistent or conflicting. He and his corporate managers gathered in federal funds through multiple conduits so complicated that he could not possibly have tracked them all.

According to a later sorting out by the General Accounting Office of Congress, Beasley's corporation took in at least $53.6 million in federal funds under ten assistance programs administered by nine federal agencies in OEO and the Departments of HEW, Labor, Housing and Urban Development, and State.[13] Only about $17 million of this was obtained directly through grants and contracts with federal agencies. The rest was obtained indirectly through intermediate organizations, among them an insurance company, Tulane University, the State of Louisiana, and various municipalities and community action agencies.

Beasley understood that the foundation's $40,000-a-year Washington attorney, former Sen. Joseph Tydings of Maryland, a liberal Democrat who had sponsored the family planning reorganization legislation before being defeated, would not be of much help rescuing him. So he retained another lawyer, a former White House staff assistant, Harry Dent of Columbia, South Carolina. HEW and the Justice Department understandably interpreted this as a bid to fix the case at a higher level in the government. A federal grand jury in New Orleans heard evidence for over a year, beginning in April of 1973.

In March, April, and May of 1974, three separate sets of criminal indictments were returned charging Joe Beasley with "conspiracy to defraud and to commit other criminal offenses against the United States through false, fictitious, and fraudulent claims."

Beasley and his comptroller, Oscar Kramer, were accused of conspiring to defraud the United States of $659,000 by filing reimbursement claims for fifteen mobile family planning clinics that were never built, and of $118,000 more by padding the cost of twenty-seven other mobile clinics. According to the indictments, some of this money was funneled to Sherman Copelin as a payoff to permit the program to operate effectively in New Orleans. When Beasley agreed to pay the money, the Mau-Maus were called off, according to the government's theory of the case.

At a birthday party for Beasley in the Saxony restaurant, according to testimony by Robert Parsons, who was on Beasley's staff, Parsons slipped $1,000 in health foundation funds, federal funds originally, in an envelope to Copelin. This was described as the first installment of $7,000 given to Copelin while he was in charge of the city's model cities program. Copelin resigned his position at the end of 1972 and went into business as a consultant. For his consulting services, Copelin allegedly received over fifty thousand dollars more in federal funds, part of a grant awarded by Beasley's foundation to SEDFRE, the Scholarship, Educational and Defense Fund for Racial Equality in New York City, for a study of day-care centers. The government said this was the last installment of the payoff. The other indictments involved the alleged manipulation, laundering, and commingling of $3,750,799 in federal family planning funds through complicated transactions with the Ford and Rockefeller foundations, Tulane University, and the State of Louisiana. According to the charges, Beasley got together with officials of Tulane and agreed that federal funds would be transferred from Tulane to the state and disguised as private donations from the Ford and Rockefeller foundations so as to be used for claiming still more federal matching funds.

Copelin was among twenty-six others who were either named as unindicted coconspirators or were granted immunity from prosecution in exchange for their cooperation with the prosecutors. Copelin was granted "use immunity" as a possible witness against Beasley, although he was never called to testify by the government or the defense at any of the trials.

The feds were after Joe Beasley, not Sherman Copelin.

A few days later, before any issues of fact had been determined by a jury, federal marshals surrounded the FHF headquarters in New Orleans and the foundation was placed in federal receivership.

In 1969, Planned Parenthood had featured Beasley and the Louisiana experience in the premier issue of its new publication, *Family Planning Perspectives*. For the cover, artist David Levine drew the figure of Margaret Sanger casting her sprightly shadow over Louisiana. Beasley wrote the lead article entitled, "View from Louisiana."[14] He began with a quotation from J. C. Furnas: "In Tinkering with Society, Good Will is Not Enough."

How true. Bigger than life in every way, Joe came to believe that this is how business was done in the cloudy regions of politics; that people who helped you had to be royally entertained and sometimes bought off. One cannot but be struck by how the tables turned on this man. Black and white politicians scurried to save their skins. With some exceptions, Democratic politicians in Louisiana acted as if they didn't know him. One interesting exception was Rep. Otto E. Passman, then chairman of the House subcommittee that controls foreign aid appropriations. A month after HEW cut off funds to FHF, Passman was pressuring the Agency for International Development in the State Department to finance a family planning project in Colombia, South America! When the blood started to flow, state law enforcement officials jumped. Beasley was brought to trial (and acquitted) in the state courts on state fraud charges similar to the federal allegations. It is not easy to understand why Dr. Hellman at HEW made no effort apparently to intervene in Beasley's defense. In the final analysis, according to Beasley's theory, the doctors at HEW are responsive to the interests of their colleagues in the state health departments and ultimately the interests of the American Medical Association. Once Beasley got in trouble, Planned Parenthood's national publications pretended that he didn't exist. Tulane abandoned him too.

The first federal court trial of the fraudulent claims for the mobile clinics and the payments to Copelin ended in a hung jury. Beasley denied personal knowledge of the phony reimbursement scheme, but admitted he had indirectly caused the payments to Copelin because he said he needed Copelin's assistance to dispel black genocide fears. The government painted Beasley to be a chiseler. He used $4,700 in federal funds that were appropriated by Congress for family planning services for the poor for liquor bills. He was accused of double-billing the foundation for personal expenses, including $16,500 of charges on his American Express card. The foundation not only paid the rent for the $960-a-month Watergate apartment in Washington but it picked up the tab for his $400-a-month apartment in New Orleans. The foundation made campaign contributions to Governor Edwards; to former Governor Big John McKeithen, then running for the U.S. Senate; to U.S. Rep. Gillis Long; and $5,000 to state Supreme Court Justice Pascal Calogero.

While Beasley was on the witness stand, the cross-examining prosecutor asked him whether he had not suggested to a congressman from Mississippi, Rep. William Colmer, then chairman of the Rules Committee, that the family planning program was desirable because it would hold down the black population. Beasley replied that the conversation had been taken out of context. If he made the remark, it is the first and only racially oriented reference to birth control he is ever known to have uttered.

At the retrial, Beasley's lawyer, former New Orleans District Attorney Jim Garrison, advised his client to rest his defense on the risk that the jury would decide the prosecution had failed to make a case, without testifying himself. That turned out to be bad advice. The jury convicted Beasley and the judge sentenced him to two years in prison.

Yet another trial of the second set of indictments ended this time in Beasley's acquittal. Awaiting the disposition of his appeal of the first conviction, and his trial on the third indictments, the defendant did not go directly to jail, as in the Monopoly game, but remained free. Volunteer lawyers from the Loyola of New Orleans University law school, a Catholic institution, handled his appeal. Let go by Tulane—and long before by Harvard—he opened a medical clinic in the lower 9th Ward of New Orleans from whence Sherman Copelin had sprung.

Douglas Mackintosh, the author of the Mau-Mau theory of Beasley's problems, sees the experience as a modern tragedy. Beasley's program, he said, "became highly popular and highly visible. It had been a thorough success while in operation and the genocide issue had quite possibly been a bogus one. Instead, what was once a beautiful dream is now a quagmire of legal trials, unindicted coconspirators, interrupted careers, paranoid theories, declining services, and disharmonious groups of Mau-Maus hiding out in the darkness."[15]

Joe Beasley may be on his way to prison, but Sherman Copelin is doing quite well. Without competitive bidding, Mayor Landrieu awarded an exclusive cost-plus contract for the maintenance services at the Superdome, New Orleans' scandal-ridden new sports arena, to a company of which Copelin was president and Don Hubbard vice president. If there is any gravy to be lapped up at either Antoine's or the Superdome, the young black leaders from the Ninth Ward will be there for their share.

7 Richard Nixon's
Catholic Strategy . . .
and the Murky Business
of Sterilization

The dividing line between family planning and
eugenics is murky.
— Judge Gerhard A. Gesell

Lonnie Relf and his wife Minnie worked on a farm in Alabama. He was paid five dollars a week. For helping the farmer's wife, her wages were an additional dollar a week. The Relfs and their six children were allowed access to the vegetable garden and given the use of a shack without electricity or running water. All over the South, machines came along to do their work more efficiently though hardly more economically. Like many other illiterate southern Negroes, the Relfs drifted to the city in search of a job. They moved to Montgomery, the capital of Alabama, where they lived for a while in the municipal garbage dump. When a newspaper publicized their living conditions in the dump, the Relf family applied for welfare and moved into a public housing project. There they were eligible for free medical care, including family planning services available under the federal Economic Opportunity Act.

Among the Relf children were two daughters, Minnie, fourteen, a seventh grade student of apparently normal intelligence, and Mary Alice, twelve, who was classified by school officials as trainable mentally retarded. It came to the attention of the Community Action Agency of Montgomery, one of the nurses subsequently explained, that "boys were hanging around" the Relf

107

household. In their later inquiries, OEO investigators could find no evidence of promiscuous behaviour, however, and commented that the teen-age boys in the neighborhood seemed more interested in the girls' older sisters. Until the drug was banned by the Federal Food and Drug Administration because of its unknown side effects, both of the Relf girls were receiving Depo-Provera, an experimental long-lasting injectable contraceptive drug. On June 12, 1973, two nurses from the Community Action Agency arrived at the Relf home and took the two girls to the hospital to be sterilized.

Sterilization is a permanent and reliable form of birth control. Sometimes, surgical removal of the uterus—a hysterectomy—is required by medical necessity regardless of whether the woman would like to become pregnant again. But healthy women can be sterilized by submitting to a tubal ligation, or tying of the fallopian tubes, which carry the egg to be fertilized, for permanent contraceptive reasons. The operation is contrary to Catholic teaching. In 1976 the Vatican reminded Catholics that sterilization to prevent pregnancy is "absolutely forbidden" even in cases where the birth of a child would result in "physical or psychic evil." For males the vasectomy is a simple operation that interupts the supply of spermatozoa without disturbing the ability to engage in sexual intercourse. For those who have no religious objections to sterilization, and who are certain that they do not wish to have children, its finality makes it an effective means of birth control. In the preceding chapter, reference was made to Joe Beasley's statement that Planned Parenthood regarded government-financed sterilization for the poor as the second of three birth control policy goals, the first being the availability of contraceptive devices and drugs, the third being abortion.

Mrs. Relf said later she was informed that the girls were being taken away for more birth control shots. She marked her "X" on a consent document authorizing the hospital to tie the tubes of both daughters. A third daughter, Katie, locked herself in a bedroom and refused to come out when the nurses returned for her. The doctor who performed the operations and the hospital where they occurred were paid with federal funds. A nurse for the Montgomery County Health Department recalled later that she had been urging the Relf parents to consent to the sterilization of their daughters so they could not produce illegitimate children but that the parents refused. At least ten other girls who were minors were sterilized with OEO funds during the first six months of 1973. Independently, the Alabama Department of Public Health, financed in part with federal HEW funds, arranged sterilizations for eighty-two other low-income women during that year. Although, as we will see later, the federal agency in Washington was officially unaware that any sterilizations were being carried out with OEO money until the necessary regulations and safeguards were issued, it was estimated that at least two thousand such presumably voluntary operations were performed with OEO funds in the 1972-73 fiscal year.[1]

The Relf girls had never given birth, and now never will, because of an operation performed without their or their parents' knowledge or consent.

A more frequent occurrence throughout the South is the induced sterilization of a mother on welfare who has just given birth to an illegitimate child. In Aiken County, South Carolina, the county's only three physicians agreed among themselves that they would provide maternity services to any mother of a third illegitimate baby only if she consented to postpartum sterilization. More than one-third of all the welfare mothers in the county were said to have been rendered incapable of additional pregnancies by the end of 1973. Shirley Brown, twenty-three, and Virgil Walker, thirty, were patients of Dr. Clovis Pierce, the only obstetrician in the county, whose income over an eighteen-month period included $60,826 for services to Medicaid (the welfare medical program) patients.[2] According to testimony given in court, Dr. Pierce told his patients in the maternity ward: "Listen here, young lady, this is my tax money paying for this baby, and I'm tired of paying for illegitimate children. If you don't want this [operation], find another doctor." Mrs. Brown refused to sign the form. The day after giving birth, she and her newborn baby were discharged from the hospital. The doctor told her not to come to his office for the customary after-care until she was prepared to be sterilized. "I had to send home suddenly to get clothes for the baby," the child's grandmother testified. Mrs. Walker said the father of the baby offered to pay for the delivery, but that the doctor refused and threatened to see to it that she would receive no further welfare payments, an allegation that Pierce denied. The day following delivery, having signed the consent form, she was sterilized.

Doctors have always been treated with almost mystical reverence in the rural South. Few black women would dream of questioning the advice of a white doctor or of seeking another medical opinion. There are black communities in the South where almost every mother of two or more children, women under thirty, have had hysterectomies, including those who are married and living with their husbands.[3] Black women who inquire about an abortion are frequently told that they should also have a hysterectomy while they are about it.

But involuntary sterilizations are not a strictly southern phenomenon nor are they directed solely at blacks. Ten Spanish speaking women sued the County-USC Medical Center in Los Angeles alleging that they were sterilized against their will. There have been many stories of the Chicano poor being pressured into sterilizations at Los Angeles County General Hospital, usually during the stress and agony of childbirth, sometimes with a vague warning that death could result if they don't submit to the inadequately explained follow-up operation.[4]

In the Brown and Walker cases, lawyers for the American Civil Liberties Union and the Southern Poverty Law Center sued Pierce and state and local officials, claiming $1.5 million damages for civil rights violations. A jury of three black women, two white women, and one white man (the foreman) heard the case in the U.S. District Court of Judge Solomon Blatt in Barnwell, South Carolina, in July of 1975. The trial lasted for two weeks, during which Pierce readily acknowledged that he would not accept welfare patients who would not agree to his conditions. The lawyer for the women, Joseph Levin, asked the jurors to award heavy damages to his clients. "There are other doctors like him in this country," he argued, "and if you don't punish him, they'll go right on imposing their social values on people." The jury deliberated eight hours, then returned a verdict of a mere five dollars in token damages to Mrs. Brown and none to Mrs. Walker (who had signed the form), a judgment that had to be interpreted as an expression of support for the doctor. The jurors decided, they said, that the women had not been significantly harmed. Before the trial, the Southern Medical Association adopted a resolution condoning Pierce's attitudes. Levin could not find a doctor in the entire state who would testify that Pierce's policies were unethical. "This matter is strictly between doctor and patient," remarked Dr. Harold Hope, the president of the medical association. "Maybe in a little more sophisticated, a little more enlightened community, with less of a history of repression, you might be able to take a case like this before a jury and win it," said lawyer Levin.

The nation's capital may or may not be more sophisticated than Barnwell, South Carolina, but attorney Melvin Belli, the famous "King of Torts" from San Francisco, filed a $25 million damage suit in the U.S. District Court of the District of Columbia on behalf of the Relfs against various public officials. Lawyers for the defendants tried understandably but unsuccessfully to have the case transferred to a more favorable setting—in Montgomery. Belli alleged that the safeguards which would have prevented the sterilization of the two girls were deliberately suppressed by the White House "for spurious political considerations."

The "spurious political considerations" to which he referred involved no less than the presidential election of 1972. The development of the "OEO guidelines" is a fascinating study of how the temporary strategic requirements of presidential politics impinged on the implementation of an extraordinarily sensitive health-care policy with consequences that reached into a hospital room in Montgomery the day that the Relf sisters were deprived of their ability to have children because some boys were reported to have been hanging around their house.

As we described earlier, the Nixon Administration encouraged both OEO and HEW to spend more for family planning grants, a goal that chanced to coincide with the desire of the Democratic-controlled Congress to increase appropriations for that special-priority purpose. Many of the social agency professionals and members of Congress may well have been inspired by a spirit of equal access to health services, but the Nixon White House was most concerned with the spiraling rise of dependency, the high incidence of illegitimacy, and the growth of the poor and/or black populations. Beginning with the first regulations promulgated by Sargent Shriver, OEO's rules prohibited the use of federal funds for either abortion or sterilization. The abortion ban was clearly in line with the conscious intent of Congress but there was little discussion then or later of the sterilization provision. Some of the family planning program officials at OEO during the Nixon years were strongly in favor of funding sterilization procedures, notably Dr. Warren Hern, a dynamic young public health physician whose title was chief of the program evaluation and development branch. Hern said many local community action agency representatives, particularly in poor white regions of Appalachia, were reporting an interest in vasectomies, the permanent male defertility operation that can be performed quickly under local anaesthesia.

When Frank C. Carlucci was assistant director of OEO in 1969, he approved the removal of the bar against sterilization. But Donald Rumsfeld, the more politically oriented director, did nothing about the request. After Rumsfeld left the agency, Carlucci became boss. Early in 1971, soon after the change of command, the recommendation was back on his desk. At a hearing before the House Education and Labor Committee, Rep. Edith Green, Democrat of Oregon, quizzed Carlucci about why family planning always "has to be only for women," a complaint then being heard more often from women. Dr. Thomas Bryant, OEO's director of health affairs, the division of which family planning was a part, added publicly what he had told both Rumsfeld and Carlucci long ago, that it was "time for us to change our policy."

Not long after that, Carlucci sent a one-sentence memo to Bryant agreeing to delete the prohibition, but remarking that "vasectomy seems like enough to me." In other words: male but not female sterilization. Voluntariness is much easier to police for vasectomies, of course, than for female operations. Bryant and his immediate superior, Wesley L. Hjornevik, the deputy director, agreed later that "nothing was ever discussed except changing the guidelines to allow vasectomies." On May 11, however, Mel Goldstein of the general counsel's office of OEO informed Hjornevik by memo: "In a conversation with me today Frank [Carlucci] has also approved the use of grant funds to permit female sterilization procedures." Hern and his immediate superior, Dr. George Contis, a pediatrician who was serving as director of the family planning program, said it was always their understanding that the change would apply to both sexes. On May 19, 1971, the italicized words below were removed from the regulation that had been in effect since 1965:

"No project funds shall be expended for any surgical procedures intended to *result in sterilizations or* cause abortions."[5]

Once the new policy had been established, Contis notified regional directors, CAA directors, and comprehensive health center directors that sterilizations were not to be undertaken until the necessary precautionary safeguards had been prepared under Hern's direction. "Please do not begin providing contraceptive services until you receive these guidelines," his memos said. State health departments were still free to follow whatever sterilization policy state law allowed, but not with OEO funds. Not many people in Washington knew about it, but HEW regulations at the time permitted sterilizations under both the family planning and Medicaid programs. Hellman estimates that approximately one hundred thousand such operations for low-income persons were paid for by HEW in fiscal year 1972-73.

It was understood at OEO that Hern would work on the regulations over the summer with the expectation that some trial projects would be funded in September to test the efficacy of the procedures. Contis and Hern, the family planners at OEO, apparently were aware of the potential for abuses if state and local authorities were allowed to use federal funds without guidance from Washington. They said they recognized from the beginning that steps had to be taken to prevent coercion, especially in the South. But preparation of the guidelines proved to be more time-consuming than had been anticipated, primarily because there were so many professional and other interested groups to be consulted. Hellman at HEW resisted the issuance of any guidelines at all because he said he did not like the idea of "practicing medicine from Washington." He told Contis it would be very difficult obtaining agreement on the provisions of the rules. Hellman was willing to allow state officials to use their own discretion.

While Dr. Hern is laboring over his guidelines, let us turn briefly to a review of the sterilization experience in the United States to see if the wise use of this discretion could reasonably be expected. Obviously anytime anyone submits voluntarily to a so-called nontherapeutic operation—that is, one not required for reasons of health—that will render him or her permanently incapable of conceiving a child, the nature of that individual's voluntary decision is extremely important. After a difficult childbirth, for example, the new mother may feel differently than she would several months later. Many of the states, moreover, had an extensive record of experience with compulsory—that is, involuntary—sterilizations.

Beginning with the first compulsory sterilization law adopted by Indiana in 1907, statutes were enacted in thirty other states providing for the sterilization of broad categories of people, among them the mentally deficient, certain of the mentally ill, epileptics, sexual perverts, and habitual criminals. Even before Indiana passed its law, many delinquents were casually sterilized at the state reformatory there on the premise that castration would be a likely if drastic cure for masturbation. The U.S. Supreme Court upheld the constitutionality of a compulsory sterilization law for the "feebleminded" in 1927 with the famous pronouncement of Justice Oliver Wendell Holmes—"Three generations of imbeciles are enough." It was not at all uncommon for a judge to grant probation to a delinquent on condition that he or she undergo sterilization. In the case of a young male this meant castration, as much to still the sexual impulse as to foreclose reproduction. Eugenic sterilization, "biomedical intervention" to improve the quality of the population by controls on childbearing, reached its zenith in the 1930s when nearly twenty-five thousand such operations were performed. Culling out the defective in the population by preventing their multiplication is an idea that has always appealed to many Americans.

In recent years, nearly half of all the compulsory sterilizations were ordered by the "Eugenics Board" in one state: North Carolina. Sterilization of the mentally retarded does make it possible, of course, for more individuals to live in the community outside of institutions. Though most mental illness is not inherited, many modern social workers seek to justify a policy of forced sterilization on the grounds that such people cannot rear children in a suitable environment, suitable for the children.

More recently, as our earlier chapters have detailed, American opinion has been swinging in favor of measures that would preclude people who cannot support themselves—especially those welfare recipients who have delivered more than one illegitimate child—from continuing to produce children. A telephone poll by the *Philadelphia Inquirer* reported 67.2 percent approval of a proposal that Americans of low intelligence be encouraged by the government to undergo sterilization. "The surgeon's knife," said Julius Paul of the Walter Reed Army Institute of Research, "still seems to have the same magical quality in the minds of some people for 'saving' America from its shame, squalor, and various miseries of human or social instigation (especially poverty) as it did over 60 years ago. . . . The racial (Negro) and socio-economic overtones of the early attacks are again heard and oftentimes not too covertly. It is conceivable that . . . the old game of *quid pro quo* (sterilization for welfare benefits) might appear again. The poor, and particularly blacks and other minority groups, are especially vulnerable to this kind of possibility. While the veneer would be *economic* (or ZPG), the underlying motivation would be otherwise."[6] During the furor over the Relf case, HEW Secretary Caspar Weinberger, a fiscal arch-conservative but a strict human libertarian in a way that most liberals aren't, referred to the sterilization movement as "a family planning sort of thing—part of the pressures for zero population growth."[7]

At a hearing conducted by Sen. Edward M. Kennedy's health subcommittee into the Relf affair, Dr. Cyril L. Crocker, a black obstetrician who was director of family planning services in the District of Columbia, made this observation:

> Those family planning programs that are essentially birth control programs have been viewed with suspicion by many blacks and other minority groups. The charge that the intent of such programs is genocidal is frequently given credence in their implementation. Where clinics function solely as contraceptive dispensaries and operate with inadequate staffing or facilities that provide neither high quality care nor respect for human dignity, the concept of family planning is debased.
> . . . While federally funded programs are designed to make family planning services available to the poor or medically indigent, they seem to have enrolled a disproportionally high percentage of minority group participants. By contrast, minorities are conspicuously underrepresented in high and mid-level positions in publicly financed family planning programs.
> Unfortunately, there are some proponents of family planning in key management positions who view birth control not as it relates to building stronger, healthier families and other individual benefits, but in terms of population control, paring the welfare rolls and maintaining the white power structure. These managers do not consider the planning of families through individual decision a right of the consumers they are presumably serving.
> Their attitudes, moreover, are frequently backed up in the rules and regulations drawn up by the fifty states. A number of states permit courts to order the sterilization of insane, retarded, or incompetent persons. Some states permit the sterilization of these persons with parental consent. Other states have seized almost any opportunity to justify

the curtailment of the fertility of minorities. A few are considering the involuntary sterilization of persons with sickle cell disease.

Although many instances of violations of the rights of the poor and of minorities have been observed in family planning programs heretofore, such transgressions have not been documented nor publicized. In some programs, for instance, not only are involuntary sterilizations being done by tubal ligation, but there are case of hysterectomies being done without patient knowledge and/or informed consent.

While it is potentially to the benefit of good family planning programs that badly run ones be publicly investigated and closed down if necessary, the airing of the current situation raises old questions about racism and government intervention in the population fight. . . .[8]

Population fight? What population fight? Nobody said anything about a population fight. He is correct, of course. In one sense, that is what the politics of population is all about: to arrange conditions that will maximize your numbers and minimize the others. If blacks, Latinos, and other groups deemed inferior, defective, troublesome, costly, etc., can be induced to stop multiplying, either voluntarily or involuntarily, the middle and upper classes think they would rest more easily.

The first American eugenicists of the early 1900s believed Negros should be forced, if necessary, to lower their birth rate, and should not be allowed to cross-breed with and adulterate the superior white stock.[9] Alyce Gullattee, a black woman psychiatrist in Washington, considered the new emphasis on sterilization in the 1960s and 1970s to be racist in origin. Whether compulsory or voluntary, sterilization programs will affect nonwhites more than whites, she contended, since they usually take place in state mental and penal institutions where minorities are disproportionately represented because of economic discrimination. "It is readily conceivable in the present climate of things," she said, "that eugenics legislation may be used to decelerate the birth rate among ethnic minorities, particularly the black minority. . . . Sterilization will save society from *poor parents* rather than *poor heredity,* or perhaps to be intellectually honest we should say poor blacks, or, again simply, blacks." She predicted ominously that liberalized abortion laws, which liberals support so enthusiastically, will provide "the legitimate vehicle for accidential sterilization" in many cases.[10] For whatever the reasons, Darity and other researchers have amply documented that even those blacks who now understand that the planned spacing of their children is in their own interests overwhelmingly fear the foolproof but irreversible step: sterilization.

One day early in the presidential election year of 1972, Wesley Hjornevik, the deputy director of operations chief of OEO, received a phone call from Paul O'Neill, an official of the Office of Management and Budget, the President's management coordinating agency that operates next door to the White House.

"You guys aren't going into sterilization, are you?" O'Neill inquired.

Hjornevik was a little taken aback by the question because Dr. Hern's guidelines had finally been completed a short time before, and on December 27, 1971, the necessary "management information" forms were approved by OMB, removing the last obstacle to publication and distribution of the regulations.

Now, however, Hjornevik—a management whiz in private industry but still learning the political nuances of Washington—was suddenly informed of the presence of "a policy interest" in the sterilization matter at the White House. It was as though an alarm had sounded in the innermost reaches of the executive branch and all kinds of people were sliding down fire poles.

Shortly thereafter, Hjornevik and Dr. Leon Cooper, who had succeeded Bryant as director of health affairs at OEO, assembled their sterilization file and hurried down Nineteenth Street to a meeting with O'Neill and James Cavanaugh at the Executive Office Building, the ornate old fortresslike structure next to the White House at the corner of Pennsylvania Avenue and Seventeenth Street.

Early in his administration, President Nixon not only reorganized the old Bureau of the Budget but also created a domestic policy counterpart of the National Security Council to be called, logically enough, the Domestic Council. John Ehrlichman was put in charge of the council. Many of the twenty-eight members of the Domestic Council staff were advance men in the triumphant Nixon campaign of 1968, efficient young fellows who could be relied upon to rein in the bureaucracy. James Cavanaugh was given responsibility for the health field. "Members of the Council staff were the president's men operating in a political environment," one study of the Nixon Domestic Council observed.[11] "They carried messages about the president's wishes in one direction; they picked up information that ought to be brought back to the president and his senior advisers. . . .They were operating in a highly political atmosphere, and they did so as agents of the president." John Kessel, the author of that study, quotes an unidentified staff member: "One thing you must be able to do is understand what the president wants"; and another: "The most important problem is to make the president's philosophy consistent at the operating level."

As the president's agent, Cavanaugh was one key actor at that meeting. Leon Cooper was another.

Cooper was an ambitious young black physician from Georgia who had been active in Democratic politics there. This record did not disqualify him for the OEO appointment because it was not easy to recruit black executives for the Nixon administration, Republicans or Democrats. By now the National Medical Association, the black equivalent of the AMA, had taken a firm position of suspicion toward family planning programs. For reasons that we have already made clear, the black doctors preferred comprehensive health-care programs with birth control only one part of the package. Any rising young black doctor who wished to acquire professional status among his peers had better speak out. So, although Cooper was not known as an ardent activist, his role in the affair was probably predestined. He did not approve of wholesale sterilization by southern white doctors because he knew almost all the patients would be poor blacks.

Even before the phone call to Hjornevik from OMB, Cooper made known his reservations about the revision in the rules. Hjornevik said later Cooper had been the target of pressure from black organizations and individuals who felt that sterilization was racially motivated. According to a later OEO investigation, "Cooper felt that implementation of the guidelines would result in the focus of all family planning grants on sterilization as opposed to family planning methods which did not result in permanent sterility."[12]

In an affidavit filed later in connection with the Relf damage suit, Cooper explained: "As soon as I learned of this planned involvement in using sterilization as a method of family planning, I had concerns as to whether such a program was in the best public interest. . . .Less drastic means of birth control were already available to OEO clients, some clients might not understand the permanent nature of the procedure, and certain minority groups might interpret a sterilization program as an act of genocide."[13] He also noted that program funds were scarce and needed to be allotted on a priority basis, sterilization being low on his priority scale. He observed earlier that "issues primarily concerning coercion and confidentiality" had arisen during OEO's first sterilization pilot project, a $246,000 grant in Anderson County, Tenn.

The jockeying for Bryant's job had been intense. Contis enlisted the assistance of a fellow Greek-American, Vice President Spiro T. Agnew, among others, in his quest for the promotion, and was bitterly disappointed when he did not receive it. Relations between the Contis-Hern family planners and the broader health affairs office under Cooper were strained from the start.

As a continuing monitoring device, the Domestic Council did not work like it was supposed to. Howard Phillips, a conservative extremist who was made an assistant to the director of OEO, was given the task of screening grants for political advantage. "In general, Nixon had no interest in the way the executive branch functioned," Phillips told me. "He regarded domestic activities as brokerable. His interests were in foreign policy. The administration had no coherent values or policy. It was zig-zag, back-and-fill, give-and-take. Social-worker-mentality bureaucrats ran the agencies, set the policies, and decided where the money was to go. I had many conversations with people at the White House. 'Don't those guys know the president doesn't want that?' they would yell at me. As far back as I can remember, it was my understanding that the administration was opposed to the use of OEO funds for abortion and/or sterilization. Whenever it came to my attention, which wasn't as often as it should have, I insisted on the administration's position. One of the problems was that the White House never did things out front. They wanted to finesse every issue. They wanted to be against abortion without upsetting the people who were for abortion. That's how they did everything."

The latest zig occured at the beginning of the campaign year.

Nixon and his ideamen, notably his Catholic liaison specialist Charles Colson, decided that the Republican president could profitably identify with "Catholic issues" such as abortion. While Moynihan was at the White House, OEO had been allowed to proceed full steam ahead with the family planning program because birth control was viewed by Ehrlichman, Colson, and the others as a necessary instrument for social control, one of the rare opportunities for liberals in Congress and conservatives in the White House to agree. Colson, who had a variety of election year assignments, as the Watergate investigations later disclosed, was in charge of the "Catholic strategy." It was soon realized that this would require closer attention to what OEO was doing. "The order went down from Colson's office to me, and from Ehrlichman's office (through Cavanaugh) to Hjornevik," Phillips recalled in an interview. "It was clear to me that, whether the reason was moral, philosophical, or political—and I'm sure it was the latter—that the administration definitely did not want OEO engaging in sterilization or abortion."

Despite his personal reservations, Cooper signed a procurement order in December for the printing of 25,000 copies of the guidelines, which were then stored in a government warehouse. Once again, Hjornevik approved the policy on January 10, the records show. But then he sent a note to Cooper: "We seem to have changed the guidelines from covering just vasectomies. Should we restrain this thing?"

At the beginning of February, when Cooper and Hjornevik went to see Cavanaugh and O'Neill, the changes in sterilization policies and the preparations of the guidelines had been public knowledge for almost a year. There were stories in the press about Carlucci's decisions at various stages. But it was not until the start of the reelection season that the president's agents awoke to the likelihood that the president's well-publicized opposition to abortion might also mean he would not want the government paying for sterilizations, which, though different from abortions, are also contrary to Catholic doctrine.

At the meeting, Cavanaugh said he and others on the Domestic Council staff had looked at the guidelines and felt they were poor public policy. Hjornevik said later: "The door wasn't closed, but they had this legitimate public policy concern. . . . The context was that this was *not the time to be doing this kind of thing* [italics mine]. We let them know we were content to sit on it. The White House definitely didn't want us to go ahead. We [Hjornevik and Cooper] agreed coming back from the meeting that we would stress Cooper's concerns rather than the White House interest."

"My purposes served their needs," Cooper later told OEO investigators.

Indeed they did. This was not the time to be "doing this kind of thing," embarking on OEO financing of sterilizations for the poor or anyone else while Nixon was courting Catholic voters—even though the very same "kind of thing"—sterilization of low-income persons—was available to the same people under Hellman's HEW-funded federal programs, probably without the knowledge, certainly without the understanding, of the president's agents. Cooper had his own reasons, his own purposes, having to do with his standing in the black medico-political community, and his aspirations for advancement in that community. However, the fact that he approved the order for the printing of the guidelines in December, would indicate that he didn't feel all that strongly about it. In any event, none of his purposes concerned the president or his agents in the slightest; as he accurately understood, they served the transitory political needs of a chief executive up for reelection.

It is of more than transitory significance that none of the four individuals involved in that meeting had any inkling, or cared in the slightest, that OEO was in fact *already* in the sterilization business. Contis and Hern knew that some local community action agencies were spending OEO family planning money to pay for sterilizations without waiting for the regulations as instructed.

On February 2, Hern was advised that the guidelines would not be issued pending "executive policy review" by the White House. Two days later, the 200 copies that he had acquired from the warehouse for distribution to the press were taken from him and lodged in a safe at OEO. The other copies were kept in cardboard boxes at the warehouse.

Subsequently, in testimony before Kennedy's Senate subcommittee, Hern said OEO received dozens of requests from Community Action Agencies for copies of the guidelines.

I might add that along in here I received a request from Dr.

Hellman's office for a copy of the guidelines, which he had reviewed on two occasions. I informed him that my understanding was that the White House was holding them up. And I said if you sent us a letter requesting them, it might get them loose. I never got the letter.

On numerous occasions I made attempts to find out when the guidelines would be issued and why they were being held up. I was told that they were being reviewed at the White House and would not be issued until after the 1972 election. . . . I was never given any explanation of what the 1972 election had to do with it.

I felt that many people's lives were at stake. We knew that some programs were going ahead without the guidelines even though we had requested them not to. And we felt this was a very dangerous situation. I told Mr. Hjornevik it was an urgent situation and the guidelines should go out immediately. He said Dr. Cooper does not think it is very urgent.[14]

In his subsequent affidavit, Cooper explained: "I decided not to issue the guidelines because I felt that it was not in the best interests of the public for OEO to engage in widespread sterilization programs without more detailed information relative to these questions."

At the end of March, Hern sent a memo to Cooper: "[This] unexplained delay is a disservice to OEO clients and programs. It places the agency in a potentially dangerous situation: Our CAAs are legally permitted to provide a sensitive service, and apparently are doing so; yet guidelines to ensure that this service is properly administered and supervised are withheld."

The next day, Cooper notified regional and CAA directors that distribution of the guidelines would be delayed indefinitely because of "unforeseen administrative difficulties in policy establishment and potential cost determination." He reminded the officials to "hold in abeyance all immediate plans for institution of such services." Later, in defense pleadings filed for the Relf's damage suit, government lawyers said Cooper had not wanted to end the sterilization program altogether because he thought OEO was on the verge of implementing a reasonable program "at some point in time." To discontinue funding of the pilot project in Tennessee, for example, would have caused severe problems, it was argued. But Belli's partner, attorney Kent Russell, contended in a brief filed with Judge Oliver Gasch on April 14, 1976, that Cooper's concerns were all "an afterthought dreamt up to cover up the White House pressure to not involve Richard Nixon in issues which could dissuade potential Nixon voters."

Hjornevik became aware later that Hern and Contis were "generating correspondence from their family planning constituency throughout the country" trying to force release of the guidelines. Growing more frantic, Hern tried to contact the office of the White House counsel, John Dean, to find out directly why the regulations were being held back. Cooper reprimanded Hern for going over his head to the White House. Fred Fielding, a lawyer on Dean's staff, told Hern he knew nothing about the matter; and, of course, he didn't because it was being handled as a political and not a legal problem. Hern was reminded by Cooper that "your work involves a number of sensitive program areas where major policy decisions are in the process of resolution." Behind all this double-talk, Hern the idealist apparently did not fully grasp the political overtones of the issue. The bickering continued back and forth between Hern and Cooper until June 2 when Hern resigned.

In retrospect, the Democratic party's nomination of George McGovern guaranteed that Nixon would receive the votes of many Catholics regardless of what OEO was doing about sterilization. After all, HEW was already doing exactly what Colson, Cavanaugh, Cooper, et al, were so determined to prevent OEO from doing.

Nixon was reelected in November. His second administration devoted itself immediately to the dismantling of OEO under Phillip's direction. Family planning programs were consolidated in HEW with the intention of turning them over eventually to state control entirely. When Hjornevik left OEO in January of 1973, the guidelines were still "under policy review." The published guidelines had been gathering dust in the warehouse in Washington for a year.

By chance, a federal evaluation team visited the Montgomery family planning center in early 1973. "The general consensus was that the family planning program there was good," Hellman informed the Senate subcommittee later in the year after the involuntary sterilization of the Relf sisters came to light in July.

HEW Secretary Weinberger was disturbed by the Relf case

revelations. He ordered a stop to all federally financed sterilizations until new guidelines were prepared that would "insure that the rights of the individual are always paramount, always observed, and always secure." The four black women members of Congress urged him not to be in a rush about resuming the funding: "The complex legal and ethical problems involved require that HEW have the advice and counsel of experts if public confidence in family planning programs is to be restored. The heart of the issue is how do we make family planning information and services available to all those who want and need them, and at the same time insure that no element of coercion creeps into programs which Congress has specifically mandated must be voluntary in nature. . . . Turning all family planning programs over to the states will merely compound the problems raised by the Relf case."

The rules that were drawn up by HEW were unsatisfactory to the family planning establishment, which considered them unduly restrictive; to lawyers for the Relfs and the National Welfare Rights Organization, who considered them "nothing more than a eugenics program";[15] and even to Dr. Hellman, who said they would "prove cumbersome" and "close an option to the poor that the rich have." Essentially these first regulations similar to those drafted under Hern's supervision would have limited nontherapeutic sterilizations (not required for health reasons) to those who are over twenty-one, legally competent, and who have given their "informed consent," all to be watched over by review committees and judges. Hellman thought the age of consent should be as low as eighteen and that states should be permitted to develop their own review procedures with only broad general direction from Washington. The National Family Planning Forum, speaking for the establishment, said the federal review requirements would be "so demanding and repetitive as to create undue hardship for the prospective patients, parents or guardians." Dr. Carl Shultz, Hellman's deputy at HEW, pointed out that the guidelines would not be fully effective anyhow because HEW lacked the surveillance and policing capability without adequate information from local programs.

This was demonstrated a short time later when the Health Research Group, an organization associated with Ralph Nader's consumer protection movement, released a report documenting how doctors were "cavalierly" subjecting women to surgical sterilization without either explaining the hazards or describing alternative methods of birth control.[16] Many of the consent forms are a farce, it was asserted, and doctors often "sell" sterilization to women without even informing them that the procedure is irreversible. At Baltimore City Hospital there were several instances reported in which women "were given sterilization permits to sign literally minutes before a caesarian section and sterilization was to be carried out." The report noted an "extraordinary increase" in sterilization procedures between 1968 and 1970. Vasectomies increased from two hundred thousand to almost a million a year, in addition to the estimated one million female sterilizations. Interns practice on charity patients, and "in many instances there is little evidence of informed consent by the patient," it was alleged. The "selling" of sterilization operations to women who had few children but were under psychological stress occurred "in a manner not unlike other deceptive marketing practices," the Nader group charged. Sterilization procedures were being "pushed" at hospitals in Los Angeles, Baltimore, Boston, New Orleans, Nashville, Chicago, and Louisville, according to the report. Dr. Bernard Rosenfeld, a resident in obstetrics and gynecology at Los Angeles County Hospital, conducted the principal research.

Most of the women involved were black and poor, Rosenfeld's group said. Of twelve cases cited from Baltimore, seven of the women were under age twenty and none had more than two chilren. In all instances the subject of sterilization was brought up by the doctor, usually when the women were in labor and under duress.

The report quoted a practicing obstetrician who had been president of the Association for Voluntary Sterilization for fifteen years:

. . . Too many people crowded too close together cause many of our social and economic problems. These, in turn, are aggravated by involuntary and irresponsible parenthood. As physicians we have obligations to our individual patients, but we also have obligations to the society of which we are a part. The welfare mess, as it has been called, cries out for solutions, one of which is fertility control.[17]

Another study funded in part by the Southern Investigative

Research Project of the Southern Regional Council quoted a physician at Grady Memorial, Atlanta's public hospital, as attributing unnecessary sterilizations more to medical greed than to racism. "If there's a doctor and a uterus around, the two will get together. Let's face it," he said, "if you're a gynecology resident, how are you going into practice if you ain't yanked some utes?"[18]

The Nader group objected to the proposed regulations, contending that thousands of female sterilizations would be conducted by money-hungry doctors who would circumvent the desired waiting period between form-signing and operation.

"They [the government] don't want to permit the propagation of a race which is defective in some way," complained Joseph Levin, general counsel of the Southern Poverty Law Center, and the same lawyer who represented the South Carolina women in the Medicaid case. This time he filed a civil action in the U.S. District Court of the District of Columbia seeking an injunction to stop the operation of the new guidelines.

Judge Gerhard A. Gesell issued the injunction, and on March 15, 1974, he held the regulations to be arbitrary, unreasonable, and insufficient protection for welfare recipients coerced into sterilizations. Here are excerpts from Gesell's opinion in the consolidated cases, *Katie Relf and National Welfare Rights Organization et al.* v. *Caspar W. Weinberger et al.*

> Sterilization of females or males is irreversible. The total number of these sterilizations is clearly of national significance. Few realize that over 16 percent of the married couples in this country between the ages of 20 and 39 have had a sterilization operation. Over the last few years, an estimated 100,000 to 150,000 low-income persons have been sterilized annually under federally funded programs. Virtually all of these people have been adults: only about 2,000 to 3,000 per year have been under 21 years of age and fewer than 300 have been under 18. There are no statistics in the record indicating what percentage of these patients were mentally incompetent.
>
> Although Congress has been insistent that all family planning programs function on a purely voluntary basis, there is uncontroverted evidence in the record that minors and other incompetents have been sterilized with federal funds and that an indefinite number of poor people have been improperly coerced into accepting a sterilization operation

under the threat that various federally supported welfare benefits would be withdrawn unless they submitted to irreversible sterilization. Patients receiving Medicaid assistance at childbirth are evidently the most frequent targets of this pressure, as the experiences of the plaintiffs Brown and Walker illustrate.

. . . Plaintiffs (in this case) argue forcefully that sterilization of minors or mental incompetents is necessarily involuntary in the nature of things. Further, they claim that sterilization of competent adults under these regulations can be undertaken without insuring that the request for sterilization is in actuality voluntary.

. . . The Court finds that the Secretary has no authority under the family planning sections of the Social Security or Public Health Services Acts to fund the sterilization or any person incompetent under state law to consent to such an operation, whether because of minority or of mental deficiency. It also finds that the challenged regulations are arbitrary and unreasonable in that they fail to implement the congressional command that federal family planning funds not be used to coerce indigent patients into submitting to sterilization. In short, federally assisted family planning sterilizations are permissible only with the voluntary, knowing, and uncoerced consent of individuals competent to give such consent.

. . . Since these conclusions are based on statutory rather than constitutional grounds, the Court need not reach the question of whether involuntary sterilization *could* be funded by Congress. It is sufficient to note that there is no indication whatever that Congress intended to do so under the existing legislation, and such an intent will not be lightly assumed in light of the fundamental interests at stake. The present statutes were passed to facilitate only voluntary family planning and thus to assist the individual in the exercise of his voluntary right to govern his own procreation. Involuntary sterilization is not only distinguishable from these services, but diametrically so. It invades rather than complements the right to procreate.

This controversy has arisen during a period of rapid change in the field of birth control. In recent years, through the efforts of dedicated proponents of family planning, birth control information and services have become widely available. Aided by the growing acceptance of family planning, medical science has steadily improved and diversified the techniques of birth prevention and control. Advancements in artificial insemination and in the understanding of genetic attributes are also affecting the decision to bear children. There are even suggestions in the scientific literature that the sex of children may soon be subject to parental control. And over this entire area lies the specter of overpopulation, with its possible impact upon food supply, interpersonal relations, privacy, and the enjoyment of our "inalienable rights."

Surely the Federal Government must move cautiously in this area, under well-defined policies determined by Congress after full consideration of constitutional and far-reaching social implications. The dividing line between family planning and eugenics is murky. And yet the Secretary, through the regulations at issue, seeks to sanction one of the most drastic methods of population control—the involuntary irreversible sterilization of men and women—without any legislative guidance. Whatever might be the merits of limiting irresponsible reproduction, which each year places increasing numbers of unwanted or mentally defective children into tax-supported institutions, it is for Congress and not individual social workers and physicians to determine the manner in which federal funds should be used to support such a program. We should not drift into a policy which has unfathomed implications and which permanently deprives unwilling or immature citizens of their ability to procreate without adequate legal safeguards and a legislative determination of the appropriate standards in light of the general welfare and of individual rights.[19]

Instead of appealing Gesell's rulling immediately to a higher court, HEW decided to try to devise guidelines that would satisfy him. At no time did the administration ask Congress to clarify its preferences regarding sterilization policy, nor did the appropriate committees of the House and Senate initiate such legislation on their own. Hellman said the subject would be too touchy for Congress to deal with. Under certain conditions HEW wanted to permit the sterilization of persons as young as eighteen, and of some mentally incompetent individuals. While the negotiations were underway, the Public Health Service (the health arm of HEW) and the Social and Rehabilitation Service (the welfare arm) agreed not to fund any sterilizations for the under-twenty-one group. Gesell not only would not accept the proposed modifications, but he also criticized HEW for being unable to

systematically monitor individual decisions to sterilize. Thus HEW must depend in substantial degree on a complex series of procedures to be undertaken by persons not realistically subject to supervision and control or otherwise responsive to Congress. The experience with other phases of the sterilization problem shows the extreme difficulty that HEW is having in monitoring even the simplest safeguards.[20]

In a follow-up survey by Ralph Nader's Health Research Group, in another report by the American Civil Liberties Union (March 1975), and in legal discovery procedures initiated by the plaintiffs in the Relf-NWRO suit, it was disclosed that HEW (and more particularly SRS, the division with responsibility for welfare programs) were failing to enforce Gesell's order or the minimal guidelines issued by the federal government. Most of the country's big university teaching hospitals were simply ignoring the waiting period, consent forms and other requirements. Doctors were using federal funds to sterilize persons under twenty-one, disregarding the federal rule, without waiting at least seventy-two hours and without assuring the woman that she would not lose her welfare benefits if she declined. There had "nothing approaching substantial compliance" with the order at SRS, the plaintiffs alleged in a brief submitted to Gesell. SRS, meanwhile, took the position that it must not meddle in state administration of welfare programs, that it was a funding source only. HEW subsequently surveyed the same hospitals covered in the other studies and confirmed that 90 percent were not following the moratorium on under-twenty-one sterilizations or the federal regulations.

By now HEW had agreed to bar federally financed sterilizations of anyone under twenty-one, or anyone incapable of giving legally adequate consent, or anyone unable to understand the consequences by him or herself. Most of the discussion then focused on the so-called borderline retarded and by the plaintiff's persistent contention that HEW had not been sufficiently vigilant policing Gesell's order. For his part, Hellman continued to maintain that "we're not getting to the heart of the matter, which is that people with money can have it done. In an effort to protect people we're encouraging discrimination." He considered it significant that Gesell had accepted the fact that sterilization is a part of family planning. "It is the logical end point of family planning for a mature couple," the doctor said. "It is part of the middle-class mores."

Indeed, as Gesell observed in his opinion, more American couples were electing to be sterilized. Voluntary contraceptive sterilization is legal in every state but Utah, though not, of course, in Catholic hospitals. According to the National Survey of Family Growth, 36 percent of the women respondents said they or their husbands planned to be sterilized before age forty-five, a stunning increase. In 1974 alone, 1.3 million sterilizations were performed in the United States, almost half again as many as the year before. "The decline of American puritanism, coupled with the growing problems of birth control, abortion, and the population explosion have made people at least consider sterilization," declared John R. Rague, executive director of the Association for Voluntary Sterilization. For many years the American College of Obstetricians and Gynecologists followed a curious standard based on multiplying the age of the woman by the number of her children. If the product exceeded 120, the operation was okay. This formula was not officially scrapped until 1969.

Nevertheless, middle-class whites were considerably more willing to terminate their ability to procreate than either blacks or Latinos, which is what bothered Hellman. As we have seen, many poor women were sterilized without knowing it. The number of sterilizations in New York City's municipal hospitals skyrocketed in the early 1970s, until rules were adopted requiring a waiting period of not seventy-two hours but sixty days between the time the consent form is signed and the operation performed.

Lawyers for a group of New York obstetrician-gynecologists attacked the federal and city guidelines in court. One of the attorneys, Roy Lucas, said the government had made an unnecessary "fertility ritual" out of sterilization. "The government should not erect artificial barriers to discourage people from being sterilized or to impede or hinder their being sterilized. Restrictions on Medicaid patients' access to sterilization seem to be predicated on the assumption that poor people aren't smart enough to make these decisions. That's a lot of nonsense. Being poor doesn't entail being dumb. The regulations are a bad example of unnecessary paternalism, of people trying to protect a group of people who don't need protection and don't ask for it."[21] Here we see another example of the weird convolutions of population politics: liberals who desire equal opportunity for the poor cry out against "unnecessary paternalism" that would safeguard their civil liberties. Dr. Helen Rodriguez-Trias, professor of pediatrics at the Albert Einstein College of Medicine suggested that the obstetricians were worried that "patients would continue to wrest some power from them."[22] She cited figures indicating that one-fourth of Puerto Rican women sterilized in New York did not know that the procedure was permanent.

Another statement of the case for safeguards was enunciated by the columnist George Will:

> Since the government is now in the business of sorting "meaningful" lives from meaningless lives, it is plausible to assume that its sterilization programs are designed to weed the population. The government does not inflict sterilization randomly. Having improved itself so much since the days of the Founding Fathers, the government now is going to improve the population.
>
> It is not surprising that most of the dismay about the Alabama sterilization centers on the fact that the bureaucrats did not observe proper "criteria" in inflicting the sterilizations. The climate of opinion is now receptive to coerced sterilizations and a lot of other programs for "population improvement."
>
> What? "Population improvement"? Who said anything about *that*? Certainly not the bureaucrats involved. But that does not mean that population improvement is not the root motive for coerced sterilization. Other professed motives are implausible.
>
> . . . The government should not do things to people, and especially should not do things involving very sensitive matters, such as coerced and irreparable physical change, unless there is a clear and compelling need to do them.
>
> Now. What is the clear and compelling need for the government to inflict involuntary sterilization?
>
> Are mentally retarded girls particularly vulnerable to impregnation? Compared with whom? Compared with men-

tally competent but socially incompetent college under-
graduates? Ghetto teenagers? Las Vegas showgirls?

. . . Frugality is not the motive of those who want the
government to sterilize little girls. The people who want this
are not misers; they are idealists. They want to sterilize
inferior people; they want to improve the population. Only
such a great project demands such a grave government
power.[23]

Indeed, as Mr. Will says, the government does not "inflict
sterilization randomly." It is the "motivational class differential"
that makes sterilization policy so important to the new politics of
population. If permanent irreversible birth control becomes
popular among the middle-class, but the poor and minorities
continue to fear it, and have to be coerced or tricked into submitting to it, the social and arithmetical implications are plain to see.
This is, as Judge Gesell observed, a period of rapid change in the
field of birth control. Family planning professionals naturally
yearn for methods that are simple and effective. There are many
dedicated public officials like Warren Hern who believe that
sterilization should be available to poor people who want to stop
having babies and who find most contraceptives too complicated.
If she has no religious or moral objections, and elects to do so fully
understanding the permanence of the procedure, a woman who
won't take the Pill because she is afraid of blood clots, or who
neglects to put in a diaphragm, or whose uterus rejects the Loop,
can be rendered incapable of conceiving another child by one
operation. But the coercive potential of such a policy is frightening. As Judge Gesell noted, the federal government should move
cautiously "under well-defined policies determined by Congress
after full consideration of constitutional and far-reaching implications." Congress has not shown the slightest inclination to openly
consider the implications. Senator Kennedy held brief superficial
hearings into the Relf matter because he sensed an opportunity to
take a cheap political shot at the Republican administration, with
no desire to inquire into the murky depths of the sterilization
question. The politics of sterilization flow beneath the surface
with scant public awareness or understanding.

CHAPTER 8 Teen Sex: Double Standards of Feasibility

It could as well have been a theater full of youngsters waiting eagerly for the Bugs Bunny cartoon to begin the Saturday matinee. The same anxious air of juvenile excitement hung over the room. But here it was time for the White Doc from Chapel Hill to pay his weekly call, and the young people in the housing project were assembling in the recreation hall. In the black neighborhoods of downtown Raleigh some of the streets were still unpaved. The public housing project provided decent if fenced-off housing for the many families and fragments of families on welfare. One evening a week, a young physician from the Carolina Population Center—Dr. Charles Arnold—drove over from the University of North Carolina to conduct an advanced seminar in sex for the youths of the project. Arnold had served a stint in the Peace Corps. Possessing Beasley's sense of idealism and dedication, but without the overgrown ego, Arnold was typical of many recent medical school graduates who were more interested in social medicine than in huge fees, young people who were conscious of the social and professional numbness of generations of American physicians before them.

Four adolescent girls from the project—already mothers themselves—were paid by the local Community Action Agency to serve as outreach workers, much the same as Beasley's recruited staff in Louisiana. Acting the role of hostesses, they passed out soft drinks and paper and pencils. The black middle class of the capital of North Carolina sanctioned UNC's federally paid-for rhetoric because they considered it useful and needed and already old hat to many of the boys and girls.

133

The doctor leaned casually against a table. Some of the boys had just finished a basketball game. They drifted into the room looking smug and worldly. This college fellow didn't know anything that they hadn't already tried upside down and sideways. Most of the youngsters were of high school age, but some of the girls in the back of the room were as young as twelve. They appeared uneasy, some of them, slouched over nervously with their hands folded in their laps. The boys and girls were encouraged to scribble anonymous questions about sex on slips of paper which were collected by the outreach workers and then answered by the doctor in tones as matter-of-fact as he could muster. His answers provoked a stream of free-wheeling discussion and more questions and comments from the audience. No euphemistic sugar-coating here, no chatter about birds and bees, no maps of confluential spermatazoa and ova.

Some of the older boys were obviously testing the doc to see how streetwise he really was, nodding knowingly at his alley idioms as though to confirm the authenticity of his expertise. When the session ended, the outreach workers stacked records on the phonograph and the young people danced and laughed and exchanged teen talk, not unlike a Sock Hop at a suburban high school. Some of them rapped with the doctor in smaller groups. One girl asked a question privately that she had been too shy to commit to paper, even anonymously.

The discussions were only a prelude to the main purpose of the course, which was to give sexually active adolescents ready access to contraceptive services. Later in the same year, 1969, management of the program was turned over to Shaw University, a local, predominantly black institution. Other doctors opened a teen clinic and prescribed contraceptives for girls before they became pregnant.

The term "family planning" is entirely euphemistic when we are talking about birth control for teen-agers. The OEO-sponsored program in Raleigh is an example of a program initiated by the government antipoverty agency to deal in time with the tragedy that occurs when an unmarried adolescent girl becomes pregnant. Too often, for girls like those in the project, the cycle of lifelong dependency begins turning there and can never be stopped. Almost invariably it is a tragedy. She will probably drop out of school. She may marry someone she would not otherwise have chosen. The cnances for the marriage to last are less promising. And, as Pat Moynihan spelled out in academic terms, an unmarried lower-class mother is likely to produce both more dependent children and more social problems.

For many reasons, among them the presence of the Carolina Population Center and the absence of any sizeable number of Catholic voters, the pine woods and red clay country of North Carolina had long been fertile ground for the birth control movement. Compulsory eugenic sterilization and state-financed birth control services were popular in that state for many years. In the late 1960s, condoms and vaginal foams—contraceptives that do not require a medical prescription—were being dispensed free to black youths as young as twelve in storefront contraceptive "stations" in Winston Salem. Clark Vincent of the Bowman-Gray Medical School, which sponsored the OEO-supported program there, explained: "These kids are so inundated with sexual stimuli that they must be protected before they qualify for their 'union card,' their first pregnancy."[1] All over the country, in big and smaller cities alike, but almost always in communities with a large black population, teen programs became an integral part of OEO's birth control activities. Almost always, the programs were initiated with a minimum of publicity and discussion.

Even slow-to-move HEW joined in the cause. Katherine B. Oettinger, then deputy assistant secretary for family planning, described for me what was being done in Miami to search out and offer help to young people who were "exposed to the dangers of pregnancy." "Mothers bring their babies . . . Babies? Their fourteen-year-old daughters, to the clinic. They say, 'I was pregnant with her at fourteen and I don't want it to happen to her. Unless she gets some protection it will.' The environment is more than they can cope with. These are places, you must understand, where the sex patterns are already set."[2]

If the solution seemed logical enough—to equip sexually active adolescents with the mechanical or pharmaceutical means to avoid becoming pregnant—the legal, moral, and political complications were far from simple. In most societies, the sexual behavior of the young, like the enforcement of moral principles, is thought to be best handled by the family without state interference. In the United States, where our leaders are freely elected, these problems are usually too tender for the political processes, as the prior chapters repeatedly illustrated, *especially* when youth is involved. Dr. Greenlee said he most resented the "pushing" of birth control pills among adolescents in Pittsburgh. The Illinois public aid policy stumbled over the legal fact that sexual intercourse with an unmarried minor was a crime in that state. Moynihan's treatise caused such a ruckus because of the implied emphasis on unrestrained extra-marital fornication by a group that did not pay all that much homage to traditional family forms. The OEO sterilization scandal exploded after the Relf sisters were sterilized on suspicion that some boys were hanging around their house.

Not everyone accepted the assumption that residence in a "project" in Raleigh or Montgomery, in the social milieu of the welfare class, where (in Mrs. Oettinger's words) "the sex patterns are already set," doomed a teen-age girl to a life of sexual promiscuity beginning at puberty. By introducing an immature twelve-year-old girl to the technology and technique of contraception, was the government somehow helping to establish random sexual intercourse as culturally acceptable or even desirable behavior? Would a suburban PTA chapter permit anything like it? Even if the sex patterns were pretty much set in that suburban high school? Would or should a family doctor supply contraceptives to minors without notifying the parents? Finally, would it work? Would the typical teen-ager do what was necessary?

At about the same time that the Raleigh program was getting underway, a similar OEO demonstration grant had to be withdrawn in Seattle because of outraged complaints from the black community. Joe Beasley, ever the astute political observer, knew better than to propose the dissemination of contraceptive services "in the absence of community consensus" to "pre-pregnant adolescents" without parental consent in Louisiana. It would be necessary first, Beasley said, to "demonstrate to the community's satisfaction that the availability of birth control services does not lead to an increase in promiscuity, but does indeed salvage the lives of numerous women and children from the stigma and disabilities of illegitimacy."[3] For Beasley to try to do in Catholic New Orleans what Arnold was doing in non-Catholic Raleigh would have been to blow his entire program out of the water, and he knew it.

Analyzing Gallup Poll data, Judith Blake reported general public disapproval of government-sponsored birth control services for teen-age females.[4] Women felt more strongly about it than men, she noted, contrary to the general sexual differences concerning birth control generally. Even among the more liberated generation of women under age thirty, only 17 percent approved. Although almost one-third of college-educated men in upper-income brackets thought it would be a good idea, the approval rating dropped to 13 percent among low-income men and those with only a grade school education. "Clearly, the extension of 'family planning' to poor, unmarried teen-agers is not regarded simply as democratization of 'health care,' " Blake commented. Subsequently, Richard Reynolds of the Ford Foundation sympathized with "Blake's concern for questions of sexual morality. It is a theme family planners hear often. However, she fails to appreciate the fact that for the teen-agers in question sexual relations are a fact of life, with or without contraception."[5]

Undeniably, in a period when birth rates were declining, the number of illegitimate births in the United States was shooting upward. Between 1940 and 1968 the rate of illegitimate births to adolescents tripled. Although the recorded gap between whites and nonwhites narrowed, the rate was still much higher for blacks. Recent statistics indicate that illegitimate births accounted for most of the black-white fertility differential between 1960 and 1970.[6] As the U.S. birth rate dipped in the 1960s, the proportion of births to teens increased from 14 percent of the total in 1961 to 17 percent in 1968. Among nonwhites, the figure went from 20 percent in 1961 to 29 percent in 1968. In the 1970s, more than one million teen-agers were becoming pregnant every year.

Truly, the problem is less visible among middle-class whites, for whom abortions or adoptions are more easily arranged. Some studies have shown that black teen-agers who get pregnant are nine times less likely than a white adolescent to have an abortion. Illegitimacy is viewed by the public-at-large as a primary contributor to the "welfare problem," which of course it is. Hence, it is an object of great public consternation—by the same people who deny the existence of a middle-class problem. In Kansas in 1971, Rep. Santford Duncan described illegitimate births to adolescents in that state as "a problem of epidemic proportions." Nevertheless the Kansas House of Representatives—male-dominated as are all state legislatures—defeated a bill that would have appropriated state funds for clinics where teen-agers could be counseled and given contraceptives. Some time later, the attorney general of that state unearthed a statute which he interpreted to prohibit the distribution of free contraceptives to any unmarried woman, even those who were adults. In another state, Michigan, efforts to repeal a law forbidding the discussion of birth control in the public schools were unsuccessful.

What we quickly discover then is that there are double moral standards: society has an interest in curtailing illegitimacy in the black housing project in Raleigh or Montgomery, but in predominantly white Kansas it is still very much a family responsibility.

California provides an interesting example of that political phenomenon in operation. It will be recalled that Congress changed the welfare laws in 1969 to require that states furnish birth control services regardless of age or marital status. An adolescent, therefore, could routinely be supplied contraceptive assistance in California or any other state without the knowledge of her parents if her family was on welfare, had been on welfare, or might reasonably be expected sometime in the future to be on welfare. In 1972, 35,000 adolescents received legal abortions in California, compared to 19,800 the year before, a trend attributed by Governor Ronald Reagan to "certain segments of the youth culture." Not many of these involved welfare recipients. Three times in three successive years, however, from 1971 through 1973, Governor Reagan vetoed bills passed by the California legislature specifying that a note from home would not be needed before a physician could safely prescribe birth control pills or another form of contraception for *any* sexually active teen-ager, on or off welfare.[7] Reagan contended that the state should not be intruding into the prerogatives of parents who happen to care about what their children are doing. "I believe parents must continue to have the right to give their consent on matters of such fundamental concern to them," his veto message of 1972 stated. "Simply because sexual permissiveness may exist among certain young people does not mean the state should make it any easier for them. . . . The state has no right to even tacitly seem to condone such behavior, particularly among children who, in too many instances, are not yet mature enough to understand the full implications of their actions."

Essentially the same double standard was reflected in President Nixon's objections to "unrestricted" distribution of contraceptive aid to minors, as he inaccurately understood this to have been a recommendation of the population growth commission. He asserted that "such measures would do nothing to preserve and strengthen close family relationships." Nixon's comments were occasioned by the proposal in the commission report that legal restrictions against access to contraceptive services by young people be eliminated. A research study conducted for the commission had estimated that nearly half of all unmarried American females have sex relations before age twenty. Fourteen percent of all fifteen-year-olds were said to have experienced sexual intercourse.

That Nixon had his finger on the pulse of middle-class opinion was evidenced by the slow pace at which state legislatures spelled out the right of teen-agers to obtain contraceptive assistance without parental consent.[8]

The same political dynamics caused Nixon to veto a bill to establish government-supported day care centers for the children of welfare mothers. Congress broadened the legislation beyond what the president had in mind by adding that working mothers who were not on welfare could pay a fee based on their incomes and deposit their preschool children at the facilities. To include other than poor children in socially integrated centers would result, declared Nixon's veto message, in "communal approaches to child rearing . . . that would diminish parental authority and involvement." What he meant, plainly, was that "communal child rearing" was all right if welfare mothers could thereby be freed to take low-paying jobs as cleaning women; but not the middle-class, even if the self-supporting parents could pay all or part of the cost. Such an arrangement, Nixon explained, would "commit the vast moral authority of the national government to the side of communal approaches to child rearing [instead of] the family-centered approach."

"Family-centered approaches" are perceived by the public, it would seem, as an unrealistic option for the black welfare class. Sociologist Phillips Cutright, who is an authority on the subject of illegitimacy, says the problem cannot be solved until the "pseudomoral barrier" is lifted and contraceptives are made easily available to all unmarried women of whatever age.[9] Many physicians are reluctant, though, to prescribe contraception for unmarried women even when the women are about to be married and can pay for it. "Unmarried women visiting physicians in general practice (rather than physicians specializing in obstetrics and gynecology), older physicians or Catholic physicians are quite likely not to get what they come for," Cutright asserts. Another study has shown that even with parental consent only 40 percent of general practitioneers and 54 percent of gynecologists will provide contraceptive information to youngsters aged fifteen to seventeen.[10] Pilpel and Wechsler (Planned Parenthood lawyers) assign additional blame to druggists and lawyers. They quote a suburban druggist who was asked whether he would sell condoms to teen-age boys: "If they're kids I know real well, I'll sell them. But not to a stranger. This community's hell on illegitimacy, and they'd run me out of town if they thought I was giving their kids contraceptives."[11] Part of the middle-class American mind-set, still, is the firmly planted notion that making it easier for young people to obtain contraceptives will encourage sexual promiscuity, loose morals, and—illogically—more illegitimacy as well. Furthermore, according to this study, lawyers who are consulted are likely, in the absence of a precise statutory provision, to advise a physician "not to touch" a sexually active teen-ager who requests birth control help without her parents' knowledge. The common law tradition inhibited physicians from furnishing medical services of any kind to a minor child without parental consent. The Supreme Court's carefully hedged opinion, by a five-to-four vote, in the abortion parental consent case indicated continuing uncertainty about the proper modern standards. But the fact remains that a far different, politically acceptable "touching" standard applies to equally sexually active youngsters who are black and poor, as demonstrated by the doctors who did considerably more than touch the Relf sisters in Alabama.

Whether to make contraceptives available to teen-agers at public expense and if necessary without parental consent was only a small part of a larger controversy that flared in middle-class communities all over the country during this period: the proper role of the public schools in sex education. Early in this century, the "social hygiene movement," as it was euphemistically labeled, began urging a more realistic and more responsible public attitude about acquainting young people with "the facts of life." Later on, the activities of Dr. Mary Calderone and the Sex Information and Education Council of the United States (SIECUS) were fastened upon by right-wing groups and religious fundamentalists as a deadly communist plot that threatened to gnaw away at the moral integrity of our youth. The Rev. Billy Joe Hargis of the Christian Crusade saw the sex education campaign as "part of a gigantic conspiracy to bring down America from within." Ronald Reagan and other rightist politicians associated sex education with a general "permissiveness" that pervaded the youth culture in the sixties and made many of the older folks squirm.

Avant-garde educators and far right-wingers, fanatics at either pole, clashed often over the issue. Mary Breasted, in her excellent study of the politics of the controversy, found that the silent majority in the middle tended to tolerate the daring new programs in the public school curriculum until the hypercritical minority on the right started screaming. Then, when the issue surfaced and became the object of angry debate, the majority was inclined to demand a curtailment of programs that were now viewed as excessive.[12] Sexually related policies stay afloat if they are permitted to cruise along quietly without making waves. But school board members, like other public officials, retreat quickly when "sex issues" enter the public arena. In middle-class circles, sex education is still very controversial. So much so that as late as 1976 Dr. Hellman of HEW said President Ford's Office of Management and Budget (with Paul O'Neill still running the health division) would not permit the preparation or circulation of government questionnaires and other information-gathering forms for the study of teen-age sex. Parents might be outraged if they knew about them.

Sex education sets off volatile forces in American society. At the peak of his power and prestige in Louisiana, Joe Beasley went trooping back to the chancery office in New Orleans to obtain church approval of a new sex education plan that he had in mind for the public schools. The bishops had no objections to such a program in the public schools as long as nobody got any fancy ideas about what the parochial schools ought to be doing. Before the program could be started, Billy Joe Hargis and his friends arrived on the scene. Protest meetings were organized. The

Louisiana legislature reacted swiftly by passing a law prohibiting *any* sex education in the schools. Incredibly, that state with its ambitious birth control program was (and is) the only state in the union where it is against the law to discuss sex in school. "The signal was loud and clear," one of Beasley's lieutenants told me. "There are some things you'd better not mess with politically in this state."

In the meantime many family planners were endeavoring to steer the focus away from a purely physiological preoccupation with genitalia and toward education ("advertising, if you will," Dr. Hellman said) about population problems in general. Baltimore was the first large-city school system to include population education in the junior and senior high school social studies curriculum. Ten years of effort by an organization called the Urban Life Population Education Institute, which was formed with the assistance of the Planned Parenthood Association of Baltimore and was funded initially by the Rockefeller Foundation, preceded the decision to make it a regular part of the social studies program there. HEW recommended further that schools instill a more effective motivation for fertility control in young people by counseling and sex education that would create less "maladaptive" values and behavior. Hellman defines population education as "the process of developing knowledge, understanding, values, and attitudes concerning population phenomena and their effect on the quality of life."[13]

If survey responses are to be believed, sexual intercourse is commonplace among unmarried adolescents today. Young people are bombarded by sexual stimuli. The family is no longer an effective restraint to such behavior. Yet middle-class parents resist sex education in the schools and become irate if a student editor publishes an article about birth control in the school newspaper. Despite these attitudes, and the unresponsiveness of most private physicians to the problem, teen clinics for the poor were able to get underway in many of the big central cities. The same parents who fought sex education classes in their childrens' schools approved contraceptive stations in the ghetto. In Chicago and Los Angeles, cities where the public schools were forbidden to discuss birth control, thousands of youths were given free contraceptives. In one recent year, four out of twelve new patients in Planned Parenthood's New York City clinics were nineteen years of age or younger.

But did the programs work? Were they effective? In 1975, according to Hellman's estimate, the number of teen-age pregnancies in the United States, including those aborted, exceeded one million, a higher rate than any other developed country in the world. One follow-up study indicated that almost one-third of the adolescent mothers who asked for and were given birth control assistance became pregnant again. "Our major problem," said Hellman, "is we really don't know why teen-agers will not use contraceptives." One reason, he thinks, is that the use of contraceptives is an admission of conscious intent. Dr. Andre Hellegers of Georgetown University predicted before the programs started that they would not work because he said a vast majority of out-of-wedlock first pregnancies occur in haphazard rather than predictable intercourse situations. There is agreement, too, that many of the lower-class girls suffer from problems of low self-esteem which are salved by the experience of motherhood. And finally there are the ambivalent feelings about the morality of the programs that cannot help but affect the political attitudes. The *New York Times* quoted a Planned Parenthood executive in that city who was also the father of a fifteen-year-old daughter: "I have told her I don't think she should have sexual intercourse. As a parent I would't provide her with contraception, but I would expect the Planned Parenthood office in my community to do something. It is now right to expect the doctor to provide help."[14]

When Hellman told the House subcommittee on Census and Population that "we have failed as a government to face up to the problem" (of teen-age pregnancies) and advocated more attention to education, the chairwoman, Rep. Patricia Schroeder, Democrat of Denver, Colorado, agreed. "But," she added, "it's a very sensitive thing . . . where you really start getting into trouble."[15] Public officials and political candidates seek to avoid the trouble by pretending that it does not exist. After President Nixon expressed his public displeasure with birth control programs for teen-agers prior to his reelection in 1972, HEW went ahead with the programs as though nothing had been said, this with the knowledge of the White House, indicating again that the public perception is more important than the public reality in the ever murky world of population politics.

CHAPTER 9 Lessons Learned,
Lessons Ignored

Our attention has focused thus far on birth control policies—
how the government goes about trying to induce selected classes
of Americans, lower-class blacks primarily, not to have so many
children. In this way the state hopes to contain the spread of
poverty and social unrest, preserve political stability and protect
the holders of power in American society, while at the same time
making available to the less privileged options that other Americans exercise routinely. Elected representatives awakened to a
new consensus—an Age of Enlightenment, many would
contend—in favor of more efficient dispensation of contraceptives and more emphasis on voluntary permanent birth control (sterilization) at a time when public assistance costs were
climbing and the segregated urban black underclass was growing
fast.

For our purposes, the new enlightenment took two forms. With
improved contraceptive technology, more Americans of all religious denominations were using artificial means of controlling
births. And they were supporting government policies of providing assistance for those who either because of ignorance or lack of
resources did not have access to contraceptive devices and drugs.
All up and down the socio-economic ladder, birth rates declined
in the United States in the 1960s, though still higher among
lower-class families than in the middle and upper classes. Except
for the problems of teen-age pregnancies, which were discussed
in the last chapter, progress could be noted generally in the
control of "excess" births.

144

While these changes were taking place, Catholic clergymen were grumbling, and fewer American Catholics were practicing their religion. The reforms adopted at the Second Vatican Council in 1962 contributed to an ecumenical spirit and raised expectations that the church would modify its position on birth control. That hope was dashed in 1968 when Pope Paul VI issued his encyclical *Humanae Vitae* reaffirming the condemnation of artificial birth control. A series of studies for the National Opinion Research Center at the University of Chicago by the Rev. Andrew M. Greeley and his associates traced changing Catholic attitudes. "In theory and to some extent in practice, a substantial proportion of the Catholic population has turned away from what is still the official sexual teaching of the church," the authors reported in 1975.[1] Artificial contraception won the approval of 45 percent of American Catholics in 1964, and 83 percent in 1974, a startling rejection of *Humanae Vitae*. Ten years before, 54 percent thought the church had "the right" to teach what views Catholics should take on birth control. In 1974 that figure had dropped to 32 percent. In a personal "Afterword" to the report, Father Greeley, himself a Catholic priest, said he did not doubt "that historians of the future will judge *Humanae Vitae* to be one of the worst mistakes in the history of Catholic Christianity—and this particularly because it seems to have nipped in the bud the splendid prospect for growth and development set in motion by the Second Vatican Council."[2] "We don't speculate that the cause of Catholic decline was the birth control decisions, nor do we simply assert it," Father Greeley commented later. "We prove [it] with the kind of certainty one rarely attains in historical analyses. If I were a bishop and saw this information I would consider it serious enough to call a panic meeting." Asked about this, Archbishop Joseph L. Bernadin of Cincinnati, president of the National Conference of Catholic Bishops, said: "Ethical values cannot be arrived at by counting noses."

These new American attitudes did not emerge suddenly. In his earlier book about the birth control practices of the poor, Lee Rainwater quoted a Catholic woman who was about to use a contraceptive and not tell the priest about it:

> Who is he to tell me how many children to have? He never has to drag about with five kids and try to make a living for

them! The way things are, it just goes on making me old and cross and sick.[3]

It was not necessary for Archbishop Bernadin to remind us, however, that bishops are not elected by their constituents nor is Catholic doctrine arrived at by popular referendum. Spokesmen for the church hierarchy slogged on through the sixties and early seventies, officially opposing most of the new birth control policies, making accommodations now and then, acquiescing only when conditions demanded. Some of the most dramatic and important cases of political interaction between policymakers and church leaders were described in the preceding chapters. There we found that in states where the influence of the church was significant, as far removed geographically and culturally as Pennsylvania and Louisiana, public and private birth control agencies took pains to assure church officials that the objectionable services would, insofar as possible, sidestep the white Catholic poor and zero in on the largely non-Catholic black community. Planned Parenthood, countless community action agencies, and Dr. Beasley all seemed to sense that their activities would go forward more expeditiously if they did not go out of their way to hustle contraceptives among the Catholic faithful. What happened in Lincoln Parish, Homewood-Brushton, Raleigh, and the South Side of Chicago was of secondary concern. Actually, the fertility rate of Americans of Spanish origin, groups that tend disproportionately to be both poor and Catholic, continued to be about double that of all whites or all blacks in the United States. Counting estimated illegal aliens in the population, the Community Relations Service, an agency of the Justice Department, reported in 1976 that the Latino population of the United States was fast approaching the black population—about 20 million Latinos and 24 million blacks.

Not long ago, I talked with a man who had been one of Joe Beasley's top lieutenants in the service delivery end of the Louisiana family planning program. He was not implicated in the corporation's financial manipulations, and now holds a high academic position, so he requested that he not be quoted by name. I inquired whether he ever had qualms about possible racial genocidal motives.

Not at the time. I must admit that now I have some reservations about the possibility there may have been some genocidal motives on the part of some people. I really don't think it was a national genocidal policy. But, as is the case with many technological and scientific advancements, there are unanticipated spinoffs. It may be that some people anticipated them. I'm not sure.

When you look at the service design, the blacks were relatively over-served. It makes you pause and wonder if that was intentional. The primary recruiting area for patients—the catchment area, we called it—was to be the postpartum ward of the large teaching hospital, the charity hospital. You get them while they're lying there, just after they've delivered. That kind of recruitment was not extended to the local Baptist hospitals or other hospitals where the medically indigent whites were delivering.

Thoughtful people should raise the questions and find out what is going on. I just have an uneasy feeling looking at some of these service patterns.

Thoughtful readers can draw their own conclusions about the experiences of the sixties and seventies. Whatever the historical background, family planning—the first of the three steps enumerated by Dr. Beasley in the national population strategy—is now supported in Congress by black representatives, male and female alike. Family planning is accepted as a necessary component in a comprehensive health service for the poor—an option that will help the disadvantaged improve their lives. The second objective in the national plan—voluntary sterilization—is more complex and more controversial. Litigation goes on in the federal courts in an effort to iron out the precautions that are necessary to protect the defenseless. The third objective—abortion on request—is still more divisive and emotional.

Abortion has never been solely or even primarily a population issue. It transcends population considerations. A book will be written someday about how the moral, legal, and political ramifications of the abortion issue were resolved in the United States, if they are. But that is not for here and now.

The counter-strategies of the Catholic leaders are nonetheless relevant to our examination of the new politics of population for at least two important reasons.

The Catholic church's role as a political force bearing directly on population policies has, I trust, been made apparent. Before plunging headlong into the political arena, their experiences in New York, Illinois, and Pennsylvania might have caused church officials to ponder carefully the course they were taking. By threatening political retribution against candidates who were unwilling to impose Catholic doctrine on citizens of other beliefs, the church disregarded the lessons of the sixties. After the judiciary committees of the Senate and House declined to recommend revision of the constitutional language that the Supreme Court interpreted to permit abortions, the bishops issued a "pastoral plan for pro-life activities." The plan called for Catholics to "infiltrate" the political parties and form "identifiable, tightly-knit and well-organized pro-life units"—political action committees—in each congressional district. In the St. Louis archdiocese, for instance, all of the 254 parishes established pro-life committees with two chairpersons. Father Edward J. O'Donnell, coordinator of the Archdiocesan Pro-Life Committee, said candidate endorsements ordinarily should not be made from the pulpit, "but this issue of life is such an overriding issue that I am not sure that an exception should not be made." Traveling troupes of haranguing demonstrators, Right-to-Life chapter members dressed as grotesque abortionists in blood-smeared surgical gowns, and carrying plumbers' helpers, followed the chairman of the Senate committee, Sen. Birch Bayh of Indiana, through New Hampshire and Massachusetts where he was campaigning in the Democratic presidential primaries. The church and its auxiliary units were clearly cranking up a major political effort. A pastoral letter on abortion was read from every pulpit on the Sunday before the anniversary of the Supreme Court decision. Then, in a twenty-seven-hundred-word statement entitled "Political Responsibility: Reflections on an Election Year," the forty-eight-bishop administrative board of the Catholic hierarchy in the U.S. went over the same ground, disavowing any thought of forming "a religious voting bloc" or of instructing Catholics how to vote.

Yet many Catholics stirred uneasily at this total concentration on Father O'Donnell's overriding issue. Writing in the Jesuit magazine America, Paul J. Webber said: "Never before in the 200 years of American independence have the bishops provided such concerted, nationwide, overt political leadership. Their pastoral plan may well signal a major shift in episcopal political efforts. If so, this new activism must be accompanied by serious discussion within the Catholic community. Stated bluntly, should the Catholic bishops as a group become so active politically?'' Webber described the pastoral statement as ''tough strategy for an all-out political battle'' and said it ''crackles with political idiom.''

''The most tragic irony of all,'' declared *America* in a previous editorial, ''would be to lose our children when seeking to gain the Congress. The growing acceptance of abortion is only one sign that the Catholic view of sex and love, marriage and the family is increasingly a minority view in the United States.'' A poll commissioned by an anti-abortion group, the National Committee for Human Rights, indicated that abortion ranked tenth on a list of seventeen pressing social issues. The Gallup and Harris polls both found considerably more than a majority of the American people in favor of the liberalized abortion system.

Commonweal, the liberal Catholic weekly, commented at the beginning of 1976 that ''the bishops have shown their indifference to the ecumenical dimensions of this issue, raised questions about the separation of church and state law and—overestimating their influence with their constituents—have promised a vote they can't deliver.'' On February 27, *Commonweal* predicted that the debate would ''dissipate the political influence of the Catholic hierarchy, who have had the poor judgment to make *this* issue *the* issue to test Catholic solidarity and political clout.'' The editorial went on to criticize the church for its ''failure to understand a generation ago that family planning and artificial birth control differed radically from abortion and were not necessarily forms of sexual immorality but potentially positive means of preserving married love and enhancing respect for life.'' The national consensus in favor of abortion may be so strong, *Commonweal* asserted, ''that those Catholics who are absolutely opposed to abortion will have to learn to live with some of the evil that has followed from the Supreme Court decision as part of the cost of living in a pluralistic and secular state.''

A committee of bishops met with Carter and Ford early in the campaign. Archbishop Bernadin and the others said they were encouraged by Ford's understanding of the need for a constitutional amendment that would give the states the authority to regulate abortion as they wished. Later the archbishop said he regretted the widespread "misperception" that this amounted to a church endorsement of the Republican candidate.

Meanwhile, Planned Parenthood took to the attack, criticizing both presidential candidates for their "cruel disregard for the rights of American women as they have curried, and curried in vain, the favors of a strident minority and the officialdom of the Roman Catholic church." The candidates were reminded of their "foremost responsibility as public officials (to) promote policies which are consistent with the needs, well-being and wishes of the majority of our people. However, the candidates appear to have abandoned that responsibility and to become supine before the unproved electoral threat brandished by the hierarchy of the Catholic church." "Our pluralistic society is now endangered" by this "brazen intrusion of the Catholic hierarchy into the political process" and by "the candidates' failure to uphold the central values of society and the rights of American women and men," Planned Parenthood fired back.

There is another reason, too, why the events of that campaign year were an extension of several of the themes of this book. Every citizen is entitled to promote orderly constitutional change, cumbersome though the amendment process must be. As it turned out, however, the federal policy debate in Congress revolved around the issue of abortion as a medical service available to recipients under the Medicaid welfare program. While campaigning for Democratic caucus delegates in Iowa, the take-off point of his drive for the presidential nomination, Jimmy Carter opposed a constitutional amendment, but said: "No active government should ever contribute to abortions. We should do all we can to minimize abortions and to favor a national statute that would restrict the practice of abortion in our country." President Ford also opposed the use of federal funds to pay for the abortions of the poor.

Just before resigning as secretary of HEW in 1975, Caspar Weinberger issued an order prohibiting Medicaid-financed abortions for the medically indigent. But the new secretary, David Mathews, former president of the University of Alabama, pulled back the order and left the policy up to the individual states. All but four states were paying for abortions under Medicaid, and these four were under challenge on discrimination grounds in the Supreme Court. The birth control implications of abortion policy cannot be ignored. In the District of Columbia, for example, there were more legal abortions (9,819) than births (9,476) in 1975. About 85 percent of the abortions were paid for by the federal government, most of them under Medicaid. Washington is a heavily black city. In the past, abortions were resorted to less often among blacks, presumably for economic rather than religious reasons. But the figures for Washington indicate that this has changed with the inclusion of abortion services in the Medicaid program. Only about 20 percent of the women having abortions in Washington were married. Nationally there were about 317 abortions for every 1,000 births in 1975; and Medicaid financed roughly one-fourth of the estimated one million legal abortions.

When the HEW appropriation bill was before Congress, the House attached a proviso sponsored by Rep. Henry J. Hyde, a conservative Republican Catholic from an almost all-white suburban middle-class district outside Chicago. The Hyde amendment barred any federal reimbursement for the cost of abortions. The Senate balked, and a protracted debate ensued in the conference committee.

On almost all particulars, the arguments were a replay of the controversy that had occurred in Illinois thirteen years before. Then the church opposed the provision of contraceptives to women on welfare because the policy would be contrary to the moral standards of Catholicism, would encourage sexual promiscuity among the unmarried, and was designed to seduce racial minorities into not having so many children. This time Hyde raised the sanctity-of-life argument and invoked the spectre of genocide, an unfamiliar arrow in his rhetorical quiver. "All of us should have a particular sensitivity to the concept of the word genocide," he told the House. "In New York City last year for every 1,000 minority births there were 1,304 minority abortions. That is one way to get rid of the poverty problem, get rid of poor people. Let us call that pooricide."[4] Hyde quoted a nonhero to his district, the Chicago black leader Jesse Jackson ("You can't just kill poor people who are in your way") and another, Dick Gregory ("I know a man in Chicago who wipes out 125 black babies a day in one of those abortion clinics. You say a poor black woman has as much right to an abortion as a rich white one. Well, then give her the right to a Cadillac, a mink, and a trip to Paris.'').

Why discriminate against the poor, liberal Democrats responded. Why should a poor woman be denied an opportunity, now protected by the Constitution, of having a safe, legal abortion that is available to anyone who can afford to pay the fee? The alternative, they foresaw, would be more self-induced (and dangerous) "coat-hanger" abortions or more unwanted children. Rep. Lloyd Meeds, a Democrat from Washington state, talked about welfare costs. "Each pregnancy brought to full term among welfare mothers is estimated to cost $2,200 in the first year alone," he said. "Therefore, we are talking about $450 million versus $45 million [in Medicaid abortion costs], an appropriation we are going to be asked to make later in the form of welfare expenditures. . . . I think every child has a right to be brought into a family that wants that child."[5]

Because our earlier case study involved voting patterns of Illinois representatives, it is worth analyzing the House vote by that state's delegation on the Hyde amendment. All five Republican representatives who are Catholics supported Hyde. The six Republicans who are not Catholics divided evenly, three for, three against. The two black Democrats and the two Jewish members from Cook County opposed the Hyde amendment. All six white Catholic Democrats in Illinois voted for the restriction. Two other Democrats (non-Catholics) opposed Hyde, one supported him.

At first, the chairman of the HEW appropriations sub-committee, Rep. Daniel Flood, Democrat of Wilkes Barre, Pennsylvania, and a Catholic critic of abortion, resisted the Hyde amendment. During the floor debate, he characterized a vote for the amendment as "a vote against poor people." But when the issue was referred to the conference committee, Flood changed into a determined defender of the restrictive amendment. Sen. Edward W. Brooke, Republican from heavily Catholic Massachusetts and the only black senator, led the fight by the Senate conferees against the restriction. All but one of the black representatives in the House—that being the elderly Robert N. C. Nix of Philadelphia—opposed Hyde, including the two black Catholics. Jesse Jackson in Chicago could side with the Right-to-Life forces ("Women don't have the right to destroy babies because they don't make them all by themselves "). But elected black politicians who depend on the support of black women as well as men had to respond to the interests their constituents have in the unrestricted availability of all medical services, now including abortion. Most of the Chicano representatives, on the other hand, supported the Hyde amendment. House conferees would not relent, and after weeks of negotiations during which the HEW appropriation bill was delayed, the senators agreed to a limitation on federal payments for abortions to those in which the prospective mother's life would be in danger if she gave birth.

The emotional and religious overtones of the abortion issue were so overwhelming that conservative Catholic legislators such as Hyde were carrying the banner for policies (and citing Jesse Jackson for a supporting authority) that would make it more difficult to prevent unwanted births of low-income blacks and result therefore in a bigger lower-class black population. Representatives of Catholic Mexican-American constituencies did the same. What this suggests, of course, is that had the Catholic church wanted to block the earlier family planning programs that were aimed primarily at blacks the evolution of federal policy might have been quite different.

Some students of the abortion controversy[6] have proposed the building of a temporary coalition based on the fact that the demand for abortion is created by unwanted pregnancies. Why not, therefore, a temporary working alliance of adversary groups—the family planners and the Right-to-Lifers—both of which want to reduce the demand for abortion? If such an alliance were found to be feasible, the two sides presumably would share a common interest in the development of more effective contraceptive technology. They ought to support more biomedical research in reproductive biology and the search for more effective contraceptives. After 1972, public and private expenditures for contraceptive research declined.[7] On June 24, 1976, the same day that the Hyde amendment was adopted, Representative Scheuer, now back in the House representing a different New York City district, offered an amendment to increase the HEW budget for population-related research by $16 million. The way to make abortions unnecessary, Scheuer argued convincingly, would be to prevent undesired conception. The black caucus supported him. The Chicanos were divided. The southern Democrats were overwhelmingly opposed. Republican conservatives opposed the amendment, too, among them Henry Hyde of Illinois. The proposal lost, 122 to 278.

CHAPTER **10**   A New Perspective
on Immigration

Throughout American history there is another form of population politics that has been most instrumental in determining the relative weight of different ethnic groups in the public affairs of the nation: immigration policy—who gets in and who does not. In an immigrant nation where each person's vote is supposed to count the same, the gatekeeper wields the power of a monarch. Although the flow of legal immigration into the United States is far less now than it used to be, new arrivals accounted for the addition of 3.9 million persons to the national population between the 1960 and 1970 censuses. That does not include an illegal alien population of unknown size. The Immigration and Naturalization Service says the illegal alien group numbers at least 8 million and could be 12 million. Some are counted in the decennial national census, but many are not. By strengthening the border guard and deploying more manpower and resources to the apprehension and deportation of illegal aliens, the government could cut off most of this traffic. But the policymakers have never chosen to do so, which is in itself an interesting political question to ponder—why?

Ample volumes have been written about the history and the politics of immigration. This is not intended to be a comprehensive study of that fascinating subject. Bringing forward the theme of the early part of the book, the treatment of birth control, our interest is chiefly the interplay of race and religion in the "new" dynamics of population policy. Specifically, we will be examining the changes that occurred because of the 1965 immigration reform act, the impact of that law and the special admission of refugees from foreign communism on two Hispanic Catholic groups whose voices are heard in the domestic affairs of the United States—the Cubans and the Mexican Americans, or Chicanos as they are now called.

Today every fourth American Catholic is of Spanish-speaking background, so the church is understandably concerned with the lives of Chicanos, Cubans, Puerto Ricans, and other Latinos in this country. Cubans and Chicanos, as it happens, exert a contrary political influence. Concentrated in southern Florida, the Cubans remain militantly anticommunist. They tend to be aggressively conservative in their social views. But the Chicanos in Texas and other southwestern states, victims of decades of economic and social discrimination, share common interests with other lower-class constituencies in the Democratic party. It may be that their similarities and their differences will help us understand the political dynamics that were present in the birth control study. It may be that the patterns of birth control and immigration politics overlap.

President Kennedy, as mentioned earlier, did not dare arouse religious discord before his reelection by toying with far-reaching family planning ventures either here or abroad. But he did believe with all his heart that the discriminatory national origins system of admissions that served his Irish ancestors so nicely was morally repugnant. Included in the batch of progressive legislation that swept through Congress after his death, under the whip of the new president, that accomplished congressional ringmaster Lyndon B. Johnson, was an immigration reform law corresponding generally to what Kennedy had in mind.

Quotas perpetuated by a succession of Nordic superiority measures beginning in the early 1920s kept the gates open to those groups whose friends and relatives were already here in large numbers and who could be easily "assimilated" into the population. Assimilation has always been the cornerstone of U.S. immigration policy: better to let in people who can learn the language and meld into the culture of America. Applicants were favored from Ireland and the other British isles, the Scandanavian countries and the northern mainland of Europe, but not from southern Europe, southern Asia, the Orient and the Pacific islands. From Canada and Latin America there were no quotas, reflecting the traditional Pan-American Good Neighbor policy.

Besides discontinuing most of the national origin concept, the 1965 law set an annual immigration ceiling of 170,000 from the "old world," the eastern hemisphere. Admissions were to be in the order of approved applications, provided that no nation could account for more than 20,000 visas in one year. Preference would go first to relatives of American citizens, extending to brothers and sisters; then to members of the professions, scientists, and artists "of exceptional ability"; and then to persons with job skills that were in short supply in the United States. Foreigners, in other words, were not to jeopardize the job security of American citizens.

Professional and technical skills were valued by the new system more than the musclepower of the huddled masses. Strong backs were no longer needed to build the railroads (although Jamaican women were welcome to fill the live-in maids' jobs that enticed few Americans at prevailing low wages). It can accurately be assumed that the typical congressman anticipated the admission of more Italians and Greeks, two groups already of political significance in the electorate, without fully understanding how a colorfree system would alter the principle of easy assimilation. The admission of more Orientals and other "colored" immigrants from eastern Asia, and more blacks from the Caribbean, stirred fresh controversies. Among others, the Irish-American patriotic societies were upset. Congressmen from New York City complained that fewer than one thousand Irish were being let in annually, a state of affairs that was said to "fly in the face of the traditions of our nation." The preference for technical skills worked to the disadvantage of the unskilled labor pool from Ireland.

Before the bill passed the Senate, the Judiciary Committee insisted on a comparable ceiling over admissions from the western hemisphere of 120,000 a year. The per-nation limit of 20,000 did not apply, however, because of the understanding that Canada and Mexico would contribute somewhat more. There already were more stringent employment certification and adjustment-of-status (the first step toward citizenship) procedures in effect for immigrants from Mexico and other Latin American countries. Now, for the first time, there would be a numerical limit on visas from other nations in this hemisphere. The conservative senators who dominated the Judiciary

Committee—southern Democrats James Eastland of Mississippi and Sam Ervin of North Carolina, and midwestern Republicans Everett Dirksen of Illinois and Roman Hruska of Nebraska—agreed with the American Legion and the American Coalition of Patriotic Societies that the door should not be left all the way open to Latin Americans.

They clearly did not anticipate, though, that 70,000 Mexicans would be admitted legally in 1973, far more than from any other single source. Plantation owner Eastland appreciated the cheap labor value of Mexican farmhands, but he and his colleagues preferred temporary seasonal migratory (non-voting) labor and wanted, above all, to be able to control the admission of dark-skinned natives from Jamaica, Haiti, and other Caribbean islands. Not only did immigration from Mexico and Jamaica shoot upwards under the new rules, but so did the entrance of "other races" from the Phillipines, Hong Kong, South Korea, Taiwan, and India. The pattern of immigration changed dramatically. Between 1965 and 1974, immigrants of races other than white or black increased from a mere 5.4 percent of the whole to 32.4 percent, or almost one-third.[1]

The table below illustrates the components of net U.S. population change, first from immigration and then from natural increase. Thus we can see, in the same context, the effects of lower birth rates and changing patterns of immigration.

Before the new immigration rules were adopted, Fidel Castro installed his communist regime on the island of Cuba ninety miles off the coast of Florida. The anticommunists in that country were seeking refuge in the United States even before the United States became involved in unsuccessful attempts to return Castro's enemies to power. Under the circumstances, President Kennedy could hardly have done other than welcome them. At the end of 1965, Castro agreed to permit twice-daily flights that transported between three and four thousand Cubans to Miami every month. They were admitted as "paroled" refugees, a curious term used to describe immigrants who are accepted without visas outside the regular quotas and rules. The refugees from Cuba were allowed by Castro to take no money and only one suitcase of possessions with them.

By the time the airlift was discontinued in 1971, nearly seven hundred thousand Cubans had been flown to the United States at

Population Change During the Year from Net Immigration

	White	Black	Other than White or Black
1960	304,000	12,000	12,000
1965	333,000	20,000	20,000
1968	317,000	33,000	48,000
1970	327,000	39,000	72,000
1973	195,000	38,000	199,000
1974	175,000	39,000	198,000
1975	167,000	40,000	*243,000

*Includes the 130,000 South Vietnamese and Cambodian refugees admitted in 1975 by special arrangement.

Population Change During the Year from Natural Increase (the Difference Between Births and Deaths

	White	Black	Other than White or Black
1960	2,123,000	429,000	46,000
1965	1,538,000	388,000	46,000
1968	1,225,000	315,000	46,000
1970	1,408,000	349,000	55,000
1973	822,000	282,000	59,000
1974	878,000	284,000	63,000
1975	891,000	285,000	63,000

Source: *Current Population Reports: Population Estimates and Projections,* Series P-25, No. 632, issued July 1976, Bureau of the Census, U.S. Department of Commerce.

a cost to the American government of over $1 billion. Each arriving family received medical care and a "transitional grant" of $100 in cash. The government also paid the resettlement costs of those who wanted to move on to someplace other than the Miami area.

For those relatively few Cuban newcomers who did not have means of support, there was a special welfare program, more generous in its benefits than the regular public assistance system. Five years after the airlift stopped—in 1976—the special Cuban welfare program still was costing $85 million a year. The director of the program, Ricardo Nunez, a wealthy Miami businessman, was accused of using its resources to organize resettled refugees and other Latinos for the benefit of the Republican party.[2]

Most of the refugees remained in the already sizable Cuban community of Miami. Once wealthy business and professional men and women started new lives. "Little Havana" along Eighth Street, *Calle Ocho,* flourished. Cubano purchasing power exceeded $1.4 billion a year in Dade County alone. The new immigrants from Cuba reversed the historic pattern by acquiring economic power first and political power second.

Their lingering dreams of returning to liberate their homeland caused many of the refugees to delay becoming American citizens. After two years they were eligible to apply for permanent resident status, and more of them did so as the hope of Castro's demise faded. Those who did register to vote tended to become Republicans. Their slowly emerging political activism, plus the expense and privileged status of the welfare program, created controversy. To offset the impact on local schools, Dade County received $14 million a year in extra federal education aid, another example of the special attention received by the refugees from the south. Two industrial cities in northern New Jersey—Union City and West New York—also qualified for additional federal school funds because of the heavy influx of Cuban refugees.

Led by Rep. William Clay of St. Louis, the Democratic Black Caucus in the House of Representatives moved without success in 1970 to cut off funds for the Cuban benefit program. A year later, the chairman of the Senate Appropriations Committee, Sen. Allen J. Ellender of Louisiana, tried to do the same, again without success. "The Cuban refugees who are unemployed receive better help than our own people," Ellender declared. "No one objects to Cubans coming to the United States through the same immigration channels as other people. My fear is that if we continue a program of this kind from a humanitarian standpoint we will be asked to take care of many people from Peru, Argentina, and Chile who are seeking other places to live."

On this issue the unlikely partnership of black congressmen and a southern white senator added up nevertheless to something short of a majority. The Cuban refugee program was politically popular. The Catholic church supported it enthusiastically. The presence of the Cubans in south Florida reinforced anti-Castro anticommunist public opinion. And while the Cubanos did not vote in large numbers, they knew what they liked and didn't like. A prominent former countryman who dared meekly suggest that it might be time to recognize the existence of Castro's government was shot and killed the next day. On that there could be no compromise. Some of the Miami Cubans who had been associated with the CIA-engineered Bay of Pigs fiasco were involved later in the Watergate burglary and other political sabotage activities carried out in President Nixon's behalf.

After the airlift to Miami ceased, other Cubans who found their way to Spain were admitted later to join their relatives in the United States. This exercise of the government's parole authority won the praise of the Catholic Conference and Sen. Edward M. Kennedy, younger brother of the late president and chairman of the Senate subcommittee on refugees.

What was not anticipated, except by Eastland, Dirksen & Co., was that the Cuban parolees would be charged against the western hemisphere quota. For every Cuban admitted as a refugee there was one less opening for other immigrants. The two senators served on a Select Commission on Western Hemisphere Immigration that looked into the matter and issued a report in 1968. A majority of the commission recommended that the Cubans not be taken off the top of the quota. But the senators flatly refused to consider any legislative clarification. They liked an arrangement that deducted one Mexican or Jamaican from the quota pool for every Cuban admitted by special arrangement. As a consequence, there developed a large backlog of applicants from Latin America. Visa delays of two years and longer were common.

Despite this and other administrative impediments, legal immigration from Mexico soared from 38,000 to 70,000 annually. For reasons already alluded to, Mexican immigration activates an entirely different set of political considerations. With or without special programs, Cubans are perceived as constructive, self-reliant contributors to the American Ideal; Mexicans are viewed as a convenient source of low-priced labor and a likely cause of social problems. Mexico itself is an impoverished nation. With half its people under age fifteen, the population of Mexico is doubling every twenty-one years. This creates a massive pressure to emigrate—even to the most unpleasant jobs across the border.

It is often forgotten that more than one hundred thousand Mexicans were living in the Southwest when that region was conquered and brought into the United States.[3] By the turn of the century, the Spanish-surnamed population of the United States neared 225,000. All through this century the long and porous border separating the two nations provided relatively easy movement, inside or outside the law, into Texas, Arizona, New Mexico, and California. The 1970 census counted almost 7 million Mexican Americans.

During the development of the western United States, Chinese and Japanese were generally ineligible for immigration. American entrepreneurs needed a steady supply of Mexicans for the back-breaking labor at little better than slave wages. By the late 1920s, however, western representatives in Congress were trying to curb what Rep. John Box of Texas called "the flood of illiterate, unclean, peonized masses."[4] Administrative restrictions were tightened a little, but farmers, cattlemen, sugar manufacturers, and the railroads were determined to preserve their source of cheap labor. For its part, the Mexican government saw emigration to the United States as a handy escape valve for that country's social problems.

Consequently, the quota proposals got nowhere in Congress. In the 1930s, though, when hard times struck the American economy, thousands of Mexican aliens were "shipped off as surplus," sent back home by local authorities and private welfare agencies with the cooperation of the Mexican government. In many cases, families were separated by the hasty, dispassionate deportations.[5]

Then, during the severe manpower shortages of World War II, the two governments entered into a different sort of contractural agreement providing for the temporary transfer of migrant farm workers into the United States—the so-called bracero program. The foreigners performed stoop labor in the fields and other unpleasant tasks left behind by Americans who were working at wartime-inflated wages in defense plants and shipyards. Instead of returning to their homeland, as they were supposed to, many of the Mexican braceros slipped off into American cities where they worked surreptitiously at the lowest paid jobs. Illegal aliens— wetbacks they were called—poured across the Rio Grande faster than border patrolmen could apprehend and deport them. The political will to interfere with this supply of marginal labor was lacking, although more than one million Mexicans were sent back home in 1954 alone.

After the war when the labor shortage no longer existed, employers wanted the bracero program to continue, and it did. Agribusinessmen were assured a flexible supply of imported labor that acted to depress wages without the necessity of adding to the permanent population of Mexican immigrants. For them it was an ideal arrangement. For organized labor it was not, however, and the unions demanded the termination of the bracero program in 1964, whereupon the volume of illegal entries increased drastically. A toughening of the labor certification required for legal admission made it harder for poor unskilled Mexicans to qualify. So, many of them sneaked across the border instead. Some obtained social security cards or applied for welfare payments. Appalling poverty and miserable public health conditions in migrant worker camps gradually came to the attention of the American public. According to a census bureau report as recently as 1975, 1.6 million of the 6.6 million Mexican Americans were living on incomes below the poverty level.[6] For many years before, the Spanish heritage residents of Texas and other southwestern states had been deprived of any opportunity to participate in the political processes. The methods of enforcing that exclusion were every bit as systematic and diabolical as those practiced against southern blacks. But the voting rights safeguards that were enacted into federal law, and Cesar Chavez's well-publicized organization of farm workers into labor unions, alerted liberal politicians to the untapped power of Hispanic voting blocs. There remained, as always, the theoretical possibility of a mighty underclass coalition across racial lines that could dominate American politics, a naturally discomforting thought to the privileged few at the top of the heap.

The bold new political activism of Chavez and other Chicano leaders, plus the surge in Mexican immigration, more public awareness of the cost of welfare, and the voting rights act all combined to make the middle class more conscious of the Chicanos in their midst. The voters now appeared to favor the imposition of numerical controls over Mexican immigration. In 1974 the House of Representatives passed a bill that would have applied the 20,000-per-nation maximum to western hemisphere immigration. Back in 1968 the Select Commission had recommended a limit twice that large—40,000—with Eastland and Dirksen dissenting. Rep. Peter Rodino of New Jersey, the liberal Democratic chairman of the House Judiciary Committee, could not persuade his committee to make an exception for the Mexicans when the issue arose in 1974. When the legislation reached the House floor, he offered a compromise amendment raising the ceiling for Mexico and Canada to 35,000 each instead of 20,000. It was defeated 203 to 174. The black Democrats voted with Rodino for the higher figure, and so did Herman Badillo, the New York congressman of Puerto Rican ancestry. Most Republicans supported the lower 20,000 ceiling, including Du Pont of Delaware, the foremost Republican advocate of bigger appropriations for family planning programs. Eastland wanted a revival of the bracero program, or something like it, guaranteeing a supply of seasonal imported labor that could be turned on and off without the necessity of offering the newcomers an opportunity for citizenship. So he refused to hold hearings on the House-passed bill and Congress adjourned without changing the law.

Just before the next Congress adjourned late in 1976, Eastland did agree to a bill that had been hurriedly passed by the House imposing the 20,000 limit on admissions from any one nation in this hemisphere, applying the eastern hemisphere preference system to all immigration (a backlog of more than 300,000 applicants had built up from the western hemisphere), and excluding Cuban refugees who become U.S. citizens from the hemisphere quota.

By then support for the cutback in legal entries from Mexico was so great that Chicano representatives did not bother to object. The bill rushed through both houses without debate.

Twice on other occasions the House approved measures seeking to deal with the more difficult problem of illegal immigration. The bills would have penalized employers who knowingly hired illegal aliens. At the low point of the recession in the mid-1970s there were 8 million Americans unemployed. Labor unions insisted that something be done to turn off the clandestine work force whose presence depressed wages by replenishing the supply of marginal-pay workers. A Gallup poll indicated that 80 percent of the American people supported measures against the employment of illegal aliens.[7]

Yet that issue too inspired strange alliances. The Republican administration endorsed the bills. Attorney General William B. Saxbe declared in 1974 that "with the manifold problems the nation faces—energy shortages, inflation, scarcity of some foodstuffs, rising unemployment—it is apparent that we are not a limitless horn of plenty." Rep. Mario Biaggi, an Italian-American Democrat from the Bronx, complained of the "silent invasion of aliens bleeding the economy." In New York City, many of the 1.5 million illegal aliens (according to INS estimates) were from the Dominican Republic, not Mexico. For reasons of their own, Zero Population Growth, the Veterans of Foreign Wars, and the International Brotherhood of Electrical Workers all clamored for enactment of the legislation.

But if the aliens could not find jobs, their families would go hungry and they would have to leave the United States. The U.S. Catholic Conference contended that amnesty (forgiveness) ought first be guaranteed all illegals already in the United States, in effect legalizing their presence retroactively. The National Chamber of Commerce and the National Restaurant Association opposed the legislation. They spoke up for employers who they said could be innocently victimized by deceptive employees. "If all illegal aliens were deported now, it would bring agriculture to a standstill," warned the American Farm Bureau Federation. As a practical consequence the National Congress of Hispanic-American Citizens and the American Civil Liberties Union cautioned that employers would hesitate to hire anyone who looked like a Mexican. Would not citizens with brown skin and straight black hair be singled out for suspicious attention, handicapping their employment opportunities? Catholic spokesmen argued further that a permanent "sub-culture" of illegal aliens would move underground, resulting ultimately in a system of internal passports for selected foreign-looking minorities. Farm worker union leader Chavez was ambivalent; he could not support discrimination against his countrymen, nor could he sanction the use of illegal aliens as strikebreakers. Alberto Garcia, president of the United California Mexican American Association, attributed all the commotion to an "alarmist and racist propaganda campaign." He proposed not only unlimited immigration from Latin America, but a preference system for those nations.[8]

Despite these objections, the dimensions of the problem were growing larger. Smuggled across the border, often at a high price, the newcomers melded into the big cities. They worked as dishwashers and janitors, barely ekeing out a living while dodging the INS officers. They were exploited by unscrupulous employers who paid sweatshop wages for the dirtiest of jobs that were repulsive to young blacks. Eastland stubbornly refused, nevertheless, to hold Senate hearings on either of the House-passed measures. His adamant attitude was blamed by Rodino on the economic interest that growers and other employers (in the Southwest especially) maintained in the supply of cheap, docile labor. Rodino's committee reported out yet another bill in 1975, but the opposition of the Catholic church prevented it from coming to a vote.

If the standard of living remains substantially higher in the United States than in Mexico, and if more resources are not devoted to enforcement of the immigration law, David S. North, a specialist in the field, predicted that the number of illegals entering the country would continue to increase. "If undeterred by more adequately enforced immigration laws," North said, "illegal immigration is likely to lead, over time, to economic dependence upon the low-skilled labor of alien workers who are essentially without rights. At bottom, a decision—by either commission or omission—to permit entry of large numbers of illegals into the work force sanctions the creation of an economically, socially, and politically disparate two-class society of legal advantaged citizens and illegal disadvantaged workers."[9]

For students of politics, there is another intriguing facet of the illegal alien controversy. The aliens often settle in the big central cities, metropolitan centers that have been losing population (and therefore congressional representation). The illegals are understandably anxious to avoid being recorded by the census-takers. At the urging of urban congressmen, the General Accounting Office issued a report recommending that the census bureau devise ways of estimating the number of illegal aliens and distributing them at the metropolitan area level in the official 1980 census. The census bureau said it would be difficult enough to make a statistically valid allocation of the acknowledged census "undercount" without sorting out those who could be thrown out of the country if they were found. The Catholic clergy wants the Hispanic illegals to stay. If they stay, urban political leaders want them taken into account in the apportionment of congressional seats and allocation of federal grants-in-aid.

Otherwise the various exceptions to the new law operated to increase legal immigration beyond what most of the legislators had foreseen. Admissions climbed from an average of about 300,000 a year to over 400,000. About half the 400,000 were believed to be in the labor force. Studies conducted for the commission on population growth estimated that immigrants constituted 12 percent of the annual growth in the labor force. Zero Population Growth, the organization dedicated to population stability, campaigned for a drastic reduction in immigration to about 40,000 a year, which would be no more than emigration out of the country.

More Americans were unhappy either with the volume of immigration or the mix or both. Their disinterest in assimilation and their lingual habits made many of the new arrivals different from those who had come through the gates before them. Chicanos congregated in Houston, where the Latino population of Harris County was doubling every seven years. Conscious of their ethnic heritage, Catholics clamored for bishops of Cuban background in Miami and of Mexican background in the Southwest. Earlier in American history, immigrants wanted father confessors who were familiar with their native tongue. But then as later, the politically adept Irish-American priests managed to land most of the bishoprics, resented by eastern European parishioners then as by Chicanos and Cubans later. Established political leaders looked on uneasily.

Much of the resentment directed at Hispanic (and Oriental) immigrants was due to the bilingual controversy. The melting pot tradition of assimilating foreigners into the national population is not as practicable with the "other races." And the Chicanos and Puerto Ricans and Koreans did not seem as eager for it to happen. Harvard sociologist Nathan Glazer has observed: "The peasants of Europe who came here have had a much stronger religious and family base than those who came up out of slave systems and peonage systems. . . . They came as male workers and their women followed. Today, the women come in as servants, and the men wander in—then they don't have anything to do."[10]

The Department of Health, Education and Welfare interpreted a decision of the Supreme Court to require that public schools offer instruction in the native language of the pupil, a revolutionary change of policy that has upset the traditionalists. Howard Phillips, the same man who was at OEO during the sterilization controversy, called bilingual education "a semantically appealing cover slogan for liberal activists who wish to emphasize those things which divide Americans . . . rather than those which unite us."[11]

The necessity of teaching courses in Chinese in San Francisco and in Spanish in New York City and Miami permits a youngster to avoid becoming fluent in English. In that way it accentuates the ethnic identity of immigrants and probably makes it more likely that young Chicano voters, for instance, will continue to behave at the polls like other Chicano voters. There has, in turn, been a revival of interest in ethnic pride and "ethnicity" by the more established European nationality groups. When the Democratic presidential candidate Jimmy Carter spoke of the virtues of preserving "ethnic purity" in the 1976 campaign, however, he was accused of using new code words for racist segregation.

After the surrender of the South Vietnamese anticommunist government in 1975, President Ford exercised *his* parole authority and made arrangements for 150,000 refugees to enter the United States. He could hardly have done otherwise, anymore than John Kennedy could have done other than welcome the Cubans. ZPG, paradoxically perhaps, did not object to the admission of the refugees from Indochina—but others did. John Tanton, the president of ZPG, observed that the normal operation of the immigration system does not give much of a chance to those who need a new start in life. Almost three-fourths of the quota openings are reserved for relatives of U.S. citizens. About 20 percent are available for immigrants whose job skills are highly valued or otherwise needed, leaving only about 6 percent under normal procedures for refugees. Outside the quotas, of course, special provisions were made from time to time for refugees from communism, notably the Cubans and before them the Hungarians. "Suppose," mused Tanton, "that Harvard University had an admissions policy that allocated 74 percent of its openings to students who were relatives of those who had attended the university in the past, another 20 percent to those who might in the future bring benefits to the university, and reserved 6 percent for those who needed a new start in life."[12]

A surprisingly vitriolic national debate ensued over whether to welcome the yellow-skinned anticommunists who had been enmeshed in a long civil war with the misguided and bungling support of the United States. The debate took an ugly, unbecoming direction that revealed the darker side of the American spirit. The discord over U.S. involvement in the war in the first place carried over to the refugee issue, swaying the humanitarian instincts of men and women ordinarily committed to helping people in trouble. It is my contention, as well, that some of the same attitudes that lay beneath the surface of the American psyche during the recent evolution of birth control policy burst into the open as the Vietnamese were about to arrive.

The black reaction in Congress is, therefore, of more than casual interest. When the appropriation to pay for the evacuation came before the House, Rep. William Clay, the black congressman from St. Louis who had led the earlier effort to discontinue the Cuban welfare program, proposed an amendment. His proposal, which was rejected, would have prohibited the resettlement of Vietnamese in any congressional district where the unemployment rate exceeded the national average. If these Orientals are to be let in, let them go to Kansas or Texas or someplace where they won't compete for jobs my people are having trouble enough finding—that seemed to be his message. The congressional Black Caucus opposed the expenditure until such time as Congress "addresses itself to jobs for all Americans." Rep. John Conyers of Michigan remarked, "It is insane to introduce this many people in this country when Detroit is in a depression."

Some of the black congressmen cited the Haitian experience.

About eight hundred refugees from President Jean Claude (Baby Doc) Duvalier's totalitarian regime on that Caribbean island had made their way to Miami in fishing boats. Claiming that their lives were in danger, they asked for political asylum. The government ordered the deportation of most of them on the grounds that they were economic and not political refugees, a distinction that infuriated many black leaders. The black-skinned Haitians were advised, nonetheless, that they must seek admission through the regular channels. The deportation of desperate Haitians from a community filled with prosperous Cuban refugees struck an uninvolved organization, the American Jewish Congress, as having "the inescapable appearance" of racial discrimination.

Somehow even the Mexican issue entered the discussion. Three Chicano Catholic bishops from San Diego, San Antonio, and Santa Fe issued a joint statement deploring the "inconsistency" of inviting Vietnamese into a country that was deporting illegal aliens to Mexico.

Clare Boothe Luce, the playwright and former ambassador to Italy, quoted from some of the mail she received in response to her statement praising the refugee plans:

—"They will all wind up on relief, adding hundreds of millions to our tax burden."

—"We already have 10 percent unemployment. They will compete for jobs our own people so badly need."

—"All their women want is husbands, and they breed like flies."

—"We have too many Orientals now. We are losing our national character."[13]

Like a discolored page out of the wrinkled past. Losing our national character by letting in people who breed like flies. The new politics of population—how like the old politics of population. "It's very troubling," commented the Harvard sociologist David Reisman. "Americans are full of self-pity. We are all justifying our grievances by striking out at others. The national mood is poisonous and dangerous and this is one symptom—striking out at helpless refugees whose number is infinitesimal."

Especially intriguing to a student of the New Politics of Immigration and Refuge was the alignment of interests concerned one way or the other with birth control programs and population growth. Black congressmen share a socio-political bond with their Chicano brethren. They support a higher quota for Mexican immigration. They vote together for economic legislation that will benefit their people. But they do not favor accommodating refugees from Cuban or Indochinese communism because unemployment is a problem and because the attitudes of these newcomers tend to be more conservative than their own.

ZPG wants net immigration reduced to zero, but believes that those most in need, like refugees, should be given a leg up.

Representative Du Pont supports birth control for the poor, and he also wants a limitation on legal Mexican immigration.

Finally, the Catholic bishop of San Antonio understands, no less than Representatives Clay and Conyers (or no less than the Carmine de Sapios and the Irish machine bosses of another age), that political power in the United States is still basically a function of arithmetic—of numbers.

But, of course, it is more than that. Power depends too on access, on man-made and manually manipulated access, to the political system. Access is a function of voting and of artificial boundaries, which is the next topic in our examination of the new political dynamics of population.

CHAPTER 11 Political Artifacts . . .
and the Right to Vote

> *We cannot give up our hold, even on a city that is*
> *dying, for a merger situation where we lose our*
> *power and poor people don't have access to sub-*
> *urban jobs and housing.*
>
> — Vernon E. Jordan, director of
> National Urban League

By any account, the Voting Rights Act of 1965 was an extra-ordinary federal intrusion into the political affairs of selected states. Most of the states singled out for the special attention were in a region—the South—that had, since the end of Recon-struction, systematically denied their black citizens the right to participate in elections. Where necessary, the new law assigned federal registrars to supervise voting registration. Literacy tests for voting were banned. And, most important, Section 5 of the act required that state and local governments covered by the special provisions submit any change in their election procedures to the U.S. Department of Justice or to the District Court in Washington for determination in advance that neither the purpose nor the effect would be discriminatory. In other words, national authority could nullify a policy that had the effect of discriminating against the black population without establishing that the action had been deliberately discriminatory.

By 1972, more than one million new black voters were regis-tered in the seven covered states—190,000 of them in Louisiana, the simultaneous scene of Dr. Beasley's national model family planning program. In 1965, 31 percent of the voting-age blacks were registered in Louisiana; in 1972, 59 percent. Yet, after ten years of federal oversight and enforcement of the voting rights law, the U.S. Civil Rights Commission reported in 1975 that "discrimination persists in the political process. The promise of

172

the 15th Amendment and the potential of the Voting Rights Act have not been fully realized."[1]

To show wnat happened after the names of black people were entered on the polling lists, the report cited a typical incident in a typical little town—Waterproof, a riverfront community in Tensas Parish about midway between Lincoln Parish and New Orleans. The only physician in Waterproof, a white man, warned his black patients that he would move away if they persisted in voting for and electing black candidates to public office, a new experience in the delta country.[2] The civil rights commission noted that the doctor's message appeared to be remarkably effective keeping voters at home on election day. Small wonder Dr. Beasley thought black clients might respond more favorably to family planning advertising featuring a black doctor than a white doctor. Small wonder either that the former official of Beasley's organization who was quoted previously began to have afterthoughts about whether something other than altruistic motives might have been involved in the design of the "catchment areas." The report of the commission went on to describe instances in which Waterproof blacks, mostly domestics and farmworkers, were advised by their white employers not to vote; and welfare recipients were threatened with the loss of food stamps if they voted for black candidates.

Once blacks became eligible to vote, the established power structure in the South turned to political artifacts—gerrymandered representative districts, at-large elections, multi-member districts, numbered places on the ballot, staggered terms, runoff elections (to give the white voters a second crack at a minority candidate who sneaked through the first time), municipal annexations, regional consolidations, and other man-made devices which diluted the voting effectiveness of minorities. "There has been," observed one student of the subject, "a shift from preventing blacks from voting to preventing blacks from winning or deciding elections; and then to preventing blacks from winning very much."[3]

Lately, as the civil rights commission report documented, whites resorted to more subtle pressures against voting: the doctor in Louisiana . . . employers intimidating their employees . . . a propane distributor in Mississippi threatening to cut off the heat of black customers who are behind with their bills if they vote . . .

a popular high school coach in North Carolina who loses his job after running for county clerk.

The "game" of politics has never been known as a charitable exercise or a character-building sport. No one ever, or hardly ever, gives away power willingly. There was no reason, certainly, to expect that the levers of power would be cheerfully turned over to black majorities in the South. If, however, the family planning programs were motivated by a desire to make health services generally available, and not by a selfish interest in containing black birth rates, is it not reasonable to expect fair representation and fair treatment for the same black population? As late as 1974, almost 76 percent of the white voters were registered in Lincoln Parish, where the Louisiana program started, as against 42 percent of the voting-age blacks, a gap of almost 40 percent, which is extremely high even by southern standards. None of the outreach workers, apparently, were also urging their clients to become voters. The gap between white and black registration in North Carolina was 17.8 points, which was greater than for the South as a whole at that time (where it was 11.2 percent).

In Beasley's city of New Orleans, no black served on the city council from Reconstruction until 1975, although the black population in the 1970 census totaled 267,000, about 45 percent of the whole. In 1972 and again in 1973 the Justice Department rejected city council redistricting plans on the grounds that the five single-member districts and two at-large districts were deliberately drawn to dilute black voting strength, having both the purpose and the effect of discrimination. All five separate districts were formulated to combine a smaller number of black voters with a larger number of white voters, not easy to do, but simple arithmetical logic from a white point of view. Litigation that reached the Supreme Court led to the appointment in 1975 of the first black member by the other council members. He was, interestingly, a black Baptist minister, typical of the old-style, easily controlled black political spokesmen, not the Copelin-Hubbard band of young militants in New Orleans with whom the mayor (and Beasley) had dealt.

Another Louisiana city, Lake Providence, tried to annex enough white suburban territory to maintain a white voting majority, but the Justice Department objected to the annexation in 1972. Blacks—67 percent of the population by now—elected the mayor and won control of the town council in 1974. Before the white council members left office, however, they attempted to transfer control of the municipal power plant to a newly created power commission, all of whose members would be white. Because the power plant happened to be the city's sole source of revenue, the transfer was stopped by federal court injunction. In nineteen different Louisiana parishes, the Nixon Justice Department objected to redistricting plans for either the school board or the police jury (county council).[4] In a typical case, to cram as many blacks into one district as possible, East Feliciana Parish contrived a racially gerrymandered monstrosity described by the federal court as "an extraordinarily shaped nineteen-sided figure that narrows at one point to the width of an intersection."

When the Voting Rights Act was extended for a second time in 1975—through 1984—Congress brought Texas and other areas with a large Chicano population under the law's provisions too. Corpus Christi, the city in south Texas that received the first OEO family planning grant, was shown later to have used multimember districts and a variety of other artifacts to prevent the fair participation of Chicanos in political affairs. The proportion of Chicanos in the city council and state legislature came nowhere near the 41 percent Spanish heritage and 5 percent black citizens in the population. Eventually the Chicanos in Corpus Christi were ceded one token seat on the school board. When a second Chicano had the effrontery to run and win, the Anglos reacted by changing the method of election to numbered posts on the ballot, a device that the federal court said discriminated against minorities by diluting their voting power. Another federal judge held that this exclusion was largely to blame for the segregation of Corpus Christi schools.[5]

Historically, the poll tax, the "white primary," and state runoff elections were used in Texas to disenfranchise the Latino minority. In 1973 the Supreme Court ruled that multimember districts for election of state legislators discriminated against Chicanos in Bexar County (San Antonio) and against blacks in Dallas County. Lower courts applied that principle later against the redistricting in Corpus Christi, El Paso, Lubbock, Fort Worth, and several other Texas counties. At the time of the House Judiciary Committee hearings in 1975 there were an estimated 2,059,000 Chicano Texans and 1,420,000 black Texans—a 31 percent minority population. In at least twenty-six counties in south Texas, Chicanos were in the majority. Nevertheless, there were no Chicano mayors and only one black mayor in any major city. In all of Texas there were only two black judges, one of a court of domestic relations and another of a county criminal court, both in Harris County (Houston).

The city fathers of Richmond, Virginia, could see the handwriting on the schoolroom wall. White movement out and into the suburbs left the central city with a much younger and slight majority black population. In the past, the whites had been able to control a system of electing all members of the city council from the city at-large. At-large elections or multimember districts allow a cohesive but slight majority to deny any representation to a substantial minority. But in 1968 the blacks managed to win three of the nine council chairs in Richmond. Subsequently the U.S. District Court surmised that Richmond's establishment recognized then that the younger black population would "translate in a few years into a black voting age majority." According to evidence in the court record, Mayor Phil J. Bagley, said "Niggers are not qualified to run the city," and vowed on another occasion, "As long as I am mayor the niggers won't take over this town."[6]

The three black members of the council were not notified of a meeting at which Bagley and the others decided to cope with the problem by annexing twenty-three square miles of adjoining Chesterfield County. A special state annexation court approved the requested addition of forty-seven thousand white suburbanites to the city's population, thereby changing overnight its racial makeup from 52 percent black to 42 percent black. The newly enlarged city elected a council in 1970. Only one black won. But by then the annexation had been challenged in a law suit that was not settled until five years later. A federal judge in the District of Columbia invalidated the 1970 election and refused to accept two alternate plans put forward by Richmond. The second of those consisted of a ward plan that would produce four majority white wards, four majority black wards, and a ninth "swing" ward with a slight white majority. Crusade for Voters, a black organization, proposed instead the creation of a "swing" ward with a 59 percent black majority.

Meanwhile, a special master who heard the evidence for the district court in Washington found that the city could offer "no economic or administrative benefits" to explain the annexation.

On that point, the court said later:

> Richmond's focus in the negotiations was upon the number of new white voters it could obtain by annexation; it expressed no interest in economic or geographic considerations such as tax revenues, vacant land, utilities, or schools. The mayor required assurances from Chesterfield County officials that at least 44,000 additional white citizens could be obtained by the city before he would agree upon settlement of the annexation suit.[7]

Referring to "the history of racial bloc voting" in Richmond, the lower court insisted that the only way the "discriminatory taint" could be scrubbed from the annexation would be through a plan resulting in the election of a black majority to the council of the enlarged community. But the court of appeals for the District of Columbia disagreed, saying that would be "substantial racial gerrymandering" in reverse, which would be equally unconstitutional.

In due course, the controversy wound its way to the U.S. Supreme Court. By now the city's lawyers had awakened to the necessity of propounding some *ex post facto* rationalization for the annexation. At a lower court hearing, the city manager testified that the annexation was needed because the city was becoming "a place of the very old and the very poor. It was losing its young affluent, what I would call the leadership group." The Ford Justice Department took the position before the Supreme Court that, under the Voting Rights Act, the city must show a legitimate purpose for the annexation in order for it to stand. It was suggested that one might well be the potential for a more racially integrated Richmond school system, something that would surely never have occurred to the city's lawyers. This was highly relevant because of another law suit that challenged the cross-district busing between Richmond and its suburbs. In a Detroit case the Supreme Court held that autonomous suburban school districts could not be brought under metropolitan areawide desegregation plans. By adding more white students to the central city school district, the municipality (inadvertently perhaps) made more racial balance in the schools possible. This is another side of the annexation coin. "Congress did not intend," argued the government's brief, "to bar all annexations that alter the racial composition of the annexing city. . . . Dilution of a racial group's political power through annexations is not, per se, in all circumstances, the abridgement of the right to vote on account of race.''

On June 24, 1975, the Supreme Court held that annexations which reduce the black percentage of the population are not prohibited if there are good reasons and if a fair election system is adopted by the enlarged city. For the five-to-three majority, Justice Byron R. White asserted: ''To hold otherwise would be either to forbid all such annexations or to require, as the price for approval of the annexation, that the black community be assigned the same proportion of council seats as before, hence perhaps permanently overrepresenting them and underrepresenting other elements in the community, including the nonblack citizens in the annexed area.''

Justice William J. Brennan wrote a dissent, joined by Thurgood Marshall and William O. Douglas. Concluding that ''the contours of this particular annexation were shaped solely by racial and political considerations,'' Brennan declared:

> Municipal politicians who are fearful of losing their political control to emerging black majorities are today placed on notice that their control can be made secure as long as they can find concentrations of white citizens into which to expand their municipal boundaries. Richmond's black population, having finally begun to approach an opportunity to elect responsive officials and to have a significant voice in the conduct of its municipal affairs, now finds its voting strength reduced by a plan which ''guarantees'' four seats on the city council but which makes the elusive fifth seat more remote than it was before.

I dwell on the Richmond case in such detail because of the recent prevalence of racially inspired municipal annexations in the South, and because of the suspicion in the minds of some that regional consolidation is likely to become a more useful metropolitan artifact in other parts of the country as more central cities acquire black voting majorities.

In 1966, Mississippi amended its constitution to make it easier for neighboring counties to consolidate, thereby allowing a majority black county to be absorbed by a larger majority white county. Simple. Except that a federal judge overruled the state action. Grenada, Mississippi, went ahead with eight successive annexations, all of exclusively white residential areas, while a black neighborhood next to the city's old boundaries was left untouched, surrounded on three sides by the city. San Antonio, Texas, about evenly divided between Anglos and Chicanos, made massive annexations, including many irregular or "finger" additions on the heavily Anglo north side. In 1974, the Justice Department objected to seven annexations that had been carried out by Charleston, South Carolina, over a ten-year period. Civil rights lawyers and the federal courts have been kept busy stamping out annexations and election changes that were discriminatory in purpose or effect.

Consolidations of cities and counties occurred frequently for rational and constructive purposes, not the least of them being the economic survival of the central city. When Jacksonville merged with Duval County in Florida, making its 841 square miles the largest land area of any American city, the voting population dropped from 41 percent black to about 20 percent black. The white establishment supported the merger. So did the Jacksonville Urban League and other black organizations which realized apparently that the economically productive, working-age white population was moving out, leaving behind a city of the very young and very old. Some black leaders did resist the consolidation, nevertheless, in some cases because they were comfortable with their subservient role in the political status quo; in others because they saw it as a white effort to dilute black power.[8] At a referendum in 1967, the merger won the approval of both whites and blacks, though the whites on the outer fringes of the old city supported it by far greater margins than the urban blacks. Before the election, blacks were assured an equitable division of the council seats and a bigger share of public jobs. John M. De Grove said black supporters struck a bargain by "opting for representation now rather than waiting to get the whole central city."[9] He quotes a black leader who understood that "someday I might have been the black mayor, but by that time I would only have been a referee in bankruptcy."

In that city, consequently, the black politicians traded away the future domination that Vernon Jordan recommended for an economically viable city and a fair, though minority, slice of municipal power. Nashville, Tennessee, carried out a similar merger with Davidson County, but only after the prospective council lines were subjected to a reverse-twist racial gerrymandering that guaranteed the election of several blacks.

Not all merger plans were so successful in the South, particularly where there were school desegregation overtones. Civic reformers in Charlotte, North Carolina, had been talking about consolidation with Mecklenburg County since the 1940s, but when a specific proposal was submitted to the voters in 1969, a countywide school busing controversy incited emotions on both sides. The plan necessarily included school board reorganization and black representation on the new board. A white antibusing group worked against the plan, which failed at the polls. Ninety-seven percent of the blacks, but only 28 percent of the whites, voted for it.[10]

Indianapolis, Indiana, is an example of a northern city where a consolidation plan (with Marion County) was put into effect more for partisan political than for immediate racial motives. A Republican mayor of that usually Democratic (and 27 percent black) city accomplished partial consolidation without a referendum by act of the Republican-controlled state legislature. The so-called "Unigov" legislation sought by Mayor Richard G. Lugar diluted the power of blacks and other Democrats in the central city without adding to the tax resource base and without disturbing the eleven separate school systems in the metropolitan area. It was a highly selective consolidation which brought white middle-class suburban voters into city elections but left the major suburban communities with some of their autonomous authority. Black politicians opposed the regional consolidation and so, oddly, did Marion County's chapter of the John Birch Society.[11]

City-county consolidations and regional councils, a form of regional intergovernmental cooperation short of consolidation, almost always cause shifts of political power. A study of trends by the Advisory Commission on Intergovernmental Relations[12] observed that some blacks feel that "black majorities in central cities must be careful not to be satisfied with gaining control of an empty purse—that is, an area with declining tax revenues." Black leaders in Jacksonville opted for the lesser of two evils. Although regional councils are voluntary ex-officio bodies and not units of government, the ACIR report noted that "black leaders tend to be suspicious of them as disguised forms of broader metropolitan area governments, leading to a possible erosion of hard-won black political power." An unidentified black leader is quoted in that study: "Whites have left most major cities and fled to the suburbs. They now realize they have given us control of many major cities. It is primarily those areas where this regionalism concept is being developed most.''

George W. Romney, the former governor of Michigan who served as Secretary of Housing and Urban Development in the first Nixon cabinet, had many traits that annoyed fellow politicians. Not the least of these was his disinclination to treat complex problems simplistically. In and out of office, for example, he persisted in speaking of the needs of the Real City, a term he used to encompass the entire metropolitan area. Race relations will never be successfully managed, he said over and over again, as long as the metropolis is partitioned into dozens of separate and autonomous governmental units all acting independently in their own interest. This multiplicity of independent political units is a segregating mechanism that makes it easy for suburbanites to divorce themselves from the problems of the central city.

The politics of regional cooperation is very much a minefield, nonetheless. Anything smacking of "metro government" is too hot to play with in most areas. When the federal revenue-sharing bill was before Congress in 1976, Rep. Benjamin Rosenthal, a Democrat from Long Island, New York, nailed on an amendment in the House committee requiring state master plans and timetables for "modernizing" and "revitalizing" state and local government. It was suggested in the legislation that the states would want to reduce the number of limited-function general governments. Republicans and southern Democrats raised such a howl about "federally dictated centralized planning and control" that the amendment was decisively stripped away when the bill reached the floor.

What this signifies is that metropolitan cooperation is a complicated subject. On one hand, many suburbanites, particularly those with financial interests in the city, would like to do what they can to prevent Julian Bond from charging them admission to go downtown. On the other hand, though, suburbia has always been leery of any consolidation arrangement that might be dominated by the central city. Race is only one factor in the equation. In the future there are likely to be more clashing considerations. Can the black population be expected to forfeit power in the central city in exchange for a restoration of the city's economic viability? If metro government makes sense (and few would deny that it does), why weren't more people pushing for it before now, when blacks are in a position to take over many of the biggest cities? How metropolitan America handles municipal annexation and regional government may well decide whether the cities survive. Unless and until there is more racial integration, the outlook is not very promising.

For a long time the casting of representative districts was a no-holds-barred political exercise in the United States. Federal judges were unwilling to enter the "political thicket" and interfere with the "rotten boroughs" that were carved out in city and countryside alike. This resulted in the stifling domination of courthouses, state legislatures and even the national Congress by a class of small-town lawyers, businessmen, and country gentlemen that an astute observer, James Reichley, dubbed the "Squirearchy."[13]

That era came to an end in the 1960s. Chief Justice Earl Warren said after his retirement that the most important of all the earthshaking decisions of the Warren Court were the reapportionment cases. It was determined, first, that the courts could consider the equal-protection implications of legislative apportionment; second, that both houses of a bicameral state legislature and the U.S. House of Representatives must be apportioned by districts of "substantially equal" population; and, finally, that the districts must be as close to exact numerical equality of population as humanly possible. The last decision held that geographic or neighborhood features—a river, a railroad, the city limits, or an ethnically identifiable community—could not be used to justify inequalities in the size of districts.

There being no automatic way of plotting district lines on a map, certain instincts traditionally govern the reapportionment process. Ordinarily the state legislatures design their own election districts as well as those for the U.S. House. Except when there are extenuating circumstances, incumbents are usually protected (given an advantage). The party in power, naturally, tries to devise districts that can elect as many of its members as possible. More interesting, and less natural, is the tendency in a marginal two-party state for the policymakers to agree on a balance of relatively safe districts for one party or the other. Rather than attaching a strong Democratic township to a district that leans Republican, Democrats are more comfortable putting it in a secure Democratic district, provided the Republicans will do the same. A multiethnic organization, such as the Democratic party of Cook County, must and does take great care in drawing districts so that the Poles, Irish, Germans, Italians, Jews, Blacks, et al., receive a fair share of seats.

Almost immediately, under the new reapportionment rules, power was diverted from the Squirearchy to the fast-growing suburbs in most of the large states. The new metropolitan legislators tended to be younger, better educated, and more expansive in their social views. This varied from place to place, of course, but the reapportioned legislative bodies were generally regarded as more progressive, less antiurban, more supportive of government action to remedy public problems.

The Supreme Court's redistricting guidelines combined with the Voting Rights Act have altered the process in several ways. After Warren's retirement, the less liberal majority on the Court backed away gradually from the stringent earlier requirements, but the political actors still have limited leeway in their drafting of district lines. The districts must be of nearly equal size—and the federal courts are available for appeal if they aren't.

States covered by the Voting Rights Act must have their redistricting plans approved by Washington in advance. The burden of proof is different, too. A group of Puerto Ricans who claim that the Chicago City Council lines discriminated against them must prove that the injustice was aimed at them deliberately. In the South, however, the allocation of districts cannot have either the effect or the purpose of reducing the voting strength of a racial minority. The new majority on the Supreme Court appeared to open a loophole in the law in 1976. Redistricting plans carried out "pursuant to court order," that is, under the supervision of the local federal district court, need not be submitted to Washington for preclearance, it was decreed.

The one-man-one-vote standard, plus the provisions in the law affording special protection in some places to groups of voters who were once discriminated against, produce some strange circumstances. *United Jewish Organizations* v. *Carey* is an example.[14] Because New York employed a literacy test for voting prior to 1970, and less than 50 percent of the voting age residents of

Bronx, Kings, and New York counties voted in the 1968 presidential election, those counties were subject to the terms of the Voting Rights Act, same as the South. A proposed redistricting of the state legislature was rejected by the Justice Department in 1972 on the grounds that the nonwhite population had been unfairly concentrated in certain districts. So the legislature drew up a new plan, one that spread black majorities over more districts. The Justice Department approved it.

A group of Jewish organizations, speaking for the Hassidic community in the Williamsburg section of Brooklyn, then went to court to challenge the new plan, which they claimed discriminated against the Jewish voters by splitting them into separate districts. No longer were the Jews a voting majority in either district, the price that had to be paid to strengthen the voting power of blacks, as mandated by law.

Like a teeter-totter, when one end comes up the other goes down. At oral arguments of this fascinating case before the Supreme Court, a lawyer for the Hassidic complainants said his clients were the victims of a "dictated quota," reverse discrimination, "a gross racial slur." Race is not part of the political process, argued attorney Nathan Lewin. "Unfortunately," replied Solicitor General Robert H. Bork on behalf of the United States, "race has been a political issue since this nation was founded."

Bork was right. At no time since the Civil War has race been more of a political issue than now. Representative districts will be redrawn, legislators will be elected from multimember of single-member districts, cities will annex territory and people, governmental units will join together for greater efficiency or build political walls against their neighbors, minority citizens will be welcomed into the normally functioning political processes or there will be a reaction against them. Political artifacts, in other words, will go on being erected and dismantled, more or less in step with the mood of the people.

12 Growth, Land Use . . .
and the Lure of the Sun Belt

Americans are a mobile people. Packing U-Haul trailers now
instead of Conestoga wagons, they pick up and move across the
land in pursuit of brighter economic opportunity, to find A Better
Life for their children, and sometimes to get away from un-
pleasantness. Changing patterns of population distribution can
portend significant shifts in regional influence and tip the balance
of power in federal and state governments. Every person's vote
should have equal weight, the courts have proclaimed. But in the
last chapter we saw that some people in some places have easier
access to the political system, and more effective representation,
than others. From the beginning, U.S. history has been marked
by important eras of national growth. Following World War II,
some trends were hardening and others were only starting to take
shape.

Heavy migration of black Americans from the rural South to
the urban North continued through the 1960s at nearly the same
rate as in the 1940s and 1950s—about 1.5 million in each of those
decades. It is probably true that the comparatively higher welfare
payments in some of the northern industrial states, such as New
York, New Jersey, and Illinois, helped to stimulate the migration.
Once they arrived, however, the newcomers were restricted by
racial discrimination to the decaying close-in neighborhoods of
the central cities. It must always be kept in mind when we talk
about the growth of the black urban population that the migrants
did not settle in the slums because they found the rats, the narcotics peddlers, and the numbers racketeers all that irresistible.

Deteriorating big-city schools hastened the flight of whites to the suburbs. The postwar growth of suburbia, fed by migration from the central city and from small towns, was facilitated by a conscious federal policy—homebuyers' mortgage insurance that took the risk out of suburban subdivisions. While the thick suburban ring circled around the increasingly black central cities, the small towns and farms lost population. Not as many human laborers were needed anymore to produce food and fiber, North or South. Metropolitan areas expanded, gobbling up productive farmland on the fringes. Many land speculators, shopping center developers, and zoning board commissioners got rich. Experts calculated that the pressures of metropolitan growth soon would consume an additional 28,000 square miles of undeveloped land.

Looking into the future, demographers predicted the interconnection of what would by then have become vast "superregions" of densely populated metropolitanism. A study by Jerome Pickard for the National Commission on Population Growth and the American Future projected that 83 percent of the American people—more than four out of five—would be living in politically disjointed and socially "atomized" urban regions of one million or more population by the end of the century.[1] For example, Pickard envisioned a Flint-Detroit-Toledo belt of 8 million people. The industrial activity along the lower Great Lakes had been occurring for many years, explained by familiar regional advantages: access to coal, iron ore, and other raw materials; ample railroads and water transportation.

But the exceptionally rapid growth of Florida and California foreshadowed another phenomenon of the sixties that would be of overriding political significance: the movement of people, jobs and capital from the Northeast and Midwest into the "Sun Belt." Florida's climate naturally attracted retired pensioners, but now something else was happening. Businesses and industries were locating more of their plants requiring scientific and technical manpower in the warm weather states. Moving vans rolled south from Philadelphia and Cleveland, following payrolls on their way to the Carolinas, to Atlanta, to booming Florida, and to Houston and Phoenix and many other sunshine cities. Oversimplifying the situation somewhat, lower-income blacks were going north, and higher-income whites were passing them going south (and west), at a time when federal spending programs were designed to redress the personal income disadvantage of the southern states because of their disproportionate numbers of poor.

Recognizing the scale of these trends, Pickard thought that by the year 2000, 5.6 million people would be living along the southeastern urban coast of Florida; and more than 3 million in the San Diego area. He said the Phoenix area would more than double in size, to 2.2 million; that more than a million people would be living in the Orlando region; Houston would be home to more than 4 million; metropolitan Los Angeles to almost 19 million.

Of course, the residents of Fort Lauderdale and Orlando might not care to have that many neighbors. The population of Florida doubled in fifteen years. In the 1970s it was still growing at a rate four times that of California. Boca Raton in Palm Beach County established a limit on the number of housing units that could be built there. Other communities along the southeastern strip and in the Tampa Bay area adopted various growth control plans. Gov. Reubin Askew recommended a state land-use law with growth controls. What little low-income housing there was in Florida consisted mostly of mobile homes. In other parts of the country as well, communities halted the extension of sewer lines, thereby putting a stop to new building. The limited-growth policies were not without their legal controversies. However, the U.S. Supreme Court declined to review a favorable lower court ruling which upheld a growth control ordinance in Petaluma, forty miles north of San Francisco. "The concept of public welfare is sufficiently broad," the lower court had said, "to uphold Petaluma's desire to preserve its small-town character, its open spaces and low density of population, and to grow at an orderly pace." One of the claims cited against the ordinance was that low-income residents would be barred from coming to Petaluma. So far the Supreme Court has not been willing to entertain the thought that a selective admissions policy—again the power of the gate-keeper!—did not square with the equal protection of the laws clause of the Fourteenth Amendment.

How volatile issues of growth and land-use policy are resolved in the years ahead will severely strain the decency and unselfishness of the American people. A basic conflict of interest separates no-growth environmentalists and social reformers who are concerned about the limited availability of satisfactory low-income housing in metropolitan areas. A conference sponsored in

1973 by the Citizens' Committee on Population and the American Future heard the environmentalist movement described as anti-urban and antidevelopment. Antigrowth sentiment thrives in people who have made it to the suburbs, who are irritated by all the cars in the parking lot, who want open space for their children to play, and who have little time left over for the problems of the inner city. Exclusionary zoning practices raise real estate values, and screen out housing for people who can't raise the sizable prevailing down payment. The population capacity of West-chester County, New York, went from 3.2 million to 1.8 million in two decades! More second homes were built in the United States in 1974 than additional units of low-rent public housing. While environmentalists castigate the villain "development," housers deplore the unwillingness to consider ways of putting more low-cost housing in the suburbs. Ernest Erber, then director of the National Committee Against Discrimination in Housing, told me: "The cutting edge of the problem is where urban growth impinges on the suburbs. A brutal examination of the issues reveals that the mass support for the environmental movement is the guy who has his house in the suburbs, is worried about taxes and schools and the like, and really wants to be the last guy in town."

All the trends of the sixties—the decline of the rural population, the black migration into the northern metropolitan centers, the explosive growth of the suburbs, the uncertainty about how much growth to permit, the shift of people and economic power to the South—were translated into the redistricting decisions of that period. Contrary to what might have been anticipated, passage of the Voting Rights Act coming on top of the Supreme Court's equal representation decrees did not automatically result in con-gressional districts from which a majority-black population would nominate and elect black congressmen. It didn't happen that way. In Beasley Land, the Louisiana legislature still carved New Or-leans into odd-shaped multiple districts containing a majority of white voters, even though the city itself consisted of almost half black voters. This does not mean that the act and the one-person-one-vote rulings had little impact. The contrary is true. Had it not been for the reapportionment decisions, for example, the central-city Democrats and rural Republican Squirearchy would have cut a deal in many of the state legislatures to preserve their respective power bases, despite their dwindling numbers, by simply denying fair representation to the suburbs. The young suburbs were the principal beneficiaries of reapportionment, bad news for the central cities but nonetheless fair.

The growth of the Sun Belt accelerated in the 1970s. "The wheel of power in this country is turning," said Governor Askew of Florida. During the first half of that decade, the population in the South and Southwest grew six times as fast as in the Great Lakes states and ten times as fast as in the Northeast. Indeed, 85 percent of the national population increase between 1970 and 1975 occurred in the South and West, most of it in the arc swinging from Virginia across to southern California. All but two of the fastest growing metropolitan areas were in Florida, Texas, and Arizona—and the two exceptions were in a western mountain state, Colorado. From migration alone, the population of Florida increased by 1.4 million in 1970-75; California and Texas by over 400,000 each. In the same period, the net out-migration from New York exceeded 500,000; Illinois, 350,000; Ohio, Pennsylvania, and Michigan, more than 100,000 each.

Northern capital and, to some extent, policies of the national government aided the industrial expansion of the South. The southern "cultural bias" against labor unions and the Protestant fundamentalist emphasis on doing things for yourself inspired businessmen to locate new operations in the South, where wages were lower and unions not yet entrenched. Air conditioning made the summer heat tolerable. Energy costs were cheaper. There was more need for service occupations, less for heavy industry. The interstate highway system opened up the South to efficient truck transportation.

After a while, it came to the attention of taxpayers in Illinois and Pennsylvania that they were helping to subsidize the economic development of Mississippi and California.[2] Tax dollars were being channeled out of their pockets into the federal treasury and on to the Sun Belt states, where the state and local tax burden is comparatively less anyhow. This regional "balance of payments deficit" was attributed partly to the superior legislative skill of southern congressional committee chairmen. Revising the federal aid allocation formulas became a top priority of those who thought they were being shortchanged. Not only are the social problems more urgent in the northern central cities, but living costs are usually greater, the burden of public safety and welfare expenditures tends to be heavier, and the recession of the 1970s struck much harder in the North. The big question is whether the urban delegations can do anything about this before their congressional clout slips away.

Inexorably, the reapportionment of House seats that occurs every ten years shifts representation away from the older central cities and into the suburban districts in their own states; and beyond that into the states of rapid growth—chiefly Florida, Arizona, Texas, California, Tennessee, and Colorado. California and Florida, which had thirty-eight House seats between them in 1950, figure to have eighty-two in the year 2000. New York and Pennsylvania had seventy-three seats in 1950 and are expected to have twenty fewer, or fifty-three, five censuses later.

Something else happened in the early 1970s, without as much attention, but possibly of even more long-run importance. For the first time in this century, the nation's rural areas and smaller cities were growing faster than big cities and their suburbs taken together. Almost 6 million more people moved out of the central cities than moved in. Those metropolitan areas with populations of two million or more experienced virtually no growth, and eight of them lost population. Only Dallas-Fort Worth among the large metropolitan areas grew faster than the national average of 4.1 percent. Although Puerto Ricans continued coming to New York, that area registered a net migration loss of 500,000.[3] Fort Myers, Sarasota, West Palm Beach, Boca Raton, Fort Lauderdale, and Fort Collins in Colorado reported big population increases.

Some, but by no means most, of the nonmetropolitan growth occurred near the edges of metro areas, signifying the expansion of those areas. The suburbs themselves were changing character. With the dispersal of many jobs from the inner city out to the suburbs, not as many could be considered "dormitory" suburbs. Now they were virtually self-contained economic units, less dependent on the central city.

Metropolitan expressways built as part of the interstate highway system made it possible for people to drive long distances from rural counties to urban or suburban jobs. There were other reasons for the rural revival. Older people preferred isolated retirement communities away from urban crime and congestion. Some young people were struck by a yearning to "return to the land" where life is simpler. Farm income picked up. Discontinuance of the military draft no longer introduced farm youths to the lure of the bright lights. State universities decentralized their expansion plans, multiplying the population of sleepy places like De Kalb, Illinois.

Not as easy to measure is the influence of race in this migration out of northern big cities and then out of metropolitan areas. The thesis of this book suggests that race was a major determining factor. The public perceptions of the social problems associated with the presence of the black population—and indeed the high black birth rates themselves—contributed to the movement from Cleveland to Charlotte (the growth of the Sun Belt) and from Cleveland back to Appalachian Ohio (the rural revival), using that city as an example.

With even less notice, another trend was reversed in the mid-seventies. A half century of massive black migration from South to North apparently came to an end. More blacks were returning "home" to the South than were leaving the South.

Consider E. J. Thigpen.[4] He is a black man who moved from Mississippi to Chicago, the land of opportunity, in 1965. He has a good job and brings home twice the average pay for a black in Chicago. As soon as he has acquired vested rights in his company's pension fund, E. J. is going to move back to Mississippi because he says his family is unsafe in Chicago. "I'd rather go back to Mississippi and buy a little place and just fish and raise my family," he told a newspaper interviewer, "because since I've been here life has been hard. In fact you can't live here. The first year I was here a young black man was beat to death in Cicero (a suburb) looking for a job. Now you have a chance of getting killed in Mississippi, but you never get beat to death looking for a job. . . . When the kids went to school, they had a tendency to 'lose' their coats, boots, hats, gloves, and lunch money. It was pretty rough living on the South Side. During the riots, we locked ourselves up in the place and sat in the windows with a pistol and said we're not going to let anybody burn the building down because we had worked too hard trying to accomplish something."

More civil rights bills were passed, including some that outlawed discrimination in housing. But there were not many suburban homes available to the Thigpens and other black families who could afford to live there. In 1970, according to the census, 70 million whites and 3.4 million blacks were living in the suburbs.[5] This 5 percent share of the total suburban population is itself deceiving because it does not distinguish between integrated and segregated suburbs. Many of the black "suburbanites" resided in traditionally segregated all-black enclaves just outside the central city. Fair housing laws notwithstanding, a white family with an income of $15,000 a year was far more likely to live in suburbia than a black family in the same income range; similarly, a black family earning $10,000 a year was far more likely to be living in the central city than a white family with the same income. Almost 78 percent of blacks in the Chicago metropolitan area were living in census tracts more than 90 percent black in 1970. The Liberal Ideal—socio-economic integration of entire metropolitan areas—proved a tough nut to crack, racism aside. There were a variety of federal housing subsidies devised to supplement the rent or mortgage payments of low-and moderate-income residents in upper-income communities. But the families who were there "on their own" resisted having even a token number of lower-income neighbors. They didn't want their children associating with the troublesome poor kids in school. They were afraid that the noisy and uncouth would disrupt the neighborhood. And they resented having near-neighbors who were being "carried" by Uncle Sam. The model "new town" of Reston in the Virginia countryside illustrates the problems. Reston was carefully planned to include some housing for low-income residents among the high-priced homes. In 1976, young gangs clashed with police; the social theories fell in a heap. Blacks living in the subsidized Fox Mill apartment project chafed at the more affluent life-style and uppity attitudes of their neighbors in fancy townhouses and ranch homes. The white citizens blamed the subsidized tenants for vandalism and violence in the schools and on the otherwise serene streets.[6]

There have been many demonstrations of the axiom that "wise" social policy is more feasible when it has been ordained from far-off Washington (by the national government) than when it is left to local, regional, and state political processes. The power of money, and the advantages that money can buy, speak loudest close to home. How land is used is a classic example.

Lawrence Sager, a constitutional law professor at the New York University School of Law, recently wrote:

Some measure of local autonomy over the control of land use is likely to be diminished in favor of regional or statewide planning. There may well be a need to substantially increase control of growth. But the great additional influence over human lives that will thereby be assumed by government will probably have to be lodged, in part, at a level of government whose constituency transcends the interests of a single community.[7]

Or, in other words, if anybody is going to pack more political wallop than the developers of Podunk, he is going to have to be bigger than all of Podunk, specifically a government whose "constituency transcends the interests" of Podunk. Under the present arrangement, land-use decisions are made by the private developers of all the Podunks of the land, with an agency of the local government exercising a veto power over those decisions. The system therefore tends to favor development. Land-use planners, conversely, are usually identified with the anticommercial preservation of critical natural resources. The United States has no population "problem" in the Malthusian sense of population pressing on the food supply. The United States exports food. Instead, in the words of the Population Reference Bureau, which speaks for the population establishment, the problem "is related to the quality and safety of our physical and social surroundings."

The best, and possibly the only, chance of establishing a balanced land-use policy rests with the federal government. Such a policy would balance the need for more low-income housing against the need for recreational sites; the interests of the established industrial centers against the sparsely settled regions that are trying to attract new industries.

Twice in recent years the Senate has passed land-use legislation, spurred on by Sen. Henry M. Jackson, Democrat of Washington and chairman of the Interior Committee. The bills established federal sanctions and penalties, in the form of financial aid forfeiture, if the states failed to conform to national standards. The standards applied to the location of parks and other recreational sites, an area around an airport, a complex of highway interchanges, power plant and garbage landfill projects, sewer lines (the "underground highways"), and areas "of more than local concern." At that time, the Nixon administration attached its "No. 1 environmental priority" to the land-use bill.

There were two important sources of opposition—one economic (people who make money off land speculation and development); the other social (people who would never stand still for some government whose constituency transcends the interests of a single community telling an entire metropolitan area how many poor and minority residents should be permitted and where).

"History warns us that a government which controls the land can control the people who live on it," declared the Liberty Lobby, a right-wing organization. The national Chamber of Commerce cried out against the "national zoning ordinance," which it said would "bring the federal government into the backyard of every American." By evoking images of The American Backyard, the Chamber reminds us of a quotation cited previously in this book from Lincoln and Alice Day.[8] If the American population is permitted to continue to grow unchecked, the Days told us "the right of eminent domain would become little more than a museum piece; the idea that a man's home was his castle, something of a wry joke."

Much milder land-use bills were killed twice in the House. There the legislation would merely have provided federal funds as an inducement for state agencies to involve themselves in the regulation of areas of more than local concern. Democratic representatives from Chicago cast crucial votes against the bill in 1973 because they said the city government would never risk sharing control over the Lake Michigan shoreline with an unfriendly governor. At the time, President Nixon was battling desperately to avoid being impeached. He withdrew his administration's support of the land-use bill at the last minute in an effort to retain the loyalty of conservative congressmen in his own party, who were firing away at the bill. Nor, for that matter, were the building trades unions very enthusiastic about the idea.

Regulation of the land *does* have a direct bearing on the lives of the people who live on it. Land is zoned for commercial ventures that generate payrolls and profits; or for parks and playgrounds; or for houses to live in. The houses can be so expensive that only the rich can afford them; or they can be so flimsy that they will soon turn into slums. At present, this mix of low- and high-priced housing, industrial activity, and open space is determined jointly by local officials and developers. The difficulty that a modest national land-use measure had getting through Congress merely underlines the absence of public support for urban social planning and coordinated national growth.

None of this can be very encouraging to the older central cities and the people who will be living in them. Those working-class whites who can have left the cities in droves, first to working-class suburbs, and now more of them are deserting the metropolitan areas altogether. More recently, the responsible and productive blacks—good citizens these communities can least afford to lose—are planning to return to the South. They are tired of having their children shaken down by fellow students and tantalized by drug dealers in the schools. Increasingly, these cities are inhabited by low-income racial minorities, illegal aliens who live in fear of detection, and the elderly poor who can never aspire to the Leisure Villages on this earth. The statistical tables in a recent federal report[9] tell the story better than words. In Representative Clay's city of St. Louis, the unemployment rate was 7.8 percent and 16.8 percent of the city population was receiving Aid to Families with Dependent Children. In Broward County, Florida, an almost all-white area hard hit by the decline of the space program, along the southeastern coast where the growth limit movement is popular, the unemployment rate was 14.9 percent, and 1.6 percent of the population was receiving AFDC.

Dependency, street crime, and poor schools are all identified with minority residents of the central cities. "The do-gooder is dead, long live Numero Uno" is supposed to have been the watchword of the social planners in the latter stages of the Nixon administration. And Numero Uno has moved away from the cities. Suburban voters don't want low-cost housing nearby. The residents of many of the fastest growing Sun Belt communities don't want much more of any kind of housing nearby. Central city payrolls have taken flight, too, for places out of residential reach of most blacks and Latinos.

Thanks to the seniority system of committee rank in Congress, senators, and representatives from the old one-party Cotton South have exercised disproportionate power in the House and Senate. It is difficult to imagine how the transfer of more seats to Alabama, Arkansas, Arizona, Florida, and Texas can possibly produce a congressional climate that is favorable to either big cities or racial minorities and the poor—especially while the redistricting process is rigged against concentrations of black and Chicano voters.

Ultimately, there is little hope for either the cities or the urban poor unless more middle-class white families can be persuaded to remain in or return to the urban centers.

The federalization of welfare would remove one of the incentives for the poor to move into the big cities, even if the payment standards varied according to the cost of living. Most southern congressmen opposed the Nixon administration's welfare reform plans (designed by Pat Moynihan) because they knew that higher welfare payments were drawing black voters out of their states and to the northern cities.

It seems to me that the changing patterns of population growth and distribution, and the problems of crime, dependency, and poor schools, are tied to the birth-rate politics that were examined earlier in this book. Discussing the concentration of the poor in the central cities, for example, Pierre de Vise, professor of urban sciences at the University of Illinois in Chicago, noted recently:

> There's a need, too, for more birth control, but this is politically sensitive. Generally, second and subsequent births have been reduced tremendously. But the rate of initial births has not gone down at all, and most surveys show that only about ten percent of low-income people use birth control, not through any lack of desire for controlling birth, but because of a lack of knowledge. It would mean teaching birth control and making it available to 12-year-olds and 13-year-olds.
>
> . . . But the big things that would induce people to come back into the city are changing the crime picture and changing the school picture—and nobody knows how to do this because, to an important extent, there is a one-to-one association between crime and quality of schools on the one hand and the concentration of minority people on the other. We don't know how to reduce crime and improve schools without *eliminating the poor blacks*. At least that's the way the middle-income whites perceive the problem. (italics mine)[10]

How to make the cities tolerable for the middle-class without "eliminating the poor blacks"—that is the problem!

As long as the minorities were politically impotent and in a state of economic servitude, this was thought to be a manageable problem, the cities salvageable. The civil rights revolution and the struggle for black political expression changed all that. The Julian Bonds, Vernon Jordans and Sherman Copelins are a new generation of black leaders determined to rule where blacks are or soon will be a majority of the voters. The white political leadership has reacted by trying to contain the minority population numerically (with government financed and promoted birth control programs) and geographically (by trying to confine them to inner-city neighborhoods); and by trying to delay the takeover, by gerry-mandering representative districts and sometimes through annexation, consolidation of governmental units, and changes in the election procedures.

CHAPTER 13 The Future . . .
and Fecundity, California

The spectre of black genocide was not compelling enough for Bouie Haden or Dick Gregory to convince black women that their interests collectively necessitated their refraining from the use of birth control. Pierre de Vise told us at the end of the last chapter that family planning had succeeded in reducing second and subsequent births to low-income minorities but not "the rate of initial births." He presumably meant, but did not consider it necessary to spell out, "initial illegitimate births," an omission interesting in itself. Married women who give birth but once, be they rich or poor, are thought to be of minimal concern to population planners in the United States.

By and large, appeals to the group political interests of blacks carried about the same weight therefore as the theological case propounded by the Catholic bishops and priests. Catholic women used forbidden contraceptives in spite of the church's dogmatic opposition. The church of Rome may have felt that the faithful masses wanted a solid rock that would stand firm against the shifting sands of public manners and taste. But, as Father Greeley has observed so well, the church's refusal to alter its position had a devastating effect on the religious participation of younger and better-educated Catholics particularly.

We see Catholic women practicing birth control in good conscience (less so, apparently, among the poor), and black women electing not to have more children than they can take care of (less so, obviously, among those who are not living with the father of their children). Even when abortions were legally available, the rate of illegitimate births remained high.

198

The fertility rate dropped below the theoretical replacement level in the mid-1970s.[1] That meant that American women would average fewer than two children each during their lifetimes, unless something happened to change the pattern of experience. The key appeared to be with childless women in their late twenties and early thirties who still talked of having children "later." But would they? And how many? Most of them entertained thoughts of having no more than two. The number of women holding jobs outside the home continued to climb dramatically. For them, babies were often a complication. On the other hand, neither The Pill nor the IUD met the test of an ideal contraceptive. Women were dissatisfied with them and skipped from one method to another. The Pill was linked to blood clotting. IUDs sometimes caused severe cramping, uterine perforations, blood poisoning, and other serious infections.

With simultaneously declining birth and death rates, there are not as many school-age children and more old people in the population. The over-sixty-five age group grew from 3.1 million in 1900 to 22.2 million in 1975 and is expected to reach 31 million by the end of the century. Only forty years ago, the sexes were represented equally in the elderly population, but in 1975 there were only sixty-nine males for every hundred females over age sixty-five.

So there are more elderly people, more wives working outside the home, not as many babies being born, fewer and later marriages, more divorces. Already elected officials can feel the heat generated by a politically active, well-organized lobby of the elderly, pushing for more social security benefits and less school taxes. A stable and older population would probably act as a brake against social change and cultural fads. There might also be more mental illness and suicides.[2] Lincoln Day says the oldsters would be less attached to the automobile, for him a happy development. But Amitai Etzioni, sociologist at Columbia, sees other effects: rising health costs, more birth defects (the older the mother, the more likely an abnormal birth), a slowdown in economic growth, and "exacerbation of political conflicts."[3] In a stable economy, no one group can get anything except by taking it from another group, Etzioni reasoned. He also predicted more ethnic and racial strain in a no-growth population because of the expectation that racial minorities and lower-income groups would be less willing to limit the size of their families than the middle and upper classes. Thus there would be pressure from the majority for the disadvantaged minority to reduce their birth rates too—by persuasion if possible, by force if necessary.

By persuasion if possible, by force if necessary. Sterilants in the water supply . . . licenses for childbearing . . . raising the legal age for marriage (and the cost of a marriage license) . . . removing the tax incentives for large families . . . free abortions . . . payment of a bonus for sterilization . . . compulsory sterilization after a maximum number of births . . . more postgraduate fellowships for women and none for married students[4]—these are a few of the persuasive and/or forceful steps that have been discussed.

One observer, Melvin Ketchel, has noted that: "Fertility control agents will ultimately become politically acceptable when they become politically necessary. If population growth continues, people will probably be willing to accept fertility control agents as the lesser of evils."[5]

A newspaper columnist in the part of Florida where growth control sentiment is strong, Ron Wiggins, wrote this satirical essay in the *Palm Beach Post* of July 23, 1975, under the headline: "Growth Is a Curse in Fecundity."

> If you have more than what the authorities consider "your share" of children, be thankful you don't live in Fecundity, Calif., where population control has become the government's business.
>
> I have this information according to a refugee who requests that I omit his last name. Something about reprisals from the Fecundity Family Planning and Euthanasia Clinic.
>
> Fred and Judy moved to Fecundity in the early 60s.
>
> "We had two children right away," Fred said. "Both times the Chamber of Commerce and our church sent flowers along with congratulations. Fecundity, you see, was very growth-oriented at the time and our young represented future buying power."
>
> In 1965, the specter of recession loomed gauntly over the Fecundity skyline when two electronics manufacturing plants closed and unemployment soared. That same year the school bond issue failed and community leaders spoke of a population surplus.
>
> "I didn't think anything of it when we didn't get any

congratulations on our third child. One fellow in the office, whose brother-in-law was out of work and lived with him, refused my cigar, saying something snide about my finding a brand my wife hates and smoking it all the time."

When the twins came, the Family Planning Clinic (an HEW pilot project) sent the following message:

"Our records show you have two more children than is morally defensible. While we certainly would be reassured to know you have taken steps to produce the 2,000,000 gallons of fresh water, 600 head of livestock, 300 acres of crop land, 5,000,000 cubic yards of oxygen and 500 tons of manufacturing your brats will squander in their long, prodigal lifetimes, we understand that accidents will happen.

"Meanwhile, won't you and your wife report to the clinic 8 a.m. sharp Tuesday for surgical alteration. To save a trip you might as well bring your extra children to the Surplus Children Home next door so we can place them with a family which hasn't used its quota."

Fred and Judy, of course, did neither, resolving to rear their children with pride and dignity no matter what the Fecundity Family Planning Clinic or anybody else thought.

"But then we started getting the pressure from all over," continued Fred. "No longer could parents take pride in a large healthy family. It got to the point where we didn't dare admit to five children.

"We disguised the oldest two childrn as Japanese domestics," Fred said. "When people discovered the truth, I found a spinster who signed over her quota to us, but even with this windfall, we were still one child over the limit."

Although the Fecundity population control authorities failed to railroad a statute for mandatory retroactive birth control, they did win passage of an ordinance requiring licenses for extra children.

"Every year we had to pay $500 for the extra child. Ostensibly, the money was earmarked for environmental replenishment. But there were dark rumors of a youth camp going up outside of town with showers to be installed by the Fecundity National Gas Co."

The last straw was a new policy on surplus children in the schools.

"The way they put it to us," Fred explained, "is that the licensed children would temporarily assume 'nonperson' status until someone moved or a death opened up a slot. Meantime, the surplus children underwent rigorous training in resource conservation.''

Here I interrupted to ask what Fred meant by resource conservation.

''They made these children hold their breaths and skip lunch.''

Fred and Judy packed their brood into the station wagon and split for Palm Beach County when the Fecundity Family Planning and Euthanasia Clinic tried to impound one of the twins after the parents failed to scrape up the license fee.

''It was really too much,'' Fred reflected somberly. ''I mean since our child was legally a nonperson, the clinic declared its intent of impounding him and auctioning him off for back taxes.''

At this point, I had to protest. Even if an agency of the government would legally impound a child, where would they find anybody to buy him?

''Well, this is only speculation, but there was a lot of talk,'' Fred said. ''On the day before the auction there were a bunch of guys in town wearing robes and flashing a lot of money. Something about needing cheap labor to tote oil barges and lift bales of money.''[6]

Wiggins' column piqued my curiosity because of where it was written—in Palm Beach, Florida, the very symbol of conspicuous affluence in American society, once the favorite winter playground of millionaire magnates who accumulated their vast fortunes in this miraculously dynamic ever-growing economy. I asked the author what had inspired his column. Nothing profound, he said, just that he had been thinking about birth control and the shortage of resources and noticed a prediction by someone that the state might someday be licensing childbirth. And where would it start? Why, California, of course, he told himself.

This book has traced an era of ''pre-Fecundity'' political change that began with the decision by Dr. Hellman and Planned Parenthood to challenge Catholic hegemony over birth control policy in the municipal hospitals of New York City. Fertility control policies were shaped in the context of rapid social change and a certain amount of disorder. The ''rising expectations'' of racial minorities were greeted by a desire on the part of the white middle class to remain apart from their problems. There followed a new middle-class awareness of black birth rates, the high cost of public welfare, and the discomfort associated with metropolitan congestion—the long lines at the movie theater, to use Pat Moynihan's illustration. Some of the more militant black leaders, young men for the most part, tried (with slight success) to alert their followers to what they saw as a deliberate genocidal campaign of keeping black birth rates down. The Catholic hierarchy took an inconsistent position, retreating here, counterattacking there, saying one thing, doing another. Social historians may well mark the end of this era of population politics as coinciding with the failure of the church to turn back the Supreme Court's abortion decision. That repudiation of the church's political role in the abortion controversy ought to teach the bishops some lessons that they should have learned in the early sixties.

We will then be in a new era of population politics. It will still be a pre-Fecundity Age of Persuasion. But for how long? Some parts of the world, in southern Asia for example, where the population crisis is immediate and deadly serious, are already well beyond the age of persuasion. Licensing of childbirth and compulsory sterilization are on the agenda now in those countries.

The nature of the danger in the United States is different. It is that population policies will continue to be pieced together in an uncoordinated fashion without the knowledge and understanding of the highest elected officials, much less the American people. Separate congressional committees, administrative agencies, and pressure groups pay little attention to one another as they make decisions about family planning funding and rules, immigration, the siting of oil refineries and airports, incentives and subsidies for people who live on farms, and in cities, the allocation of slices of the federal budget.

In the years ahead there will be vitally important questions to be asked, guidelines to be watched. There is a need for population education in the public schools, but is the typical program "alarmist propaganda" or objective scholarship? Can family planning services be made readily available without selective coercion? How can teen-age pregnancies be prevented without prebranding entire social groups as hopelessly sexually promiscuous at puberty? Where is the line between eugenics and the promotion of sterilization? How can the ignorant and the defenseless be protected against involuntary sterilization? Why should the tax system continue to reward large families? Is there a population crisis in the United States? What is the answer to the illegal alien problem? If "adjustments" are made in the immigration preference system, are they clearly stated and clearly understood by the American people? Where is the boundary between discriminatory gerrymandering of representative district lines that should be constitutionally forbidden, and the normal operation of the political decision-making processes? How can the constitutional guarantee of equal protection of the laws be applied to birth control? What is the proper balance of public incentives to help the cities, the suburbs, the rural areas? Should public policy be directed at keeping the metropolitan areas from losing jobs and population, or at distributing people and payrolls over the entire country more evenly? After all is said and done, was the federally financed program of family planning for the poor and uneducated genocidal in its design? Its motivation? Its impact? What can and should be done to safeguard the voluntariness of these programs in the future?

Vigilance and openness are the two essential requisites of wise social policy, it seems to me. Almost always, if the American people are informed about what is happening, they will do what is best, or what is almost best. Too often in the past the politics of fertility control and population were allowed to operate without public knowledge and understanding. Unless we are careful, that road leads to Fecundity, California.

Appendices

COMPONENTS OF POPULATION CHANGE FOR THE UNITED STATES,
1960-1975

White

	Pop. Beginning of Year*	% Change	Nat. Increase per 1,000	Births	Deaths
1960	158,959	1.52	13.3	22.7	9.4
1965	170,336	1.09	9.0	18.4	9.4
1970	178,692	0.96	7.8	17.2	9.4
1975	185,095	0.57	4.8	13.8	9.0
1976	186,151				

Black

1960	18,817	2.23	22.6	32.9	10.3
1965	20,889	1.87	18.4	28.5	10.0
1970	22,617	1.70	15.3	25.3	9.9
1975	24,366	1.33	11.6	20.6	9.0
1976	24,690				

*In thousands.

Source: *Population Estimates and Projections*, Current Population Reports, Series P-25, No. 632, July 1976, Bureau of the Census, U.S. Department of Commerce.

APPENDIX B

PUBLIC ASSISTANCE

	AFDC Recipients	*AFDC Expenditures*
1950	2,233,000	$ 556,000,000
1960	3,073,000	1,055,000,000
1965	4,396,000	1,809,000,000
1967	5,309,000	2,280,000,000
1969	7,313,000	3,565,000,000
1970	9,659,000	4,857,000,000
1971	10,651,000	6,203,000,000
1972	11,069,000	7,020,000,000

Source: Statistical Abstract of the United States.

PERCENTAGE OF RESIDENTS RECEIVING AFDC

	1971	*1976*
New York City	11.1%	11.0%
Chicago (Cook County)*	6.1	10.9
Philadelphia	11.3	14.5
Detroit (Wayne County)*	5.8	11.5
Baltimore	12.5	15.6
Washington, D.C.	8.6	14.2
Boston (Suffolk County)*	12.0	14.0
St. Louis	11.0	16.8
New Orleans	11.2	11.2

*The statistics for Chicago, Detroit, and Boston are for the entire counties.

Source: "Recipients of Public Assistance Money Payments and Amounts of Such Payments by Program, State and County," February 1971 and February 1976, DHEW Publication No. SRS 76-03105 and NCSS Report A-8, 2-71.

APPENDIX C

PERCENTAGE OF TOTAL PUBLIC SCHOOL ENROLLMENT

	White		Minority	
	1955	*1975*	*1955*	*1975*
Baltimore	58%	27%	42%	73%
Chicago	70	30	23	77
Philadelphia	61	33	39	67
New York City	72	32	28	68
Los Angeles	76	40	24	60
Detroit	71	22	29	78
Dallas	84	41	16	59
Houston	77	37	23	63
Washington, D.C.	36	3	64	97

Source: Report by Irving Anker, Chancellor of New York City public schools, to conference of the Council of the Great City Schools, May 20, 1976, Washington, D.C.

Notes

CHAPTER 1—INTRODUCTION

1. Speech at Mississippi State University, Starkville, Miss., United Press International news report, October 8, 1970.

2. See Peter Bachrach and Elihu Bergman, *Power and Choice: the Formulation of American Population Policy* (Lexington, Mass., 1973); and Thomas Blau, "Politics, Pundits and Population" in *Political Issues in U.S. Population Policy*, Virginia Gray and Bergman, eds. (Lexington, Mass., 1974), pp. 17-35.

3. Judith Blake, "Population Policy for Americans: Is the Government Being Misled?" *Science*, May 2, 1969, pp. 552-529. See also Kingsley Davis, "Population Policy: Will Current Programs Succeed?" *Science*, November 10, 1967, pp. 730-739.

4. See Lee Rainwater, *And the Poor Get Children*, (Chicago, 1960).

5. John F. Kantner, *Studies in Family Planning*, Population Council, May 1968.

6. James A. Sweet, "Differentials in the Rate of Fertility Decline: 1960-1970," *Family Planning Perspectives* 6, no. 2 (Spring 1974): 104.

CHAPTER 2 — PRELUDE TO CHANGE

BLACK BIRTH RATES . . . AND THE POWERHOUSE

1. Samuel C. Busey, *Immigration: Its Evils and Consequences* (New York, 1856), p.88.

2. *Nation*, October 16, 1866, p. 312.

3. David M. Kennedy, *Birth Control in America* (New Haven, Conn., 1969), p. 124.

4. Philip Appleman, *The Silent Explosion* (Boston, 1965), p. 80.

5. C. Thomas Dienes, *Law, Politics, and Birth Control* (Chicago, 1972), p. 87.

6. Ibid., p. 95.

7. Margaret Sanger letter to Mary Lasker, January 20, 1942, in the Sanger Papers, Library of Congress. Quoted in Kennedy, *Birth Control*, p. 259.

8. Margaret Sanger, *The Pivot of Civilization* (New York, 1922), p. 262.

9. Kennedy, *Birth Control*, p. 119.

10. Ibid., p. 121. See generally chapter 4, "Revolution and Repression: The Changing Ideology of Birth Control."

11. Eugene Genovese, *Roll, Jordan, Roll: The World the Slaves Made* (New York, 1976), p. 459.

12. Much of the statistical material in this section is from Reynolds Farley, *The Growth of the Black Population* (Chicago, 1970).

13. *Family Planning Perspectives*, 2, no. 4 (October 1970): 10.

14. *Washington Post*, Nov. 11, 1976, p. A-10.

15. Sweet, "Differentials," p. 104.

16. Ernest B. Attah, "Racial Aspects of Zero Population Growth," *Science*, June 15, 1973, pp. 1143-1151.

17. "The Anatomy of a Victory," Planned Parenthood Federation of America, New York, 1959, p. 25.

18. *Commonweal*, September 12, 1958, p. 583.

19. "Anatomy," p. 26.

20. Louis M. Hellman, "One Galileo is Enough: Some Aspects of Current Population Problems," *The Eugenics Review* 57 (December 1965): 161-166.

21. "Anatomy," p. 33.

CHAPTER 3 — ILLINOIS:

THE POLITICS OF CHURCH AND STATE

1. Most of the research for this chapter was conducted by the author while preparing an unpublished case study in 1964 and 1965 for the Eagleton Institute of Politics series of case studies in practical politics. The author covered the events as a newspaper correspondent in Springfield, Ill. Later the participants were reinterviewed in more detail, and the documents reexamined, to reconstruct what happened and why.

2. Some years later, in 1975, Imbiorski left the priesthood and married a woman who had been on his staff.

3. See Herschel W. Yates, Jr., "American Protestantism and Birth Control: An Examination of Shifts Within a Major Religious Value Orientation" (graduate thesis, Harvard University, 1968).

4. See Phyllis Tilson Piotrow, *World Population Crisis: The United States Response* (New York, 1973).

5. John J. Rohr, S. J., "Birth Control in Illinois: A Study in Church-State Relations," *Chicago Studies* 4, no. 1 (Spring 1965): 40.

6. Philip M. Hauser, *Look*, November 21, 1961, p. 29.

CHAPTER 4— FROM EISENHOWER TO NIXON: THE EVOLUTION OF FEDERAL POLICY

1. Phyllis Tilson Piotrow, *World Population Crisis: The United States Response* (New York, 1973). Her book deals with the politics of family planning in the context of the foreign assistance program as well as social programs in this country. Although the political dynamics in Congress are similar for both subjects, my inquiry is limited to topics that affect the U.S. population only.

2. Sar A. Levitan, *The Great Society's Poor Law* (Baltimore, 1969). See generally chapter 8, "Fighting Poverty with a Pill," p. 207. Also see book review in *Family Planning Perspectives* 1, no. 2 (October 1969): 51.

3. Anthony R. Measham, *Family Planning in North Carolina: The Politics of a Lukewarm Issue*, Monograph 17 (Carolina Population Center, University of North Carolina, Chapel Hill, 1972).

4. Measham et al., "Physicians and Contraception," *Southern Medical Journal* 64 (1971): 499.

5. David M. Kennedy, *Birth Control in America* (New Haven, Conn., 1969), p. 172. See Kennedy generally, chapter 7, "Birth Control and American Medicine."

6. Frederick S. Jaffe, "Public Policy on Fertility Control," *Scientific American* 299, no. 1 (July 1973): 17.

7. Christopher Jencks, "The Moynihan Report," *New York Review of Books*, October 1965, pp. 216-218, reprinted in Lee Rainwater and William L. Yancy, *The Moynihan Report and the Politics of Controversy* (Cambridge 1967), p. 444. See also Daniel P. Moynihan, "The Negro Family: The Case for National Action," U.S. Department of Labor Office of Planning and Research (U.S. Government Printing Office, 1965); and Charles V. Willie, ed., *The Family Life of Black People* (Columbus, 1970).

8. Charles V. Willie, undated position paper presented to the President's Commission on Population Growth and the American Future.

9. Eugene Genovese, *Roll, Jordan, Roll: The World the Slaves Made* (New York, 1976), p. 149.

10. *Chicago Sun-Times*, October 29, 1967, p. 24.

11. *Washington Post*, May 4, 1969, p. G8.

12. *New York Times*, September 22, 1969, p. 35.

13. Dr. Louis M. Hellman, "The Impact of Family Planning Services and Population Research Act of 1970 on the Population of the U.S." Printed proceedings of the 1971 annual meeting of the American Assn. of Planned Parenthood Physicians.

14. Elihu Bergman, "The Politics of Population U.S.A.: A Critique of the Population Policy Process." Population Program and Policy Design Series No. 5 (Carolina Population Center, University of North Carolina, Chapel Hill, 1971).

15. Lincoln H. Day and Alice Taylor Day, *Too Many Americans* (New York, 1965), p. 5.

16. Ibid., pp. 67-69.

17. Garrett Hardin, "The Tragedy of the Commons," *Science*, December 13, 1968, pp. 1243-1248.

18. *New York Times*, September 22, 1969, p. 35M.

19. *New York Times*, October 5, 1969, op ed page.

20. *New York Times*, May 11, 1969, p. 5E.

21. Samuel M. Wishik, "Population Programs and Policy," *Villanova Law Review* 15, no. 4 (Summer 1970):813.

22. Dr. Louis M. Hellman, lecture, Center for Population Studies, Harvard University, December 10, 1975.

23. "Has Legal Abortion Contributed to U.S 'Birth Dearth'?" *Family Planning Perspectives* 4, no. 2 (April 1972):7.

24. H. Yuan Tien, "National Population Problems and Poverty Reduction," *Villanova Law Review* 15, no. 4 (Summer 1970):807.

CHAPTER 5 — BLACK GENOCIDE AND HOMEWOOD-BRUSHTON

1. B. William Austin, "Population Policy and the Black Community," report of the national Urban League, July 1974, p. 43.

2. William A. Darity, Castellano B. Turner, H. Jean Thiebaux, "Race Consciousness and Fears of Black Genocide as Barriers to Family Planning," paper presented to April 1971 meeting of the American Association of Planned Parenthood Physicians, Kansas City, Mo. Darity's work also is summarized in Austin, "Population Policy," p. 63.

3. Charles V. Willie, undated position paper presented to the President's Commission on Population Growth and the American Future.

4. Austin, "Population Policy," p. 71 ff.

5. "Family Size and the Black American," *Population Bulletin* 30, no. 4 (1975). For a description of the Homewood-Brushton dispute, see also *New York Times*, December 17, 1967, p. 71, and August 11, 1968, p. 44.

6. J. Mayone Stycos, "Opinion, Ideology and Population Problems: Some Sources of Domestic and Foreign Opposition to Birth Control," in National Academy of Sciences, *Rapid Population Growth: Consequences and Policy Implications* (Baltimore: 1971), p. 558.

7. Telephone interview, August 11, 1975.

8. Clinton Jones, in Bergman's *Political Issues in U.S. Population Policy*, (Lexington, Mass., 1974) pp. 151-166, uses three categories: civil rightism, radicalism, black nationalism.

9. Darity, Turner, Thiebaux, "Race Consciousness."

10. Jackson testimony before Commission on Population Growth and the American Future, Chicago, June 27, 1971.

11. Stycos, "Opinion," p. 555.

12. Joseph F. Martin, "Is the Black Physician Being Heard?" proceedings of the 1969 annual meeting of the American Association of Planned Parenthood Physicians.

13. See *The Thrust*, Pittsburgh Catholic Diocesan newspaper, December 22, 1967, for Monsignor Rice's column, "The Pill and the Black Poor." See also Stycos, "Opinion," p. 553; and the *Pittsburgh Press*, August 7, 1968, p. 1. For the maternity ward closing statement, see *The Thrust,* March 2, 1969.

14. In 1975 there were 916,854 black Catholics in the U.S., about 4 percent of the black population and 2 percent of the U.S. Catholic population. The largest black Catholic dioceses were Lafayette, La., and Chicago.

15. *New Courier*, March 8, 1969.

16. Julius Paul, "The Return of Punitive Sterilization Proposals: Current Attacks on Illegitimacy and the AFDC Program," *Law And Society Review* 3, no. 1 (August 1968):89.

17. Ibid., p. 90.

18. Samuel F. Yette, *The Choice: The Issue of Black Survival in America* (New York, 1971), pp. 111-113.

19. Paul, "The Return of Sterilization," p. 92.

20. Perry Deane Young, "A Surfeit of Surgery," *Washington Post*, May 30, 1976, p. B1.

21. Ibid., p. B2.

22. *The Family Planner*, Syntex Laboratories, Palo Alto, Calif., (May 1969), p. 1.

23. Johan W. Eliot, "Fertility Control and Coercion," *Family Planning Perspectives* 5, no. 3 (Summer 1973):132.

24. *Time*, July 4, 1969, pp. 16-21, cover story on Cesar Chavez. For a discussion of Mexican-American fertility, see also Stycos, "Opinion," p. 551, and Helen B. Shaffer, "Zero Population Growth," *Editorial Research Reports*, November 24, 1971, p. 923.

25. For discussions of Jewish-black relations, see Robert G. Weisbord and Arthur Stein, *Bittersweet Encounter: The Afro-American and the American Jew* (Westport, Conn., 1970), and Lenora E. Berson, *The Negroes and the Jews* (New York, 1971).

26. *Time*, July 14, 1975, p. 39. Neidorf's letter of reply is in the August 4, 1975, issue. See also "Birthrate Lag Called Threat to Jewish Survival," *Washington Post*, March 17, 1975; Milton Himmelfarb, "A Plague of Children," *Commentary* 51, (April 1971):37; S. Solomon, Ulster Community College, Stone Ridge, N.Y., paper presented to meeting of World Population Society, Washington, D.C., February 7-9, 1974, on Hassidic Jewish attitudes.

27. Phillips Cutright, "Voluntary Controls on U.S. Population," mimeographed (Joint Center for Urban Studies of MIT and Harvard, 1970).

28. Norman A. Hilmar, "Population Control, Family Planning, and Planned Parenthood," address to Planned Parenthood-World Population, Southeast Council/National Board Meeting, Savannah, Ga., May 7, 1970.

CHAPTER 6—BIRTH RATES IN THE BAYOUS . . . THE SAGA OF JOE BEASLEY

1. The biographical information and most of the quotations with Beasley's views are from the transcripts of Beasley's lectures at Harvard University in 1973 and from a personal interview by the author in New Orleans on August 24, 1976. His experience with the family planning program in Louisiana was used as a case study in Prof. Graham T. Allison's John F. Kennedy School of Government course in law and public policy. I am grateful to Professor Allison for making available his course materials. The statement about Beasley's reaction to his career as surgeon is on page 1 of the Beasley transcript.

2. Harvard-Beasley trs., p. 23.

3. Beasley interview, New Orleans, August 24, 1976.

4. Harvard-Beasley trs., p. 7.

5. For a detailed summary of the Lincoln Parish experience, see Beasley, "Louisiana: Developing and Managing a Statewide Family Planning Program," *Family Planning Perspectives*, October 1971.

6. Harvard-Beasley trs., p. 10.

7. Harvard-Beasley trs., p. 14.

8. Douglas Mackintosh, "How Family Health Foundation was Mau-Maued," *New Orleans*, May 1975, p. 45.

9. Harvard-Beasley trs., p. 82.

10. Harvard-Beasley trs., p. 83.

11. Harvard-Beasley trs., pp. 11, 82.

12. Harvard-Beasley trs., pp. 96, 97.

13. "Administration of Federal Assistance Programs—a Case Study Showing Need for Additional Improvements," Report to Congress by the Comptroller General of the United States, July 28, 1976.

14. Beasley, "View from Louisiana," *Family Planning Perspectives*, Spring 1969, p. 2.

15. Mackintosh, "Family Health Foundation," p. 45.

CHAPTER 7 — RICHARD NIXON'S CATHOLIC STRATEGY . . . AND THE MURKY BUSINESS OF STERILIZATION

1. See Hearings, Subcommittee on Health, U.S. Senate Committee on Labor and Public Welfare, on "Quality of Health Care—Human Experimentation, 1973," part 4, July 10, 1973, pp. 1446 ff.

2. *Washington Post*, July 22, 1973, p. 1.

3. Perry Deane Young, "A Surfeit of Surgery," *Washington Post*, May 30, 1976, p. B1.

4. Claudia Dreifus, "Sterilizing the Poor," *The Progressive* 39, no. 12 (December, 1975): 13.

5. For the section on the OEO guidelines, I am indebted to Mark Bloom's excellent article, "Sterilization Guidelines: 22 Months on the Shelf," in *Medical World News*, November 9, 1973, p. 53. Other material is taken from the Senate hearings, from the pleadings in *Relf* v. *U.S.*, 74-224, U.S. District Court, District of Columbia, and from my own interviews.

6. Julius Paul, "The Return of Punitive Sterilization Proposals: Current Attacks on Illegitimacy and the AFDC Program," *Law and Society Review* 3, no. 1 (1968). See also Jonas Robitscher, ed., *Eugenic Sterilization* (Springfield, Ill., 1973).

7. Louis Kohlmeier, "Why Should Government Be in the Sterilization Business?" *Chicago Tribune*, December 2, 1973, p. 12, Section 2.

8. Senate hearings, "Quality of Health Care—Human Experimentation," p. 1616.

9. Florette Henri, *Black Migration: Movement North 1900-1920* (Garden City, N.Y., 1975), p. 220.

10. Alyce Gullattee, "The Politics of Eugenics," in Jonas Robitscher, ed., *Eugenic Sterilization* (Springfield, Ill., 1973).

11. John H. Kessel, *The Domestic Presidency: Decision-Making in the White House* (North Scituate, Mass., 1975), p. 27. Other quotes are from pp. 30 and 50.

12. Senate hearings, p. 1573.

13. *Relf* v. *U.S.* (The case had not yet been brought to trial early in 1977.)

14. Senate hearings, p. 1510.

15. Associated Press, February 6, 1974.

16. Health Research Group, "Study on Surgical Sterilization: Present Abuses and Proposed Regulations," October 29, 1973, Dr. Bernard Rosenfeld, Dr. Sidney M. Wolfe, Robert E. McGarrah, Jr.

17. Identified only as "Dr. Wood." From *Contemporary Ob/Gyn* 1:31-40, 1973.

18. Young, "Surfeit of Surgery."

19. Memorandum opinion in civil actions No. 73-1557 and No. 74-243.

20. Gesell memorandum in above cases filed October 22, 1975.

21. The Lucas remarks are from a thorough and objective summary of opposing arguments in Patricia Donovan's "Sterilization and the Poor: Two Views On the Need for Protection from Abuse," *Family Planning/Population Reporter* 5, no. 2 (April 1976):28.

22. Letter to the editor, *New York Times*, February 18, 1976, p. 32.

23. *Washington Post*, column page, July 23, 1973.

CHAPTER 8 — TEEN SEX: DOUBLE STANDARDS OF FEASIBILITY

1. *Chicago Sun-Times*, March 2, 1969, Section Two, p. 1.

2. Ibid., p. 3.

3. Beasley, "View from Louisiana," *Family Planning Perspectives*, Spring 1969, p. 5.

4. Judith Blake, "Population Policy for Americans: Is the Government Being Misled?" *Science*, May 2, 1969, pp. 522-529.

5. *Science*, July 11, 1969, p. 121.

6. John E. Anderson and Jack C. Smith, "Planned and Unplanned Fertility in a Metropolitan Area: Black and White Differences." *Family Planning Perspectives*, November-December 1975, p. 281.

7. Subsequently, Reagan's successor as governor, Edmund G. Brown, Jr., signed the California legislation into law.

8. See Eve W. Paul et al., "Pregnancy, Teen-agers and the Law, 1976," *Family Planning Perspectives*, January-February 1976, p. 16. On July 1, 1976, the U.S. Supreme Court struck down a Missouri parental consent law involving abortions but indicated that a carefully limited state statute would be constitutionally permissible.

9. Phillips Cutright, "Illegitimacy: Myths, Causes, and Cures," *Family Planning Perspectives*, January 1971, p. 25.

10. *Ortho Panel 3: Report and Commentary on Current Problems in Medical Practice* (Ortho Pharmaceutical Corporation, 1968). Quoted in *Family Planning Perspectives*, October 1969, p. 47.

11. Harriet Pilpel and Nancy Wechsler, "Birth Control, Teen-agers and the Law," *Family Planning Perspectives*, Spring 1969, p. 29.

12. Mary Breasted, *Oh! Sex Education!* (New York, 1970).

13. Hearing before House Subcommittee on Census and Population, Committee on Post Office and Civil Service, February 9, 1976.

14. *New York Times*, July 10, 1972, p. 26-C.

15. House subcommittee (note 13 above).

CHAPTER 9 — LESSONS LEARNED, LESSONS IGNORED

1. Greeley et al., "American Catholics—Ten Years Later," *The Critic*, January-February 1975, p. 18.

2. *Washington Post*, March 24, 1976, p. A-13.

3. Rainwater, *And the Poor Get Children* (Chicago, 1960), p. 39.

4. House debate, August 10, 1976. See *Congressional Record*, p. H-8641 for roll call and discussion of motion to refuse to recede from the Hyde amendment.

5. Ibid., p. H-8637.

6. See Elihu Bergman, "Resolving the American Abortion Controversy: A Case for Political Coalition Building." Paper prepared for Notre Dame Conference on Abortion, Morality, and Public Policy (March 1975).

7. Koblinsky, Marjorie A., et al., "Funding for Reproductive Research: The Status and the Needs," *Family Planning Perspectives*, September-October 1976, p. 212.

CHAPTER 10 — A NEW PERSPECTIVE ON IMMIGRATION

1. *Current Population Reports: Estimates and Projections*, Series P-25, No. 632 issued July 1976 (Washington, D.C., Bureau of the Census, U.S. Department of Commerce).

2. *New York Times*, August 8, 1976, p. 17.

3. Julian Samora, "Immigration Provides Key," *Agenda Quarterly*, National Council of La Raza, Winter 1973, p. 4.

4. Ronald Wyse, "The Position of Mexicans in Immigration and Nationality Laws," Leo Grebler et al., *Mexican Immigration to the United States: the Record and its Implications*, Mexican-American Study Project Advance Report (University of California Graduate School of Business Administration, 1966), p. D-10.

5. Grebler, *Mexican Immigration*, p. 29.

6. *New York Times*, September 7, 1975. Comparable figures for Puerto Ricans living in the United States 545,000 out of 1,671,000 living in poverty; and for Cubans: 106,000 of 743,000 below the poverty level.

7. *Intercom*, August 1976, p. 13.

8. Ibid., p. 11.

9. Ibid., p. 12.

10. "Latest Wave of Immigrants Brings New Problems to U.S.," *U.S. News and World Report*, April 5, 1976, p. 25.

11. "Bilingualism Masks Leftist Drive for Cultural Separation," *Human Events*, September 28, 1974, p. 8.

12. John Tanton, "Immigration: An Illiberal Concern?" *Zero Population Growth National Reporter*, April 1975, p. 4.

13. *New York Times*, May 11, 1975, op ed page.

CHAPTER 11 — POLITICAL ARTIFACTS . . . AND THE RIGHT TO VOTE

1. *The Voting Rights Act: Ten Years After*, Report of U.S. Civil Rights Commission, January 1975, letter of transmittal.

2. Ibid., p. 187.

3. Armand Derfner, testimony before House Judiciary Committee, March 17, 1975, published hearings, Part 1, p. 629.

4. *Ten Years After*, p. 293.

5. George J. Korbel, testimony before House Judiciary Committee, March 13, 1975, printed hearings, Part 1, p. 360. See also Charles L. Cotrell testimony, p. 398 of the hearings.

6. *City of Richmond, Va.* v. *United States*, 376 F. Supp. 1344, p. 1350, No. 29 (D.D.C., 1974). Bagley quotes cited also in *Ten Years After*, p. 302.

7. *Ten Years After*, vol. 2, p. 1285.

8. John M. De Grove, "The City of Jacksonville: Consolidation in Action," *Regional Governance: Promise and Performance* (Washington, D.C. Advisory Commission on Intergovernmental Relations, 1973), pp. 17-25.

9. Ibid., p. 72.

10. For a discussion of the Charlotte experience, see *Regional Governance*, p. 4.

11. For a discussion of the Indianapolis experience, see *Regional Governance*, p. 72.

12. "Minority Perspectives," *Regional Decision Making*, (Washington, D.C., Advisory Commission on Intergovernmental Relations, 1973), pp. 129-138.

13. See James Reichley, "The American Squirearchy," *Harper's*, February 1966, p. 98.

14. *United Jewish Organizations of Williamsburg, Inc.* v. *Hugh L. Carey*, U.S. Supreme Court Docket No. 75-104.

CHAPTER 12 — GROWTH, LAND USE . . . AND THE LURE OF THE SUN BELT

1. Jerome P. Pickard, Appalachian Regional Commission, "U.S. Metropolitan Growth and Expansion, 1970-2000, with Population Projections." Research Paper.

2. *Business Week,* May 18, 1976. See also *New York Times*, February 8, 1976, p. 1.

3. *Population Estimates and Projections*, Series P-25, No. 618 (Washington, D.C., Bureau of the Census, U.S. Department of Commerce).

4. Justin M. Fishbein, "Fear Forcing Family Back South," *Chicago Tribune*, July 24, 1976, p. 8.

5. Karl E. Taeuber, "Racial Segregation: The Persisting Dilemma," Annals of the American Academy, November 1975. Quoted in *Congressional Record*, May 20, 1976, p. S 7644.

6. See *Washington Post*, July 23, 1976, p. C1, and July 26, 1976, p. C1.

7. Lawrence G. Sager, "Keeping the Cities Down to Size," *New York Times*, August 29, 1976, p. 18E.

8. Lincoln H. Day and Alice Taylor Day, *Too Many Americans* (New York, 1965), p. 69.

9. See "Recipients of Public Assistance Money Payments and Amounts of Such Payments, By Program, State, and County, February 1976." U.S. Department of Health, Education and Welfare Publication No. (SRS) 76-03105, p. 2.

10. Pierre de Vise, "Cities are Becoming Dumping Grounds for Poor People," *U.S. News and World Report*, April 5, 1976, p. 54.

CHAPTER 13 — THE FUTURE . . . AND FECUNDITY, CALIFORNIA

1. For characteristics of U.S. population in 1975, see *Current Population Reports*, Series P-20, No. 292 (Washington, D.C., Bureau of the Census, U.S. Department of Commerce).

2. Edwin D. Driver, *Essays on Population Policy* (Lexington, Mass., 1972) p. 193.

3. William Raspberry, "The Negative Effects of ZPG," Quoted in *Washington Post*, July 30, 1973, op ed page.

4. See Daniel Callahan, *The American Population Debate* (New York, 1971).

5. Ibid., chapter 20.

6. Page B1.

Bibliography

I. GENERAL POPULATION POLITICS

Ames, John S., "The Politics of Population Policy: Lessons for the Population Pros." In *Population Policymaking in the American States: Issues and Processes*, edited by Elihu Bergman et al.

Appleman, Philip. *The Silent Explosion*. Boston: Beacon Press, 1965.

Bachrach, Peter, and Bergman, Elihu. *Power and Choice: The Formulation of American Population Policy*. Lexington, Mass.: Lexington Books, D.C. Heath, 1973.

Berelson, Bernard. "Beyond Family Planning." *Studies in Family Planning* 38, February 1969, pp. 1-16.

_____. "The Great Debate on Population Policy: An Instructive Entertainment." An occasional paper of the Population Council, New York, 1975.

Bergman, Elihu. "The Political Analysis of Population Policy Choices." Mimeographed. 1974.

_____. "The Politics of Population USA: A Critique of the Policy Process." Population Program and Policy Design Series, no. 5. Carolina Population Center, University of North Carolina, Chapel Hill, 1971.

_____. "Resolving the American Abortion Controversy: a Case for Political Coalition Building." Published in the proceedings of the Notre Dame Conference on Abortion, Morality and Public Policy, March 1975.

_____. "Some Consequences of Population Movement on the American Political System," Mimeographed. Carolina Population Center, Chapel Hill, N.C., 1969.

_____. "Some Political Dimensions in American Population Policymaking." Discussion paper prepared for the World Population Seminar, Vassar College, Poughkeepsie, N.Y., November 17, 1974.

————, et al., eds. *Population Policymaking in the American States: Issues and Processes*. Lexington, Mass.: Lexington Books, D.C. Heath, 1974.

Blake, Judith. "Population Policy for Americans: Is the Government Being Misled?" *Science* 164 (May 2, 1969): 522-529.

Blau, Thomas. "Politics, Pundits, and Population." In *Political Issues in U.S. Population Policy,* edited by Gray and Bergman, pp. 17-35.

Blaustein, Albert P. "Arguendo: The Legal Challenge of Population Control," *Law and Society Review* 3, no. 1, August 1968.

Breasted, Mary. *Oh! Sex Education!* New York: Praeger, 1970.

Callahan, Daniel, ed. *The American Population Debate*. New York: Doubleday, 1971.

Campbell, Angus; Converse, Philip E.; Miller, Warren E.; and Stokes, Donald E. "Population Movement and Political Behavior." In Charles B. Nam, *Population and Society*. Boston: Houghton Mifflin, 1968.

"Catholic Perspectives on Population Issues," *Population Bulletin* 30, no. 6. Population Reference Bureau, Washington, D.C., 1975.

Clinton, Richard L., and Godwin, R. Kenneth, eds. *Research in the Politics of Population*. Lexington, Mass.: Lexington Books, D.C. Heath, 1972.

Clinton, Richard L. ed. *Population and Politics*. Lexington, Mass.: Lexington Books, D.C. Heath, 1973.

Cutright, Phillips. "Illegitimacy: Myths, Causes and Cures." *Family Planning Perspectives* 3, no. 1, January 1971, p. 25.

————. "Voluntary Controls of U.S. Population." Mimeographed paper, Joint Center for Urban Studies of M.I.T. and Harvard, June 1970.

Davis, Kingsley. "Population Policy: Will Current Programs Succeed?" *Science* 158, November 10, 1967, pp. 730-739.

Day, Lincoln H., and Day, Alice Taylor. *Too Many Americans*. New York: Delta, 1965.

Driver, Edwin D. *Essays on Population Policy*. Lexington, Mass.: D.C. Heath, 1972.

Gray, Virginia, and Bergman, Elihu, eds. *Political Issues in U.S. Population Policy*. Lexington, Mass.: D.C. Heath, 1974.

Greeley, Andrew M.; Saldahna, Shirley; McCready, William; and McCourt, Kathleen. "American Catholics—Ten Years Later," *The Critic* (January-February 1975) 33, no. 2, p. 14.

Hardin, Garrett. "Multiple Paths to Population Control." *Family Planning Perspectives* 2, no. 4 (October 1970).

————. "The Tragedy of the Commons." *Science* 162: 1243-1248.

Hauerwas, Stanley, and Roos, L. John. "Ethics and Population Policy." In *Political Issues in U.S. Population Policy*, edited by Gray and Bergman, pp. 189-205.

Hauser, Philip M. *The Population Dilemma*. Englewood Cliffs, N.J.: Prentice-Hall, 1970.

_____. "America's Population Crisis." *Look*, November 21, 1961, pp. 30-31.

Kessel, John H. *The Domestic Presidency: Decision-Making in the White House*. North Scituate, Mass.: Duxbury Press, 1975.

Levitan, Sar A. *The Great Society's Poor Law*. Baltimore: Johns Hopkins Press, 1969, Chapter 8, "Fighting Poverty with a Pill."

National Academy of Sciences. *The Growth of U.S. Population*. National Research Council Publication 1279, Washington, D.C., 1965.

_____. *Rapid Population Growth: Consequences and Policy Implications*. Baltimore: Johns Hopkins Press, 1971.

Pilpel, Harriet F. "Limiting Population: The Voluntary Approach." *Civil Liberties*, November 1971.

Piotrow, Phyllis Tilson. *World Population Crisis: The United States Response*. New York: Praeger, 1973.

Pohlman, Edward, ed. *Population: A Clash of Prophets*. New York: Mentor, 1973.

Population and the American Future. Report of the Commission on Population Growth and the American Future, March 1972, U.S. Government Printing Office. Also published by the New American Library, New York.

Price, Daniel O., ed. *The 99th Hour*. Chapel Hill: University of North Carolina Press, 1967.

Schur, Edwin M. *The Family and the Sexual Revolution*. Bloomington, Ind.: Indiana University Press, 1964. See Part 3, "Birth Control."

Segal, Aaron. "The Rich, the Poor, and Population." In *Population and Politics*, edited by Richard Clinton. Lexington, Mass.: Lexington Books, 1973.

Shultz, Dr. Carl S. "Federal Population Policy: A Decade of Change." *Villanova Law Review* 15 (1970): 788-800.

Sklar, June, and Berkov, Beth. "The American Birth Rate: Evidence of a Coming Rise." *Science*, August 29, 1975.

Sulloway, Alvah W. "The Legal and Political Aspects of Population Control in the U.S." *Law and Contemporary Problems* 25, no. 3 (1960).

Tien, H. Yuan. "National Population Problems and Standardization of Family Size." *Villanova Law Review* 15 (1970): 801-807.

Weiner, Myron. "Political Demography: An Inquiry Into the Political Consequences of Population Change." In N.A.S. *Rapid Population Growth: Consequences and Policy Implications*, pp. 567-617.

Wishik, Samuel M. "Population Programs and Policy," *Villanova Law Review* 15 (1970): 808-817.

Young, Louise B. *Population in Perspective*. New York: Oxford University Press, 1968.

II. FAMILY PLANNING PROGRAMS

Ambrose, Linda. "Sex Education in the Public Schools: The Need for Official Leadership. *Family Planning/Population Reporter* 5, no. 5 (October 1976), p. 78.

"The Anatomy of a Victory." A panel discussion of a public controversy, Planned Parenthood Federation of America, New York, 1959. Mimeographed.

Beasley, Joseph D. Transcript of lectures, John F. Kennedy School of Government, Harvard University, 1973.

————. "United States: Utilization of a Family Planning Program in a Metropolitan Area." *Studies in Family Planning*, no. 59, November 1970.

————. "View from Louisiana." *Family Planning Perspectives* 1, no. 1 (Spring 1969), p. 2.

————. "Louisiana: Developing and Managing a Statewide Family Planning Program." *Family Planning Perspectives* 3, no. 4 (October 1971).

————. "The Orleans Parish Family Planning Demonstration Program." *The Milbank Memorial Fund Quarterly* 47 (1969): 225-253.

Dennett. Mary Ware. *Birth Control Laws—Shall We Keep Them, Change Them or Abolish Them*. New York: The Grafton Press, 1926.

Dienes, C. Thomas. *Law, Politics and Birth Control*. Chicago: University of Illinois Press, 1972.

Djerassi, Carl. "Birth Control after 1984," *Science* 169 (September 4, 1970), p. 949.

Eliot, Johan W. "Fertility Control and Coercion." *Family Planning Perspectives* 5, no. 3 (Summer 1973), p. 132.

Finn, J. "Controversy in New York." *Commonweal*, September 12, 1958.

Fryer, Peter. *The Birth Controllers*. London: Secker & Warburg, 1965.

General Accounting Office. "Administration of Federal Assistance Programs—a Case Study Showing Need for Additional Improvements." Report to Congress by the Comptroller General of the U.S., July 28, 1976.

Gustaveson, Patricia B. *Implementation of Family Planning Policy by Public Welfare*. Monograph 8, Carolina Population Center, Chapel Hill, N.C., 1970.

Harkavy, Oscar; Jaffe, Fred; and Wishik, Samuel. "Family Planning—Public Policy: Who is Misleading Whom." *Science* 165 (July 25, 1969), p. 367. A response to Judith Blake article.

Hellman, Louis M. "The Impact of the Family Planning Services and Population Research Act of 1970 on the Population of the U.S." Printed proceedings of the 1971 annual meeting of the American Assn. of Planned Parenthood Physicians.

_____. "One Galileo is Enough: Some Aspects of Current Population Problems." *Eugenics Review* 57, no. 4 (December 1965), p. 161.

Hilmar, Norman A. "Population Control, Family Planning and Planned Parenthood." Address to Planned Parenthood-World Population Southeast Council, Savannah, Ga., May 7, 1970.

Himmelfarb, Milton. "A Plague of Children." *Commentary* 51, no. 4 (April 1971), p. 37.

Jaffe, Frederick S. "Public Policy on Fertility Control," *Scientific American* 299, no. 1 (July 1973), p. 17.

_____. and Polgar, Steven P. "Family Planning and Public Policy: Is the 'Culture of Poverty' the New Cop-Out?" *Journal of Marriage and the Family* 30, part 2, May 1968.

Kennedy, David M. *Birth Control in America*. New Haven, Conn.: Yale University Press, 1970.

Koblinsky, Marjorie A.; Jaffe, Frederick S.; Greep, Roy O. "Funding for Reproductive Research: The Status and the Needs." *Family Planning Perspectives* 8, no. 5 (September-October 1976), p. 212.

"Louisiana Story." *U.S. News and World Report*, July 28, 1969, p. 55.

Mackintosh, Douglas. "How Family Health Foundation was Mau-Maued." *New Orleans* 9, no. 8 (May 1975), p. 45.

Measham, Anthony R. *Family Planning in North Carolina: the Politics of a Lukewarm Issue*. Monograph 17, Carolina Population Center, Chapel Hill, N.C., 1972.

_____; Hatcher, R. A.; and Arnold, C. B. "Physicians and Contraception." *Southern Medical Journal* 64 (1971):499.

Pilpel, Harriet F., and Wechsler, Nancy F. "Birth Control, Teen-agers and the Law." *Family Planning Perspectives* 1, no. 1 (Spring 1969), p. 29.

Rainwater, Lee. *And the Poor Get Children*. Chicago: Quadrangle Books, 1960.

Rohr, John A. S.J., "Birth Control in Illinois: a Case Study in Church-State Relations." *Chicago Studies* 4, no. 1 (Spring 1965).

Sanger, Margaret. *The Pivot of Civilization*. New York: Brentano's, 1922.

Sheppard, Harold L. "Effects of Family Planning on Poverty in the U.S." Staff paper, W. E. Upjohn Institute for Employment Research, Kalamazoo, Mich., October 1967.

Silver, Morton A. "Birth Control and the Private Physician." *Family Planning Perspectives* 4, no. 2 (April 1972), p. 42.

Spingarn, Natalie Davis. *National Journal* 3, no. 47 (November 20, 1971), p. 2288.

Stycos, J. Mayone. "Opinion, Ideology, and Population Problems: Some Sources of Domestic and Foreign Opposition to Birth Control." In N.A.S., *Rapid Population Growth*, p. 533.

Watts, Daniel H. "Birth Control." *Liberator*, May 1969. p. 3.

Weinberg, D. "Family Planning in the American States." In *Population Policymaking in the American States*, edited by Bergman et al.

Westoff, Charles F. "The Decline of Unplanned Births in the U.S." *Science* 191 (1976):38.

Whelpton, Pascal K.; Campbell, Arthur A.; and Patterson, John E. *Fertility and Family Planning in the U.S.* Princeton: Princeton University Press, 1966.

Yates, Herschel W. Jr. "American Protestantism and Birth Control: An Examination of Shifts Within a Major Religious Value Orientation." Unpublished graduate thesis, Harvard University, 1968.

III. THE BLACK GENOCIDE ISSUE

Attah, Ernest B., "Racial Aspects of Zero Population Growth." *Science* 180 (June 15, 1973), p. 1143.

Anderson, John E., and Smith, Jack C. "Planned and Unplanned Fertility in a Metropolitan Area: Black and White Differences." *Family Planning Perspectives* 7, no. 6 (November-December 1975), p. 281.

Austin, B. William. "Population Policy and the Black Community." National Urban League, July 1974. Unpublished report.

Bernard, Jessie. *Marriage and Family Among Negroes*. Englewood Cliffs, N.J.: Prentice-Hall, 1966.

Berson, Lenora E. *The Negroes and the Jews*. New York: Random House, 1971.

Darity, William A.; Turner, Castellano B.; and Thiebaux, H. Jean. "An Exploratory Study of Barriers to Family Planning, Race Consciousness and Fears of Black Genocide." Proceedings of the 1971 annual meeting of the American Assn. of Planned Parenthood Physicians.

"Family Size and the Black American." *Population Bulletin* 30, no. 4. Population Reference Bureau, Washington, D.C., 1975.

Farley, Reynolds. *The Growth of the Black Population*. Chicago; Markham, 1970.

Genovese, Eugene D. *Roll, Jordan, Roll: The World the Slaves Made*. New York: Vintage Books, 1976.

Henri, Florette. *Black Migration: Movement North 1900-1920*. Garden City, N.Y.: Anchor Press/Doubleday, 1975.

Jones, Clinton. "Population Issues and the Black Community." In *Political Issues in U.S. Population Policy*, edited by Gray and Bergman, p. 151.

Martin, Joseph F. "Is the Black Physician Being Heard?" Proceedings of the 1969 meeting of the American Assn. of Planned Parenthood Physicians.

Moynihan, Daniel P. *The Negro Family: The Case for National Action*. U.S. Department of Labor, Office of Policy Planning and Research, 1965.

Rainwater, Lee, and Yancy, William L. *The Moynihan Report and the Politics of Controversy*. Cambridge: MIT Press, 1967.

Sweet, James A. "Differentials in the Rate of Fertility Decline: 1960-1970." *Family Planning Perspectives* 6, no. 2 (Spring 1974), p. 103.

Weisbord, Robert G. *Genocide? Birth Control and the Black American*. Westport, Conn.: Greenwood Press, 1975.

_____, and Stein, Arthur. *Bittersweet Encounter: the Afro-American and the American Jew*. Westport, Conn.: Negro Universities Press, 1970.

Willie, Charles V., ed. *The Family Life of Black People*. Columbus, O.: Charles E. Merrill, 1970.

Woodson, Carter G. *A Century of Negro Migration*. New York: Russell & Russell, 1969.

Yette, Samuel F. *The Choice: The Issue of Black Survival in America*. New York: G. P. Putnam's Sons, 1971.

IV. STERILIZATION

Bloom, Mark. "Sterilization Guidelines: 22 Months on the Shelf." *Medical World News*, November 9, 1973, p. 53.

Donovan, Patricia. "Sterilization and the Poor: Two Views on the Need for Protection From Abuse." *Family Planning/Population Reporter* 5, no. 2 (April 1976), p. 28.

Dreifus, Claudia. "Sterilizing the Poor." *The Progressive* 39, no. 12 (December 1975), p. 13.

Gullattee, Alyce McL. C. "The Politics of Eugenics." In *Eugenic Sterilization*, edited by Jonas Robitscher. Springfield, Ill.: Charles C. Thomas, 1973.

Health Research Group. "Study on Surgical Sterilization: Present Abuses and Proposed Regulation." Washington, D.C. October 29, 1973. The Health Research Group is a nonprofit public interest group associated with Ralph Nader and funded by Public Citizen, Inc.

Health Subcommittee, Senate Committee on Labor and Public Welfare. *Quality of Health Care—Human Experimentation, 1973*. Printed hearings, Part 4, July 10, 1973. Montgomery, Ala., sterilization case.

Morrison, Joseph L. "Illegitimacy, Sterilization and Racism: a North Carolina Case History, 1965." *The Social Service Review* 39, no. 1 (March 1965), pp. 1-10.

Paul, Julius. "The Return of Punitive Sterilization Proposals: Current Attacks on Illegitimacy and the AFDC Program." *Law and Society Review* 3, no. 1 (August 1968).

"Sterilization Without Consent: Teaching Hospital Violations of HEW Regulations." Report by Health Research Group, January 21, 1975.

Woodside, Moya. *Sterilization in North Carolina: a Sociological and Psychological Study.* Chapel Hill: University of North Carolina Press, 1950.

Young, Perry Deane. "A Surfeit of Surgery." *Washington Post*, May 30, 1976, p. B-1.

V. IMMIGRATION

Abbott, Edith. *Historical Aspects of the Immigration Problem.* New York: Arno Press, 1969.

Agenda Quarterly. National Council of La Raza, Winter 1973. Special issue on Mexican immigration.

Busey, Samuel C. *Immigration: Its Evils and Consequences.* New York: DeWitt and Davenport, 1856.

Grebler, Leo et al. "Mexican Immigration to the United States: the Record and its Implications." Mexican-American Study Project Advance Report. Los Angeles, University of California Graduate School of Business Administration, 1966.

Handlin, Oscar. *The Uprooted: the Epic Story of Great Migrations That Made the American People.* New York: Grosset & Dunlap, 1951.

Keely, Charles B. "Immigration Composition and Population Policy." *Science*, August 16, 1974, p. 590.

Tanton, John. "Immigration: an Illiberal Concern?" *Zero Population Growth National Reporter*, April 1975, p. 4.

Western Hemisphere Immigration, select commission on. Report of January 1968. Washington, D.C., Government Printing Office 937-839.

VI. VOTING RIGHTS, REGIONALISM, REDISTRICTING

Advisory Commission on Intergovernmental Relations. *Regional Governance: Promise and Performance,* May 1973, No. A-41, Washington, D.C.

Cotrell, Charles L. "The Effects of At-Large Elections on the Political Access and Voting Strength of Mexican-Americans and Blacks in Texas." Paper presented at the Rocky Mountain Social Science Convention, April 25-27, 1974, El Paso, Tex.

De Grove, John M. "The City of Jacksonville: Consolidation in Action." In ACIR *Regional Governance*, p. 17.

Derfner, Armand. "Racial Discrimination and the Right to Vote." *Vanderbilt Law Review* 3, no. 26 (April 1973), p. 552.

Graham, Gene. *One Man, One Vote: Baker v. Carr and the American Levellers*. Boston; Atlantic-Little, Brown, 1972.

Lawyers Committee for Civil Rights Under Law. *Ten-Year Report*. Washington, November 1973. See p. 42, "Opening Up the Political Process."

Voting Rights Act Extension, 1975 hearings. Committee on the Judiciary, Subcommittee on Civil and Constitutional Rights, U.S. House of Representatives. Two printed volumes. U.S. Government Printing Office Washington, D.C.

The Voting Rights Act: Ten Years After. A Report of the U.S. Commission on Civil Rights, January 1975, Washington, D.C.

VII. LAND USE, GROWTH, AND URBAN AFFAIRS

De Vise, Pierre. "Cities are Becoming Dumping Grounds for Poor People." *U.S. News and World Report*, April 5, 1976, p. 54.

Glazer, Nathan, and Moynihan, Daniel P. *Beyond the Melting Pot: The Negroes, Puerto Ricans, Jews, Italians and Irish of New York City*. Cambridge: MIT and Harvard Press, 1963.

Kain, John F., and Persky, Joseph J. "Alternatives to the Gilded Ghetto." *The Public Interest*, no. 14 (Winter 1969), p. 74.

Olson, Mancur, and Landsberg, Hans H., eds. *The No-Growth Society*. New York: W. W. Norton, 1973.

Pickard, Jerome. "U.S. Metropolitan Growth and Expansion, 1970-2000, With Population Projections." Research paper for Commission on Population Growth and the American Future.

U.S. Commission on Population Growth and the American Future. Research reports, vol. 4, "Governance and Population: the Governmental Implications of Population Change," and vol. 6, "Aspects of Population Growth Policy."

Index